Testimonials

"A remarkable, life-affirming story from a truly remarkable woman."
Journalist and Novelist Ray Connolly

"Angie McCartney is smart, witty, mischievous and smart as a whip. Her zest for life which is reflected in her remarkable book is infectious."
William J. Bratton, CBE, former NYPD Police Commissioner and Chief of the Los Angeles Police Department

"Angie McCartney is a woman I describe as a freedom fighter."
The Reverend Jesse Jackson

"About time this book was written! Open it now and come on a journey, this wonderful woman has a wealth of stories. I am so pleased she has put some of them down on paper at last."
Comic and broadcaster Peter Price

"Angie and I shared many hours sifting through Paul's fan-mail when she brought it to me. They were very happy days."
Freda Kelly, Brian Epstein's Assistant and Beatles Fan Club Secretary

"Having known Angie for many years, I always appreciated her kindness and friendship whenever our paths would meet on our long and winding roads."
May Pang, John Lennon's Muse

ANGIE McCARTNEY

My Long and Winding Road

The *first* 82.9 Years

To Paul
Enjoy!

Angie
McCarthy

Foreword by Cynthia Lennon

ROK BOOKS

First hardcover edition printed 2013 in the United Kingdom

A catalogue record for this book is available from the British Library.

ISBN (Hardcover): 978-0-9575029-0-1
ISBN (eBook): 978-0-9575029-1-8

Published by ROK Books Limited, ROK House, Kingswood Business Park, Holyhead Road,
Albrighton, Wolverhampton WV7 3AU

For more copies of this book, please email: info@rokbooks.com
Tel: 01902 374896

Edited by Paul Simpson
Book Design by Amazing15

Printed in Great Britain

Acknowledgement

**The publishers would like to thank Angie and Ruth McCartney and
Martin Nethercutt for their unstinting support on this project**

Dedications

For Ruth

This book is dedicated to my darling daughter Ruth. My world, my reason for living, my buddy, my salvation. Someone who never puts herself first, who strives to be the best, despite life's setbacks. Her sense of humour never fails to brighten a dark spot in life, and her tenacity and vigour for life are an inspiration. Oh, and she makes a fine shepherd's pie too.

She even forgave me for trashing her Andy Pandy shoes.

I pray that life will eventually bring you all the rewards you so richly deserve. Now shut up, and put the kettle on!

From your devoted Mum. (W.W.W.I.L.)

(P.S. she's such a control freak, she actually corrected a grammatical error in this very dedication)

For Martin

And to Martin, who didn't know when he married Ruth that if you "buy one, you get one free." Whose artistic input in building my cyber-world and branding has been invaluable and much appreciated.

It will *always* be my turn to fold your laundry. As long as you take me to The Harbor Room whenever I ask.

Love from Madge, The Mighty Midget.

Contents

Foreword by Cynthia Lennon

My friendship with Angie McCartney dates back many eons, and memories of times shared, laughs along the way, good times, and some not so good, but always our strongest bond has been the similarity of our relationships with our kids, mine with Julian and hers with Ruth. Although Angie and I are ten years apart in age, our kids were only separated by three years, and so as Mums of young kids in the middle of Beatle madness, I think we immediately saw something in one another about trying to retain our Hoylake values. Angie was born in Hoylake and I grew up there so we had shared experiences on a few different levels.

She walked into our house, Kenwood, in St. George's Hill, Surrey one evening in 1965 with Jim, Paul, Jane Asher and some other friends, and immediately asked me if she could do anything to help in the kitchen. I said, "No thanks" and she went to sit on one of our 18-foot sofas, which seemed to swallow her up. But don't let Angie's stature fool you... she's small but mighty.

Like me, Ange and Ruth have been around the globe once or twice, and never failed to keep their sense of humour, work ethic, loyalty to each other, friends and family, no matter how dysfunctional. In fact, it was Angie who once told me she put the "fun" in "dysfunctional."

In the Seventies, I witnessed her devotion in nursing Jim, and the unselfish support of young Ruth who, as a teenager, was always by her side, helping in whatever way she could to ease his suffering. Ruth's school in West Kirby was close to our house and they would often stop by for a natter on the way home – and of course – a cup of tea!

The Beatles fell apart but somehow we've always managed to stay in touch throughout the years and the miles. Since then, I've watched and read about their global travels, various jobs, projects, and company McCartney Multimedia, in sunny California.

When she asked me to write to the foreword to her book, I was delighted, and although we now communicate across the miles by telephone, she never fails to make me laugh when we share experiences, and it will be fun to see the names of Lennon and McCartney together again – if only in print!

I sincerely wish her every success with this, her first book, which has only taken her a little over eighty-two years to complete, and she is even threatening a second one – I can hardly wait! Oh, but I do expect a signed copy!

Lovingly, Cynthia Lennon

MARCH 1976

My daughter Ruth has "donated" a piece of her writing to set the tone for what most readers will surely consider the "heart of the matter" of my life's long and winding road... an essay she penned some years back called "The Chemistry of Lennon and McCartney". It's a child's eye view of the dynamics of The Beatles observed while she was growing up in the eye of the hurricane. I thought it was an appropriate way to set the tone for my journey. Enjoy. Angie

The Chemistry of Lennon and McCartney
By Ruth McCartney

"It's a drag." Paul McCartney, England, December 8, 1980.

My beloved step-brother was never one to deal with soul-wrenching grief in a practical manner. He was brought up in the guilt-ridden Catholic mindset of "bury-your-head-in-the-sand.com." "Let's not talk about it, son," a la father Jimmy Mac.

He and the world had just lost someone very dear to them. I had lost my Uncle John, the myopic, misunderstood, manipulative, mystifying Mop-Top who had helped me to learn to ride a bicycle; Julian and Sean had lost a father; Cynthia, her knight in shining armour; Yoko, a fellow artist, contemporary and house husband... and Paul? Well, call me crazy, but he lost the wife. I'm certainly not implying anything of a carnal nature here, but to almost all intents and porpoises (as John would have put it), what they had was a marriage.

Mark David Chapman's selfish quest for his Warhol-esque fifteen minutes of fame was the fatal wound to an injured relationship that had lasted almost twenty-three years. This unconventional partnership, much like a paradigmatic marriage, had endured its sundry situations... its honeymoon period; its seven year itch; the adoption of its offspring by Northern Songs and sometime foster parent Michael Jackson; the tender temptations of Jane, Cynthia, Yoko, Linda, May Pang and others; the psychedelic side-trips; the jesters in the High Court; a very public airing of some dirty laundry lyrics; and finally, like two great lions in a butcher's shop who have matured enough to realise there's enough meat in the market for both of them... a mutual, if grudging respect. It was a drag alright.

On a dank, blustery evening in October 1940 at the Oxford Street Maternity hospital in Liverpool, Julia Stanley Lennon gave birth to a bouncing bundle of boy joy whom she named John Winston. The boy's father, Alfred, a professional coward and merchant seaman was away on a voyage. He would return *six years later* and attempt to make amends with the young lad by offering to take him to New Zealand.

Hitler's Luftwaffe was extremely interested in this industrialised zone with its munitions factories, rail network and busy seaport, but despite the young John's pleas to Julia, Freddie was sent packing and John Winston was returned to the care of his house-proud Aunty Mimi and dairy farmer Uncle George, at Mendips on Menlove Avenue, where he'd been living for a year.

Almost twenty-one months after John Winston had screamed his first protest, a thirty-two year old Mary Patricia Mohin McCartney would experience the same set of emotions and circumstances at her place of work – she was a nursing sister at Walton Hospital – only difference being that her husband, (a.k.a. "me Dad"), was there at 2.05 a.m. to welcome his first born, James Paul, into the world.

The family grew within eighteen months to include brother Peter Michael, and they resided in various houses in Allerton and Speke from Roach Avenue to Ardwick Road, before finally settling at 20 Forthlin Road in 1955.

The following year, mother Mary died of breast cancer, leaving the emotionally immature Paul to ask, upon hearing the news of the tragedy, "What are we going to do without her money?" My brother Mike has been quoted as opining that it was this pivotally catastrophic event that caused an inwardly devastated fourteen year old Paul to pour his passion and pain into his music, which paradoxically became a blessing for all of us.

Across town, John Winston would be the victim of the same disastrous occurrence just two years later. Julia was killed by a car driven by an off duty policeman on July 15, 1958. The deprivation of his Mother's friendship would affect John deeply and bond these partners in rhyme for years to come. Paul had already suffered the loss of his mother, and although two years younger, and infinitely less experienced than John, it would prove to be a mutually morbid situation in which they could commiserate.

Almost a year before the sudden passing of Julia Lennon, a coincidental collision of cosmic proportions took place at St. Peter's Parish Church in Woolton Village.

On the afternoon of July 6, 1957, right across the street from the ossuary of a certain spinster called Eleanor Rigby, an unsuspecting schoolboy named Ivan Vaughn, lad about town, villain of Vale Street and part-time tea chest bassist, took a chubby fifteen year old Paul McCartney to listen to local "legends in their own lunchtime" – the band they called The Quarry Men.

The group was headed by a sexy, sardonic closet nice-guy – the almost seventeen-year-old John Winston Lennon with his £17 guitar. Paul remembers: "It was at Woolton Village Fete I met him. I was a fat schoolboy and, as he leaned an arm 'round my shoulder, I realised that he was drunk."

Not a very glamorous account of an event that was to change minds, music, marketing, merchandise and mania as we knew it. This completely unremarkable set of circumstances would lead to an alliance, that although inconsanguineous, would ultimately disprove the old adage "blood's thicker than water". That may be, but shit's thicker than blood. And these guys went through their fair share of shit together.

To encapsulate their relationship, you most definitely "had to be there". I was very fortunate in that regard. I may have only been a child, but with the 20-20 vision of hindsight I can safely say that even though I suffered the rigours of having my hair chopped off by teenage souvenir seekers as a tot; going to the school cloakroom and finding my raincoat and wellies missing because they had the name McCartney embossed inside them; being told never to give my name or phone number to any strangers in case they were kidnappers, or worse – *journalists*; growing up never knowing if my friends wanted to play with me for me or if they had the ulterior "meet a Beatle" motive; and a jillion other put downs that have turned me into the psychotic, co-dependent mental case that I am today (*not !!!*) I wouldn't have missed it for the world!

I would never have the memory of John and Paul arguing out a song together in the attic at Cavendish Avenue; the honour of having "Blackbird" written for my maternal Grandmother, Edie; the photos of a four-year-old me with Paul in the Bahamas on the location of *Help!*; the recollection of a "blind without his glasses" John wakening up at Rembrandt to be told by mother Angie that they were number one in the charts – again; the birth of all my nieces and nephews; the look on Jim's face when he heard Paul had recorded his one and only musical composition ("Walking in the Park with Eloise") with Chet Atkins and Floyd Cramer; and a jillion other pick-me-ups too numerous to mention. The reason I'm most grateful to have been there is, still to this day, that Jim chose to give me his name. It's a responsibility I take very seriously. McCartney is a fairly common name, as is Lennon, and if you look in any telephone book in most major cities in the world, you'll find a slew of 'em.

I remember Jim's words "toler and moder"... toleration and moderation, and try to live by them (except when it comes to buying shoes!). I clean my teeth, say my prayers, don't do drugs, don't smoke, *try* to pay my bills on time and completely believe in Karma. The significance of being there through the "Beatle Years" is only just now beginning to dawn on me. Having finally realised the value and responsibility of "the name" I must say, it's certainly a helluva perk to be related to Paul.

But it's a helluva privilege to be related to Jim. Why? Coz there's no hairs on a seagull's chest!

Looking back across the years, the synchronicitous world events, the alignment of the planets and a whole host of other spooky things – all I, with my high school education, can conclude is this... John and Paul were meant to meet, meant to create and one was designed to play sturm and drang to the other's yin and yang.

One Romulus to the other's Remus. Ladies and Gentlemen, The Nurk Twins, live without the aid of a net, ably backed up by their band The Oedipus Guilt Complex.

They were the product of a wartime town, a depressed economy, a "things-can't-get-any-worse-luv" society, and they struggled for years to become an "Overnight Success". There was something about being a Scouser that is still undefinable to this day. Our little city has spawned show business legends such as Arthur Askey, Ken Dodd, Glenda Jackson, Rex Harrison, Derek Nimmo, Willy Russell and even *Wayne's World*'s funnyman Mike Myers.

It seems that a free sense of humour kit is handed out at birth to every child born on 'Pool soil.

Is it stranger than fiction that the two Beatles, Stuart Sutcliffe, born in Edinburgh, Scotland, and Pete Best, born in Madras, India – who undoubtedly had an impact on both the group's look and sound – didn't stay the course?

Certainly in the case of John and Paul – two wartime babies, growing up without mothers in fairly, what could be considered upper working to middle class circumstances, the Scouse-glue bonded and stuck.

The combination of John's irreverence and Paul's naiveté; of John's panoply and Paul's privacy; John's perspicacious pessimism vs. Paul's seemingly guileless gyp created the oil and vinegar that tasted so good to our ears. The Brothers Grimm of the musical manuscript. The Abbot & Costello of press conferences. The Orville & Wilbur of melodious travel.

That is not to decry the phenomenal contributions of George and Ringo – it was all part of the package that not only survived, but dictated the Zeitgeist, but the motherless boys certainly managed to find an *anschauung* – a way into each other's souls, bosoms and brains, a way for one to discern the true nature of the other. Alike, yet different. Compatriots yet adversaries.

I'm sure there's a fascinating psychoanalytical clinical explanation for their kinesis, but I just like to think of them as a needle and a thread in a haystack who were lucky enough to find each other and stitch together a tapestry of musical memories which has decorated the walls of the world, and, like those fine pieces of art, will only continue to improve with age.

Like the tragic deaths of Julia and Mary, and as the Death card in the Tarot signifies "change", the equally untimely demise of JFK left America in a depressed, emotional turmoil. The civil rights problems of the early Sixties, the social unrest after World War II and the Korean war served, in my opinion, to act as a tunnel from which it appeared there was no escape.

Then on February 9, 1964, Ed Sullivan shone the proverbial light on the viewing public. The long night was over. The Beatles had conquered America. For the next two and a half years, John and Paul, (together with George and Ringo), would travel, eat, rehearse, write, play, record and "sleep" (again, not literally) together.

The magic eventually had to wear off. On Monday, August 29, 1966 , after endearing youth and enraging society, they played their penultimate concert together at Candlestick Park in San Francisco.

The Scouse glue was coming unstuck. Their next and final gig was to be on the roof of their Savile Row headquarters in London on January 30, 1969.

The glue had turned flaky. The honeymoon was over. The divorce lawyers had moved in. But the legacy remains. From the four on the floor, skiffle-inspired raw rock 'n roll songs of the Hamburg days, to the sophisticated psychedelic tales of public works excavations in Blackburn, Lancashire – it's all still there for us to reminisce, regret and rejoice over.

The Bonnie and Clyde of rock 'n roll had pulled their last job. Busted. Caught red-handed with lives, wives and children of their own. Finito. Sayonara. Later dude...

And so we move into the era of Oasis, Green Day, The Smashing Pumpkins, Nelly, Dave Grohl and various other really groovy types with piercings in places I have to look up in a medical dictionary – but d'ya know what? Ask the songwriters of today who influenced them and eight out of ten will tell you The Beatles. So it goes, and in the end, the music you make is equal to the kudos you take. Now *that's* not such a drag after all !!

Now to my story... or in the words of Joan Rivers... "Enough about me talking about me.... What do you think about me?"

Childhood: 1929 to 1945

The beginning of this book goes as far back as November 1929. That's when I made my first appearance, weeks after the Wall Street crash that begat the Great Depression. I have to rely on research, because unfortunately, I didn't have a Facebook page then or even an iPad – poor underprivileged child.

It was a time when songs such as "Happy Days Are Here Again" were being played, albeit rather inappropriately, and "Makin' Whoopee", and "Ain't Misbehavin'" (take your choice), which was probably all people could afford to do in those days. Belts began to tighten and soup kitchens opened up. And in England, people pulled together like they always do in times of trouble.

When Dad lost his job he'd put cardboard in his shoes to cover the holes while he was trekking around trying to find work. He was a pharmaceutical salesman at a time when people really just wanted razor blades – you can understand why. He eventually got a job with Dr. Eric McAlpine in Norris Green, Liverpool, as a pharmacist, for which he was qualified.

Neville Chamberlain did his best to appease Adolf Hitler, but in the end, was unable to stop World War II. Once again Great Britain huddled together, made the best of it and eventually got through. Keep calm and carry on.

And better times were on the way...

When I Was a Little Girl, Way Back Home in Liverpool

Before embarking on this book, I sat down to list my recollections of childhood. Having recently read Bill Clinton's *My Life* in which he graphically writes about his entire childhood, his memories were a great inspiration for me to finally take action.

This book was autographed and given to me personally by this great man in July 2005. I consider it one of the most memorable occasions of life. This man has charisma that you just cannot describe until you experience it first-hand. I whispered to him, "Are there any microphones here?" When he assured me that there were not, I whispered to him, "You are the reason why I became an American citizen." He hugged me and kissed me on the cheek.

Talk about an "I'll never wash that side of my face again" moment.

I was born Angela Stopforth, in Hoylake, on the Wirral in Great Britain on November 14, 1929. Mum gave birth to me at home at 19 Grosvenor Road, Hoylake, Wirral, Merseyside. A few days later, my Dad was dispatched to take me to be christened at a nearby Catholic church, as she was still bedridden from my birth. She told him to have me named Angela Lucy. Lucy Pemberton, Mum's friend, was to be my godmother.

However, the priest deemed that Lucy was not a saint's name and insisted it be changed to Lucia. But when Dad got back home, he jokingly said he couldn't remember the chosen names, and that the baby had been named Mary Ellen. Mum flew off the handle and screamed, "Take her back! I want it changed!" Mary Ellen was the handle given to the "shawlies" – ladies who wore black woolen shawls and sold flowers, fruit and vegetables off barrows in Clayton Square in Liverpool. He relented and told her he was just joking, and that I did in fact bear the regal names of Angela Lucia.

My own earliest recollection is of standing inside the wooden gate of 3 Carr Lane, Norris Green, Liverpool, where we had just moved from my birthplace in Hoylake, ("over the water", as we called it). My frequent bouts of asthma had originated the plan – made by my dad and his employer, Dr. McAlpine – that we should move to a less moist area. Dr. Mac pulled some strings with the Liverpool housing folks and arranged for us to rent a modest three-bedroom house on the outskirts of the city, and close to his surgery, where Dad worked as a freelance pharmacist.

Dad's Moustache

My Mum was as feisty as they come.

Before I was born, there was an incident on their wedding anniversary. Dad was a Sergeant Major in the British Army, an instructor in the use of mustard gases in World War I. Stationed in Otley, Yorkshire, Mum lived off base in a rented house belonging to a Mrs. Burnell. My oldest sister, Mae, was a baby, and as their wedding anniversary was coming up, Dad asked Mum to organise a babysitter so he could take her out to dinner. That was a big deal in those days.

So, Mrs. Burnell came in to sit with Mae, Mum got all gussied up, ready for her big night out. Nine o'clock came, then ten o'clock. As Mum's hopes dropped, and her embarrassment grew, she and Mrs. Burnell sat in the two armchairs, one each side of the fireplace. Eventually, they heard the sound of the key trying to find the lock. Dad staggered in, quite jovial, completely oblivious of the fact that he had broken his promise. With a nice buzz going, he bid everyone goodnight and toddled off to bed.

Mum calmly went in the bathroom and got his cold-water razor. She then shaved off just one half of his Sergeant Major waxed moustache as he slept in his blissful stupor.

Next morning, she awoke to the sound of him shaving in the bathroom. He removed the other half of his moustache, took a cup of tea to Mum in bed, kissed her goodbye, and never mentioned the incident. Then he went off to war for another day.

From that day until the day that he died, he never mentioned it. Neither did Mum. 'Tis better to shave face than save face.

My Dad

Fathers are special people, especially to their little girls. His memory conjures up so many recollections and never fails to bring a smile to my face. He was a pipe smoker, and in my mind's eye I can clearly see him cleaning it out with pipe cleaners. He used to ride his bicycle very majestically, wearing a bowler hat at all times.

In the doctor's free clinic in Norris Green, Liverpool, where he worked as a pharmacist, some of the women would come in and ask to see "the red fella" as he had auburn hair.

Every Friday he brought Milky Way bars for us kids. We used to cut them into slices to make them go as far as possible. He created in me a love of crossword puzzles, which I still have to this day.

One of my earliest recollections is of him picking me up out of bed and bringing me downstairs to play the piano to me on a pillow on his lap after he and Mum got home from the theatre. He'd say, "This one may not be pretty, but by God, she'll grow up loving music." He got that right.

Our Lady

My long-suffering sister Joan was plagued with having to take me everywhere. One Sunday afternoon when we were kids, we were upstairs at 3 Carr Lane, and Joan had her friend Lily Gould over to play. I was, as usual, the little nuisance. They dressed me up in a lace curtain, and had me hold a rosary and stand on the bedside table. They told me to be quiet and that they would come back for me soon enough.

They went out into the garden to read their comics and forgot all about me. Ages after, Mum wondered where I was, went upstairs and found me almost asleep, swaying. She asked, "What on earth are you doing?" In hushed tones I replied, "Shhhh... don't talk to me. I'm Our Lady."

A Mighty Wind

As kids we always looked forward to our annual trip to Menai Bridge, Anglesey, in North Wales. My Dad's boss, Dr. McAlpine, dispatched his chauffeur to drive us from Carr Lane in Norris Green to the rented cottage for a three-week holiday. It was a big moment when we would drive off, and Dad would throw pennies into the street to the kids who were whooping at us as we moved away.

I have a lasting memory of we kids all being treated to a Lyons ice cream when we went across the bridge into Anglesey. Little round patties of ice cream in white greaseproof paper, which they popped into a cone. The wonderful vanilla smell is still in my nostrils.

Every year we rented the same cottage from a Mrs. Williams, who would move out to give us the run of the place. She stayed in the house next door, which was a disadvantage for her. You see, the cottage had paper-thin walls, when Dad came back from the village pub at night, he would dispense his excess gas in the bedroom, which caused a mighty rumble. Mum would say, "Bob, stop it! Mrs. Williams will hear you."

"Oh, don't worry about it," he replied. "I have told her that my wife is a martyr to wind."

They were lazy, relaxing times, and about the most exciting thing I remember was that frogs would leap around our ankles when we were drawing water from the pump in the outside yard to fill up bowls of cold water to wash in. Shower? Bathtub? Not on your life.

On Starting School

Due to my constant battles with asthma, pleurisy and pneumonia, I didn't start school until I was six. The normal age at that time was five.

From day one, I absolutely hated it with a passion (Ruth followed in my footsteps on that one), and was scared stiff of everyone, particularly the nuns. In those days, they wore full black habits and were covered down to their ankles. Their wimples were stiff white things, like the protective collars that vets put on dogs and cats to stop them scratching themselves. Their rosary hung from their waist, and clanked as they walked. They had no compunction whatsoever in whacking us with a ruler, either on the palm or the back of the hand, or the back of the knees. My chief transgression, which got me into the most trouble, was giggling. At least my sense of humour was not retarded.

Classes at St. Teresa's consisted of about sixty children, mixed boys and girls, and as far as I remember, the girls used to be disciplined far more than the boys. We had two wags in our class named Casson and Downey, the Butch and Sundance of their day. They were very mischievous, scared of nothing, always up to pranks, yet full of fun. I always wished I could be more like them and less timid. Mind you, my parental upbringing at that stage, although loving and kind, was strict, and I was always urged to remain in the background and not to be forward, voice any opinions, complain, or attract attention. That stayed with me for a long time, and I think it was only when I came to live in America that I fully grasped that it was OK to have a personality.

If ever I went home and told my mum, "I got the cane today" she would slap me across the back of the legs and say, "Well, you must have deserved it." Should have kept my trap shut.

I was always pretty bright when it came to marks in class. Usually, Casson and Downey came first and second, and frequently, I came third. I was crushed when it came time to give out letters for the best students to take home to their parents about the possibility of a scholarship to a better school. I haltingly asked if I could have one, only to be told that, yes, I was good enough, but that there was no way my Mum would be able to afford the uniform and books.

On Monday mornings, when the register, or roll call, was run, we were told to put up our hands if we had missed Mass the previous day. Woe betide you if you put up your hands. You were made to stand up and explain why you had committed this transgression. In my case, it was usually because I was not well. I was a real sickly, wimpy kid. And it was all marked down in a book. I never found out what they did with that book. Probably showed it to the Mass Police.

I guess bullying was something we took for granted and didn't even think to complain. My main one related to my wearing glasses, and sometimes if I would ask if I could join in a game in the playground, they'd just sneer and say, "Oh, go away speccy four eyes." But I didn't do anything about it.

When I was seven and my Dad died, Mum was thrown into very difficult straits and depended on the priests to bring us vouchers to spend at a general shop at Broadway in Norris Green. This didn't do anything for my self-confidence. It was almost a relief in a way when the war broke out and everything changed. No more school, and heaven knows only how or when we slept, between the bombing, the sirens, the Air Raid Wardens shouting to people to put their lights out, and the occasional visits from soldiers asking if we could squeeze another couple of people into our shelter if theirs had been damaged or an incendiary or unexploded bomb had landed in their garden. It was never dull, that's for sure. But I can honestly say we didn't think we were having a hard time. We just got on with it.

Ah, the jolly old British.

The Kerry Dance

My sister Joan, with whom I shared a bed for many years in childhood, wasn't musically gifted at that point in her life. However, that didn't stop her from giving impromptu performances. Whilst in a deep sleep, she'd often sit bolt upright in the bed and loudly sing "The Kerry Dance" from start to finish.

At this point you're probably wondering how that marvellously intriguing song goes. Let me teach you:

Oh the days of the Kerry dancing
Oh the ring of the piper's tune,
Oh for one of those hours of gladness
Gone alas, like our youth too soon...

When the boys began to gather
In the Glen on a summer's night
Oh, the Kerry piper's tuning
Made us dance with wild delight

Oh to think of it
Oh to dream of it
Fills my heart with tears (Repeat – from the top!)

For some reason her butchering of the song used to rile me no end. I would wake up and yell, "Mum, she's doing it again!" Mum would come into the room and shush me, telling me to let her finish. In her estimation, it might harm her, like waking a sleepwalker before they had finished their journey.

To this day, if you ask Joan to sing "The Kerry Dance", she swears she doesn't know the words. Not sure if I actually believe her, but I'll sleep on it.

She later blossomed out and developed quite a good singing voice. In fact, she cut her first CD at the ripe young age of 82!

Mae and Ralph – The Not-So-Handy Man

When my Dad travelled to London in 1937 for his throat operation, a journey from which he would never return, the last words he said to Mae and her fiancé Ralph Butchard were: "If anything happens to me, I want you two to get married and help to keep the home together."

They kept their promise to him and had a very low-key wedding at St. Teresa's Church in Norris Green. Ralph duly moved in to live with us all at 3 Carr Lane, where they both remained until they went to that big car park in the sky.

Ralph came from a family of farming folks and was a good guy. He was very basic in his interests and skills, and worked for a company in Warrington called Arthur Monk and Company. They were somewhat revolutionary in that they gave shares in the company to all of their employees. What a real incentive for them to work hard and be loyal.

Ralph's skills didn't lend themselves to domesticity. I remember Mae patiently pleading with him to decorate the toilet with a new material called Congowall, which was a heavyweight wallpaper type of material, rather like linoleum. When he had finished and called us all to come and view his handiwork, it looked as though he had used rocks for pasting it on, which made the lumps and bumps look like a mountainous surface. Mae patiently stripped it and re-papered it properly, lump free.

Another time, when she was nagging at him to help with the gardening, he offered to cut the hedges but the end result looked like a blind man with a band saw had cut it. Curiously, it looked like a figure of eight. Again, Mae to the rescue. She was delighted (silly girl) when Ralph triumphantly presented her with a wedding anniversary present of a brand spanking new pair of hedge cutters to right the wrongs and make it all shipshape.

On another wedding anniversary he said, "I have brought you a present, love, come out to the van to see it." Lo and behold, there was a ladder, a bucket and a set of chamois leathers. It was an invitation for her to clean the upstairs windows. How she kept her cool I will never know.

He would frequently spoil her with delightful gifts like a spirit level, a new set of screwdrivers, or a packet of sandpaper, and she always accepted them like the lady she truly was. I really don't think he thought he was doing anything wrong, or that she might have liked a bottle of perfume or a jar of hand cream. They loved each other and made a good marriage. They also helped us keep the home together after our Dad had died.

Mae gave birth to three lovely kids, Bobby, Jill and John, who are all now in the Brisbane area living happily ever after. I hear from them all the time.

Mickey, my First Pet

After my Dad died, my asthma escalated, no doubt due to stress, and Mum thought it might be nice to get me a puppy, something to lavish my affection on. He was a lovely little black and white mongrel, and followed me everywhere. Mickey. I can see him now.

There was a family party at Carr Lane one night, with lots of revelry, and a barrel of beer in the back kitchen.

That was the night that Ralph stood at the bottom of the stars, with his back to the pantry cupboard, and yelled to my cousin who was emerging from the toilet at the top of stairs: "Come on, run at me." So she did, ran down for the first few stairs and launched herself in the air for the following ones, intending to land in Ralphs arms. Turned out he was just kidding, and by the time she landed, he had stepped aside, leaving Rosalind with a cut head and lots of bleeding. Such was the degree of craziness going on that night.

As a little 'un, I was forced to go to bed while the proceedings were still in full swing, and next morning, I was up and about early, came downstairs, and found little Mickey lying underneath the dripping tap of the beer barrel, with his little paws wrapped around his obviously aching head. He had lain underneath it all night and consumed heaven knows only how much beer. Poor baby must have been nursing the mother and father of a hangover.

A little while later, after Mum had lit the fire in the kitchen grate, he ran in, jumped on the fire, and killed himself. In answer to my screams, Mum, Mae, Ralph and others crowded in, wrapped him in wet towels, but it was too late. I was inconsolable. First my Daddy, now my beloved Mickey. It had a lasting effect on me. I don't remember what happened to his remains, I only know that I was emotionally scarred. I never had another pet as a child. I got on with life as a solitary child, but I never felt lonely. I think that deep down I am still the same, I am happy to be alone, but never lonely.

Mae had a series of cats over the coming years, beginning my continuing love of these amazing creatures. But even now, I am aware of trying not to love them too much because of the inevitable parting that I must face.

Recently, someone asked me why we named our cats Thelma, Louise, Butch Cassidy, and Sundance all after characters that hurled themselves off cliffs at the end of movies... perhaps subconsciously now I know the answer!

Choir Convictions

I was a proud member of the school choir at St. Teresa's, and it gave me a lasting memory of my friend Kathleen Murphy. Kathleen could not pronounce the word "chimney". We used to sing a sacred song called "Bless This House" which included the words "bless the roof and chimney tall."

Kathleen, who stood behind me in the choir line-up, would always sing "chimbley" which never failed to crack me up. I patiently tried to teach her to say "chim" and "nee". She could pronounce each word separately with no problem, but when she combined chim and nee, it would still come out "chimbley". Our Choir Master, Gerald Kieron, used to get so mad at me for giggling.

More laughter, no resolution.

I've Got The Music in Me

Growing up, I was fortunate to have a wonderful piano teacher, Mrs. Foley. We were too poor to pay full-price for lessons, but she settled for a very small amount of money. I delivered the morning paper for about four shillings a week, and I used that to pay for the lessons. She kindly donated much of the sheet music and instruction manuals to enable me to study for the Victoria School of Music examinations, which I ultimately achieved and became a Licentiate of just before my fourteenth birthday in 1943.

On the day I took my final exam I nervously entered the examination room at Central Hall on Renshaw Street in Liverpool, and promptly fell down the two steps in the entry way. I dropped my examination card, fished it out from underneath the piano, covered in dust, but still managed to perform successfully to qualify for my teaching certificate.

I thought I was hot shit that day due in no small effort to dear Mrs. Foley. I still hold those certificates with great pride. Like me, they've been around the world.

I tried to make a few bob by giving piano lessons to one or two locals, but realised I didn't have the patience for it. I frequently had an overwhelming desire to slam the piano lid down on their little knuckles. One of my pupils was my friend Freddy Walsh, and I quickly concluded that my attitude was: "Well, if I can do it, why can't he!" So my potential career as a music teacher came to an abrupt halt quick smart.

World War II

One of my wartime experiences makes an interesting recollection. In September 1939, my brother Bob, who was in the Territorial Army (the equivalent of the US Army Reserve), was called upon to don his uniform and report to a centre in a nearby school. We all waved him off on the number 14 tram from outside St. Teresa's School, and watched the anti-aircraft protection balloons (barrage balloons), appearing in the sky. These were supposed to prevent enemy planes getting close enough to drop bombs. Nice try. Didn't work.

Shortly after, our school, St. Teresa's, on Utting Avenue East, was commandeered by the government to house folks who had lost their homes to Hitler's bombs, and anyone who had a spare bed was also forced to take in munitions workers who were drafted in from other parts of the country to work in the factories whose employees had gone off to war.

My Mum took in two lodgers, Mr. Polly, and George Butler. Mr. Polly would toddle off to the Dog & Gun pub every night, as would George, irrespective of air raid warnings. Mum would be ensconced in our little Anderson air raid shelter in the back garden of 3 Carr Lane, along with my two sisters and I. Mae would fill up a big square Smith's Crisps tin every afternoon with whatever food she could muster: jam sandwiches, her wonderful scones, (I still have the recipe), and any other titbits that were left in our meagre kitchen. Empty lemonade bottles were filled with tap water for our nightly sojourn.

When I look back, I don't think the Anderson shelters would have helped much had a bomb dropped near them. Made from six curved sheets bolted together at the top, with steel plates at either end, and measuring 6ft 6in by 4ft 6in, the shelter could accommodate six people. These shelters were half buried in the ground with earth heaped on top. The entrance was protected by a steel shield and an earthen blast wall.

Anderson shelters were given free to poor people with a valid ID card. (I guess we were officially poor). Men who earned more than £5 a week could buy one for £7. Soon after the outbreak of World War II, over two million families had shelters in their garden. By the time of the Blitz this had risen to two and a quarter million.

They were installed by young soldiers, and had wooden slatted bunk beds around three sides, and a somewhat rickety door on the fourth side. The floor was just the dirt of the actual ground where they had dug down to put us partly below ground. Then soil was piled up on top of them for extra protection. Some folks were lucky enough to also have sandbags on top. We didn't. We had matches and candles to light our way. Not posh enough to own torches (flashlights) in those days. I shudder to think what a fire hazard that was. Never mind the bombs.

We would do crossword puzzles, spelling bees, play word games etc., and I always attribute that to my early desire to be a published writer. That only took me eighty-two years!

One night, George Butler came back from the pub about 10.30 p.m. and banged on the air raid shelter door. Mum opened it gingerly, and there he stood, swaying, obviously more than happy after his nightly trip, with a bottle of sherry in his hand, saying: "Here you are Mum, by Christ, them buggers is moving tonight, if they had come any closer they would have singed me bloody moustache orf!!" Mum, fearing that we would soon hear "put that light out" from the Air Raid Wardens who constantly patrolled the streets, tried to grab George's arm to get him into the shelter, and as we all looked upwards, there in the beam of the searchlights we saw a huge parachute, with what looked like a big metal drum swinging underneath it, swaying towards us. Then, miraculously, a gust of wind came and blew it a few hundred yards away, where it made a direct hit on Dr. McAlpine's house at the bottom of Utting Avenue East, and when we walked down there the next day, all that remained was a smoking crater and piles of rubble. That's something I still have nightmares about.

On the other side, I was delighted that we could no longer go to school, and were only needed to assemble for a half a day each week for roll call, or "The Register" as it was called.

There was precious little formal schooling after that until we officially left school at the age of fourteen. And for me, that was it. I reckon I am becoming more and more educated by the day with all the stuff that I can research on the Internet. Google is my friend.

Brazilian Breathing Treatment

When I was about twelve, I began exchanging letters with a Brazilian pen pal I found in a magazine. Her name was Marie Alice Mencarini and she lived in São Paulo, Brazil's capital.

It seemed very exotic for me to be corresponding with someone so far away. Heaven only knows what drivel I must have written to her, probably about my adventures in the air raid shelters, or some other aspect of my fairly non-eventful life.

However, I remember telling her that I suffered from asthma. She kindly sent me a bottle of something called "Vapo Cresoline", which my Mum used to burn on a shovel of hot coals from the fireplace. It would emit fumes that miraculously cleared my clogged bronchial tubes, and at the same time filled the room with black smoke. I wonder what a danger to the environment it must have caused, not to mention my lungs?

But I will forever remember the kindness of someone whom I had never met. If she ever reads this, she can be assured that she helped me immeasurably. Environment be damned!

Pool Pump

During the war, Mum was forced to take in many lodgers, which meant that I was relegated to sleeping on the couch in the living room at 3 Carr Lane (which we called the kitchen). I was excited to learn that our class at St. Teresa's was going to visit Norris Green Baths near Broadway at the bottom of Utting Avenue East.

Somehow Mum managed to scrape up enough cash to buy me a swimming costume, a delightful affair with black and yellow stripes. I looked like a tubby little bumblebee.

We duly arrived and were ushered into the changing rooms by our teacher, who was going to guide us through basic swimming lessons. When I ventured forth out of the cubicle someone ran up behind me and pushed me into the deep end of the pool, which was frightening at seven feet deep.

I still have nightmares of the experience. I can recall it now as if it played out in slow motion, arms and legs all around me, greenish water, bubbles, my struggles and panic, and surfacing a couple of times. I can't recall who got me out or how. The next thing I remember was lying face down on a tiled floor in an office, with someone pumping at my lungs. A messenger was dispatched to get my Mum, who eventually dressed me in dry clothes and walked me home. She had lit the fire in the grate at home and I laid there trembling and feeling very sorry for myself.

Over the years I have made several attempts at learning to swim, the only successful one being in Brisbane, Australia, when I was visiting family a few years back. That only lasted a few minutes. I would love to be able to swim, but until then, my visits to pools are still restricted to the shallow end.

I'm waiting for my friends the Speakmans – who can conquer all one's fears in a session – to pay a visit when it's warm enough for a dip!

The Dockers Umbrella

During school holidays when I was a wee one, I used to take a penny tramcar from outside St. Teresa's to the Pier Head, then another one on the Overhead Railway, affectionately known as "The Dockers Umbrella".

For a penny you could ride all the way out to Seaforth and Litherland Docks. I would look down in amazement at the ships loading and unloading, the lorries dropping off their goods to be shipped around the world. It all seemed so magical to me then. That's what kick-started my fascination with America. I remember playing with an empty cardboard box in our house at 3 Carr Lane. If I could fit, I'd clamber into the box and sit underneath the kitchen table. If anyone tried to speak to me I'd say, "Ssshh, I'm going to America." It was my private ocean liner. Fantasies abounded and my imagination took over. I never dreamed I would really do it. It took me a good while, and I had to go via King's Lynn, London and Australia, but I finally made it.

My Uncle Frank Pennington, a captain on Cunard ships like *The Empress of Britain*, sometimes docked in Liverpool and I would get so excited to visit him on board. He'd pull out a dresser drawer for me to sit on in his cabin. The Mersey Docks and Harbour Board ran the Port of Liverpool, and its greatest rival was the Manchester Ship Canal. Today they work in tandem. Compared to how primitive the operation was in the early Thirties, it's now a hugely streamlined project, handling millions of tons of cargo yearly. The ill-fated *Titanic* was registered to the Port of Liverpool. Uncle Frank was an artist and would create etchings of ships, foreign ports of call, and places of interest like the Bridge Of Sighs in Venice. I left them all behind with family when I left England.

The actual overhead railway cars were really rickety, and if I close my eyes, I can still conjure up the smell. It was a mixture of tobacco, sweat, stale food, beer, and other unmentionable odours. After World War II, the cruise lines began to operate out of Liverpool, giving it even more cachet.

If I still had a few pennies left, I would then take a trip across the Mersey on *The Royal Iris* or one of the other ferries. I vividly recall the thrill of seeing them pull up the gangplank and set off across the water. It's no wonder that Gerry Marsden's song "Ferry Across The Mersey" has such a special place in the memories of ex-pat Scousers. You can always hear it played on jukeboxes in the British pubs in Santa Monica, California.

Today when I go back, I see a much more streamlined, modernised seaport, still bustling and full of stories... but it will never have more mystery and excitement than it did when I just a little school kid with big dreams and a vivid imagination.

The Colours of My Life

Now here's a strange thing: when my oldest sister Mae was alive and we lived under the same roof in Norris Green in my younger days, every day, without fail, we would emerge from our respective bedrooms and both be dressed in the same colour.

Cut to: grown-up life, living with daughter Ruth, here, there and everywhere. Almost without fail, when we meet up in the mornings, we are always dressed in the same colour.

Don't ask me how it happens, but it does. Even when we are continents apart, she in Germany or Russia, me in America, when we either email or speak on the phone and ask, "What are you wearing?" (Yes, I know... that sounds like an opening for a dirty phone call.)

It's always the same result. Maybe there's just a little trace of 'Witchy Poo' in both of us.

Play The Piano Angela

Not being as self- confident then as I am now, I would cringe when my Mum would say, "Play the piano Angela" every time we had visitors.

She was of course very proud of my achievements, having delivered newspapers to make about four shillings a week to pay for my piano lessons with the very patient Mrs. Foley, who was more than generous to me, both with her time and financial support.

My first big achievement was in learning to play The Warsaw Concerto, from the film *Dangerous Moonlight*, which I learned later was also an inspiration to Sir George Martin, who couldn't read music at that stage, but who taught it to himself by just listening to it over and over on a record. However, I practised it so long and at all hours of the day and night that it became known as "The Bloody Warsaw Concerto" in our house, Mum, Joan and Mae were so fed up listening to it.

Then, I wanted to tackle Grieg's Piano Concerto in A Minor. However, during wartime, sheet music was extremely hard to find, and finally, in desperation I wrote to one of my musical heroes, Eileen Joyce, the concert pianist, having gone to great lengths to find an address in London. I asked for her advice as to where I might buy a copy. To my delight and surprise, she sent me a copy in the mail, which I treasured, and which became extremely dog-eared over the years as I laboriously thumped my way through it, until I had mastered the entire thing.

My other party pieces were Beethoven's Moonlight Sonata and "Für Elise" (which I called furry knees). Hence my Mother's gut-busting pride at her asthmatic, wheezy little fourteen year old, and wanting to put me on parade. At that stage in my life, I could think of nothing worse.

Another oddball thing I once did was play the piano in a shop window for a week. It was National Piano Week at a piano store on Bold Street, and like a silly sod, I would dress up in an evening gown (courtesy of sister Joan) and play all manner of stuff on a revolving plinth, while bemused passers-by pressed their noses to the window, and muttered rude comments. I don't think many of them dashed in and bought a piano. Oh, and I lost the lovely white lace dress, which Joan has never forgiven me for. I guess I must have left it in the changing room when I finished the project. I thought I was a star, and earned a few shillings a week for making a complete prat out of myself in public. It was especially exciting when the cops came as the crowds were spilling out from the pavement into the roadway, making it a danger to motorists. It was my moment of fame and I loved it.

My confidence was boosted a little when I worked at Littlewoods Pools, where they had Concert Parties in each of their branches, and I hooked up with a man called Tom Coward. We eventually became a double act called – what else – "Tom and Angela", and we would play to captive audiences in the canteens of the various branches. We even spread our wings and would play at old peoples' homes (poor things) and hospitals occasionally. We weren't so much *X Factor* as "*Why*" Factor. But it was all good fun, and we even got our photos in Littlewoods' magazine which made us feel like broken down variety artists. It's a good thing we weren't miked up, as we used to tell one another dirty jokes to pass the time!

Aunty Emily

My Dad's family, the Stopforths, adopted Emily Parsonage, who ultimately became Mrs. McClarty. She and her sister Mae were choral singers in the Liverpool Philharmonic Society. It seemed that everyone was musical in those days. My father was a pianist, and my mother a choral singer also.

Emily had the appearance and demeanour of Queen Mary, the rather severe-looking wife of King George. She had a booming voice, always wore lots of furs (imitation), jewels (fake), and used a lorgnette. She would carry either an ornate umbrella or walking cane, which she didn't hesitate to use to prod unsuspecting shop assistants or delivery boys if they incurred her wrath.

During World War II, when meat was rationed, she was standing in a queue at a London butcher's store when she heard a woman at the front saying, "Could you put it on my account please, I'm Mrs. McClarty." At this, Emily couldn't contain herself: here was the strumpet her husband had run off with. She yelled out, "No, you are not Mrs. McClarty. You are the slut who is living with my husband!" Yes, always a crowd pleaser was Aunty Emily.

Mum used to visit her in London, which resulted in some hilarious stories. On one occasion they went to the Savoy hotel for afternoon tea. When Aunty Emily saw the prices, she decided on a visit to the ladies room whereupon she proceeded to take down the gold velvet curtains and stuff them into her voluminous handbag. When Mum protested, she said, "Damn them to hell! If we have to pay seven shillings and sixpence for their paltry afternoon tea, I am taking something home with me."

Then they went to the cinema. When a man sitting behind her protested about her large hat, she boomed at him, "Sir, if I take this hat off, my bloody hair comes with it. Now sit down, be quiet, and let's enjoy the film."

No doubt the manager didn't have the nerve to ask her to leave.

She came to visit us in Liverpool and wanted to have her hair done. My sister Mae took her over to Scargreen Avenue, our local shopping centre, where she intimidated the hairdresser who dared to ask her: "Madam, is this your natural colour or have you had it tinted?" "My good woman," she replied, "I have had my hair every colour but heliotrope, and I *hate* heliotrope." Exit one gibbering hairdresser for a lie down in the back room.

When she was in Liverpool she went shopping with me and my then-fiancé, Eddie Williams. We were in one of Liverpool's classiest stores, Bon Marché. Emily picked up a handbag and asked the assistant, "How much is this?" The answer came back: "Three pounds twelve shillings and sixpence, Madam." "Bloody ridiculous!" shouted Emily, throwing it back across the counter. "This rubbish would only be fifteen shillings in Selfridges." Eddie and I tried to sink into the carpet.

There was a Royal Wedding taking place in London, the marriage of the Princess Royal at Westminster Abbey. Aunty Em decided she wanted some of that action, so she dressed in some of her finest stage clothes and fake jewellery, feathery toque hat, silver lorgnette around her neck, and silver beaded bag, got herself into a taxi and set off for the Abbey. When the driver reached the farthest point he was permitted to access, she regally exited the cab and said to the nearest policeman, "Excuse me my good man, I am Lady Inverclyde, my husband has already arrived. Can you please escort me to my position in the Abbey." He was, of course, utterly bamboozled by her majestic presence, and called out to the nearest usher. "Lady Inverclyde" who in turn, down the line called out, "Lady Inverclyde" which was echoed all the way across the red carpet and up the steps to the Abbey, where she was finally ushered in. She plonked herself down in the first empty pew she saw.

She didn't have the courage to try to crash the reception, and did the same thing in reverse, getting herself a taxi back to her little one room flat across town.

Truly, a regal lady who had known better times, but lived with dignity and panache to the end.

Young Life: 1945 to 1964

When World War II ended, we all felt there was a new beginning, although we still had to clear up the mess, the rubble from the air raids. At fifteen years old I had my first real job, at The Automatic Telephone Company, along with my sister Joan, and then on to the Royal Court Theatre, which I loved. Having access to shows, rehearsals, music, ballet etc. I had the time of my life.

We listened to the big American Bands on the radio like Les Brown, saw movies with fun people like The Andrews Sisters, went jiving and jitterbugging at the local ballrooms, I began my foray into the secretarial world of shorthand, typing, book-keeping, and all the fun stuff which I still practise today. I had a variety of jobs, and became a fan of Frank Sinatra.

How we all swooned to this dear, hungry looking young man and wanted to mother him. We were beginning to get to see American movies in England and aspired to live the exciting life of the housewives of the United States with their incredible kitchen gadgets, tea in little mesh bags, vending machines, poodle skirts, cars with the top down, drive-ins, and a million things we English dreamed of but never thought we would achieve. We got to watch movies from America like *The Bells of St. Mary's*, *Mildred Pierce*, *Spellbound* and *The Lost Weekend*.

They played the National Anthem before the start of movies in the cinema. Everyone stood to attention and sang along very respectfully.

I met and married my first husband, Eddie Williams, who was a fireman in the railways, gave birth to my darling daughter, became a widow for the first time, struggled, survived, became stronger, (hello?) met Jim McCartney who would change our lives, and moved in to the crazy world known as Beatlemania.

My Brother Bob

My brother Bob was my personal hero. When he was away during his military service in World War II, I'd write him regularly with what I considered was riveting news from home. He would dutifully respond but would often mark my letters with a red pen or pencil. He took it upon himself to correct spelling, syntax or grammatical errors, and went so far as grading them.

"Six out of ten," or "Could do better," or "Needs improvement," he'd write.

I was mortified. *I sweahr to this day that it made me an eggcellent prewfreader and spellor extraordinairy.*

Of the odd things that live in this weird mind of mine, I still remember his Military ID number in The Royal Corps of Signals: 2578142! How's that for a useless piece of trivia.

Recollections of the Royal Court Theatre from a Commoner

I worked in the box office of the Royal Court Theatre from early 1943 to late 1945. At the time it was owned by Howard & Wyndham Ltd, a respected theatre management company.

We would open the windows to the public sharp at 10 a.m. and take up our positions. Sooner or later, somebody would come up to the window and ask, "Have you got any tickets?" Of course we had flaming tickets. Whoever got the simpleton would lean back to fellow workers and say, "Got one." It was almost a guarantee that everyday someone would ask this stupid question. The silly question was usually followed by an equally silly request. "I need centre gangway seats...my sister/aunt/granny has a bad leg." If we asked them which leg it was, they were usually flummoxed.

The job also required a good amount of mind-reading on our parts. Which production they wanted to see sometimes took a little detective work given the ridiculous clues. "Oh, the one with that girl in that was in that thing with wotisname. You know, where she fell in love with a married man." Or, "Oh, you know, the one that has the cat and dog in it...." It was like pulling teeth some days.

Then there was the memorable occasion when we were completely sold out, although we used to mark the seating plans with red lines to keep the best seats reserved for last minute VIPs. Just before curtain up we were permitted to sell them to the plebs.

On one occasion, a man asked, "If Prince Philip wanted to see the show, would you have a seat for him?" "Of course," I replied. "Well, he's not coming, so can I have his seat?" Some of the customers were sharper than others.

Mr. Mason was the manager, and to me, he seemed to live upstairs in an ivory tower. The box office clerks rarely saw him, but he was always resplendent in evening dress each night in the auditorium. I remember a lovely young lady called Kay Swords, a raven-haired beauty worked there, whom I admired tremendously.

I answered the phone one day to a lady who imperiously asked for two box seats for that night. We were sold out, but that didn't dissuade her. "But this is Mrs. Topham of Aintree Race Course, you *must* have seats for me." After going around once more, she demanded to be connected to Mr. Mason. But not before doling out a parting shot. "What is your name? I will report you." Ah, the customer is always right (sometimes).

On May 8, 1945, the night World War II ended (VE night), my friend, Rita Harrison and I had planned to go over to the Liverpool Empire to see Frankie Laine. However, when we heard the news about the war, and the fact that Noel Coward was planning a party on stage after the show, we gave away our tickets.

Next thing I knew, I was being summoned to Noel Coward's dressing room. He was starring in his own show, *Sigh No More* with Graham Payne and wife Madge Elliott. It also starred Cyril Richard and Joyce Grenfell. I entered the great man's dressing room with trepidation. He motioned me to sit down. I could almost hear my knees knocking. He asked me my name, and promptly wrote a little note to my Mum, asking if I might be allowed to stay for the festivities. He sealed it up in a big square white envelope, together with a big white five-pound note, for me to take a taxi home at the end of the proceedings.

I jumped on the first tram available, went home to my Mum, proudly bearing the note (and the moulah!). Of course, she gladly said yes. Bear in mind I was only fifteen years old at the time, and this was quite something.

Upon reflection, I often wondered how they pulled a party together so quickly, but after the final curtain, the stagehands and other staff jumped to action. They put up trestle tables, set them out with food and drinks galore (I think they may have got them from the Adelphi hotel where Mr. Coward was staying). The orchestra got up on stage with their instruments, and it was, as far as I recall, a rocking party.

When I was working there, during my break time, I would sometimes sneak into the auditorium during matinees to watch the shows. I remember Sir Michael Redgrave in Oscar Wilde's "The Importance of Being Earnest". There was a whining, whimpering child in the orchestra stalls, and after putting up with it for a few minutes, Sir Michael went to footlights and peered over. "Madame, either that child goes, or I do," he said. There was a shuffling sound, and the embarrassed mother and her baby got up and left. After which, he returned to his position mid-stage and said to his startled fellow performers: "Let's take it from the line where I say…"

It was quite an afternoon.

If we had a fair amount of empty seats, we were allowed to call Broadgreen Hospital so that the nurses could bring in some of the World War II vets from their burns unit. It was heart-breaking to see these brave young men with horrendous burns, still happy to turn out for a couple of hours of entertainment. One of them was so grateful that he sent me a box of biscuits (cookies to the Americans!) as a thank you. I was so touched.

We often worked late into the evening. After closing, we wrote up our daily reports and balanced our cash. No credit cards in those days. The rats would run along the overhead hot water pipes, and it was funny to see them, jumping and even trying to lick their paws as the heat struck them. We would throw books of tickets up in the air to scare them away. They would scamper off through the spaces above into heaven only knows where.

In later years, our dear friends Reflections, a singing and dancing group, were appearing with Ken Dodd in pantomime. We spent several hilarious nights watching the show. At the wrap party we witnessed boxes and boxes of Crawfords (or was it Jacobs?) four-pound biscuit (cookie) tins lined up in Doddy's dressing room. They were a gift from the manufacturers for a show he and the Diddy Men had done for the staff and their families.

I often regret that I didn't take as many pictures as I would have liked, for the Royal Court Theatre will always have a very special place in my heart. It has been restored to its former glory in 2012 and I can't wait for my next visit to Liverpool to see it.

Happy memories indeed.

Mount Pleasant, Liverpool

I worked for a time at Conlon & Sons in Mount Pleasant, Liverpool. This group of opticians was the family business that had belonged to my Mum's family. When her father, Bernard Conlon, died, the Will was never found, so the business then automatically belonged to his oldest son, William.

My Uncle Willy, as we called him, was to me the epitome of success and wealth. They lived in Heswall, on the Wirral, and had a swinging couch on the lawn! He would stay at the Adelphi hotel in the City all week and go home at weekends.

After he passed away, he left the business to his daughters, Wyn and Marjorie, and my cousin Wyn ran the business.

She was kind enough to give me a job, where I did the menial junior stuff, taking care of the showcases of spectacle frames and lorgnettes (wish I had one of those now!) in the glass fronted showcases and windows at 22 Mount Pleasant.

I did the filing, answered the phone, and took pairs of glasses to the specialists who had prescribed them when they were returned to Conlon's by the manufacturers to be verified. This entailed hoofing it by foot up the hill every day to Rodney Street. I was about fourteen and terribly impressed with all the majestic houses that I visited with my precious cargo.

I also noticed an imposing building on Rodney Street called Pitman's Training College, and ventured in for a brochure.

This began my quest to become the killer secretary, which I still aspire to be. I managed to finagle a few bob to pay for classes to begin learning Pitman's shorthand, typing, and the bare bones of basic double entry bookkeeping. This would keep me in good stead over the coming years. To this day I think in shorthand often when I am watching the news or listening to the radio.

On my lunch hour I would pop next door to the sweets and tobacconist shop run by Muriel and Edward Hagen. They lived in Childwall, which was very posh by my standards. Muriel would occasionally have me hold the fort in the shop when she and Edward had to go shopping, or to trade-related events. I met a wonderful variety of people there, including my first prostitute. I was shocked and amazed when this girl told me what she did for a living. I realised that she was a poor, lost soul, trying to make a few bob to support her young illegitimate child. It opened my eyes to a broader world after the somewhat sheltered life I had led up to then.

The Hagens also broadened my outlook socially, and took me to functions relating to the catering trade, where I met lots of very grown up people who impressed the heck out of me.

Edward was Polish and had been stationed in Blackpool in the North of England during World War II. He was a very warm man who possessed a teddy-bearish quality, and became like a father to me. There always seemed to be an air of mystery about him. I can remember a night when he knocked on the door of 3 Carr Lane and said he needed to visit a house just up the road, where there was something buried in the garden, which he needed to retrieve. Never did get to the bottom of that one.

I remember going to their house in Childwall on my eighteenth birthday for a little celebration tea party. It was a Sunday, and on the bus back home, the conductor told the passengers that the Queen had just given birth to a son, Prince Charles. That was on November, 14, 1948. It was quite an exciting time.

Muriel and Edward mixed with a lot of Polish ex-airmen. I dated one for a time, Kazmish Zharlikovski, who had a great sadness in his life. He had witnessed his wife being taken into the gas chambers in a concentration camp in Poland.

He was an ice skater. I used to go to the Liverpool Ice Rink to watch him play ice hockey and we used to go to the pictures together. A very nice, gentle young man, but with an air of resignation about life.

Next door to Muriel and Edward's shop was an advertising agency owned by Arthur Maiden. I became friends with some of the boys there. I particularly remember Cyril Cross, who was a devoted friend. I told him one day that I was going on a date that night at the Grafton Rooms with a local hottie and had forgotten to bring my dance shoes. Bugger me if he didn't take the tram up to 3 Carr Lane and ask my sister Mae for my shoes. She was a bit confused as she thought I was going out with someone other than him, but he duly turned up back at Conlon & Sons before we closed with my dance shoes. What a gentleman! They don't make them like that anymore.

There was another young man there who was way out of my league, but I had a terrible crush on him. When I found out he was a devotee of Oscar Wilde, I too became a fan of the controversial writer. In fact, I sometimes quote him: "We each finish up with the face we deserve." How true that has proven to be.

Spike Milligan

As a youngster, listening to *The Goon Show* on the radio in England, I became a fan of Spike Milligan, and loved his characters, such as Bluebottle, Eccles, Minnie Bannister and Count Jim Moriarty. In those pre-television days, we were subjected to a wonderful variety of characters and could personally envision our own private idea of what these people looked like. My favourite was Eccles.

I took the plunge and wrote a fan letter, my first, to the BBC, never really thinking I would get a reply. But after a few weeks, I received a sepia picture postcard picture of Spike, standing in front of a very shabby looking curtain at a microphone, in a suit and brown checked carpet slippers.

On the back he had written: "To Angela, with all my love, Spike Milligan. Get undressed with the light on, I have my telescope trained on Liverpool."

Aunt Annie's Wooden Leg

In my mid-teens my Mum was helping to nurse Aunt Annie in Birkdale, together with her sister, my Aunty Hylda, who was Aunt Annie's housekeeper.

After Aunt Annie's eventual demise, it fell to Mum and Aunty Hylda to carry out the formalities. This included laying her out in preparation for the undertaker. Aunt Annie had a wooden half-leg, which they removed and placed on top of a dresser in the room where she lay.

After the formalities were concluded and the body was dispatched to the mortuary, I decided to purloin Aunt Annie's wooden leg and take it home. Not sure why, but it seemed too good an opportunity to miss.

This object became a running gag (pardon the pun). My sister Mae sent it to my friend, Freddy Walsh, who was in the Air Force in Kasfareet in the Middle East. He in turn mailed it back to me on my twenty-first birthday, which I excitedly opened at the café where I daily took my lunch in Clayton Square, Liverpool when I worked at Littlewoods. It subsequently traversed the world, being sent from family member to family member. My only sadness now is that I don't remember where it finished up. Maybe the Smithsonian? I think I'll try to Google "Aunt Annie's wooden leg". Or maybe a search on eBay would turn it up?

Either way, I deserve a good kick in the arse!

The Last Waltz

Ballroom dancing was one of my passions growing up. One night while staying in Birkdale, in the era of the famous Aunt Annie, I was dancing at the Floral Hall in Southport, when this gorgeous hunk asked me for the last waltz.

As we danced, I felt a "ping" which was the elastic in my knickers going south, and much to my dismay, felt the garment slipping down my legs. Fortunately the dance floor was packed, making movement minimal. So when the offending kecks landed around my ankles, I managed to step out of them, leaving them on the dance floor for some bewildered cleaning lady to no doubt find the next day.

It was my best move of the night!

Bewitched, Bothered and Bewildered

In my early twenties I went to the Liverpool Empire with my fiancé, Eddie Williams, and among the acts on the variety bill was a hypnotist.

When he asked for volunteers I decided to step up. I was the only girl in a group of six.

I had always been curious about hypnotism and was not afraid to give it a try. After all, I figured that as this demonstration was in public, he wasn't going to do anything harmful. Much to my consternation, it took no time at all to put me under.

Once the hypnotist had me fully under his spell, he ordered a couple of the boys to lift me up by the ankles and suspend me between two wooden chairs. The space below my shoulders and body was totally unsupported.

Then, I am told, he asked the same two boys to stand on my stomach, which remained completely rigid. I'd like to see them try it now, it would be like rowing on a sea of jello.

During his spiel he gave the command that whenever we heard the song "Bewitched, Bothered and Bewildered" at the Empire Theatre, we would go to sleep. Because we were under his spell, we were all unaware of this caveat. After a short spell, he brought us all back to consciousness, thanked us, and we returned to our seats.

At the intermission, Eddie and I went to the bar for a drink. As we were returning to our seats for the second half of the show, the pit orchestra stuck up "Bewitched". All I remember was an overwhelming desire to go to sleep. In fact, I sat down on the stairs leading to the auditorium, and the usherette had great difficulty in wakening me. This evidently happened to all of the folks who had taken part in the demonstration. The house lights went up, he came back on stage, and said whatever command was necessary to bring us all back to consciousness. Eddie led me back to my seat, and we continued watching the show.

The hypnotist's command seemed to extend beyond the reach of the Empire Theatre. I remember after the show, a very worried tram conductor shaking me at the Terminus at Lower House Lane. It seemed I had gone to sleep again. The tram was going back down the same route and dropped me off my regular stop but I felt pretty weird.

The next day I went to work at Littlewoods Pools on Walton Hall Avenue, and halfway through the morning, my colleagues found me fast asleep at my desk. Somebody telephoned the Empire Theatre, and the hypnotist said that if I would come back right away he would help me get out of this state. I made the trek back to the theatre's dressing room where the hypnotist explained that he was going to put me out, then bring me back. The idea scared me but I didn't really have any option but to comply.

I eventually went back to work and was okay. But I didn't want to go the Empire for a long time. I was lured back when a lot of American acts started coming to Liverpool. I saw Frankie Laine, Danny Kaye, Sammy Davis Jr., and Frank Sinatra among others. And fortunately, none of them performed the dreaded song.

Even now when I hear it, I hold my breath. As I am writing this, I am listening to dear Steve Tyrell on iTunes, and he just performed the song but I am still awake. Mind you, nobody would want to go to sleep when Steve's singing!

Frank Sinatra

All my life I've been a huge Frank Sinatra fan, right up until we lost him in 1998.

He was at a low ebb in his career when he appeared at the Liverpool Empire on July 27, 1953, when his marriage to Ava Gardner was rocky. He abruptly left the stage in the middle of singing "Night and Day" and the audience sat in silent shock. The curtain was eventually lowered, the house lights went up, and a voice over the loudspeaker system said: "Ladies and Gentlemen, that concludes this evening's performance."

I had, in my naiveté, imagined that if I waited outside the stage door I might get his autograph. Silly twisted girl, as Peter Sellers might have said on *The Goon Show*!

He was later to appear in Blackpool, so I mailed my treasured autograph book to the theatre there. Can you imagine being so trusting? I had amassed a wonderful collection of autographs in this leather-bound book while working at the Royal Court Theatre. The mere idea that I would drop it in the mail was just crazy. But sure enough, after about a week, back it came with Frank Sinatra's autograph. I was so proud.

The sad thing is I don't really remember when was the last time I had that book. I do remember a decade later sitting with friends and going through it to marvel at some of the ones I had managed to snag. It included the autographs of Johnny Ray, Frankie Laine, Danny Kaye, Sir Michael Redgrave, Noel Coward, Arthur Askey, Ted Ray, Frankie Vaughan, Engelbert Humperdinck, Sammy

Davis Jr., Mary Hopkin, Billy Connolly, Bob Monkhouse, Roy Rogers – who rode in through the front of house at the Empire Theatre on Trigger – and hosts of others. I realise that many of these names won't mean a thing to the younger generation, but they sure meant a lot to me in those times. It would probably fetch a pretty penny in today's auction market.

Perhaps the most valuable item I have is an invitation to Frank Sinatra's memorial service. I keep it safely in a fireproof box, along with my originally signed photograph of Four Lads Who Shook The World.

Way back when The Beatles were first making their mark on the United States, there was an occasion when Brian Epstein told them he had arranged a flight back from Palm Springs to Los Angeles on somebody's private plane. He didn't say whose. They got to the landing strip and were excited at the prospect of a private plane.

They were even more excited when they boarded, buckled up, and prepared for take off. John was sitting across the aisle from Paul, and leaned over and whispered, "Psst, look who I'm sitting next to." It was Sinatra. When the boys had regained some of their composure, Paul evidently said to Old Blue Eyes, "Wow, my stepmother won't believe me when I tell her I've met you." As soon as he had said it, he had that awful realization: "Oh Lord, did I say that out loud?" "Don't worry about it pally, I did exactly the same thing when I first met John Wayne," Sinatra said with a smile. I guess everyone has their heroes.

Eviction with Conviction

When Eddie Williams and I were first married, we lodged with a Mrs. Gray in Anfield, who ran a tight ship. She had a television set and would occasionally invite us into her sitting room to watch one of the two channels available in Britain at the time. Believe it or not, this was a big deal. We would buy her a box of sweets or chocolates, and she would ceremoniously invite us to partake of one (or maybe two if she was in a particularly good mood). She kept them locked in a writing bureau. She would unlock it, offer us a choice from the box, take one for herself, put the box back in the top of the cabinet, lock it, get a duster and polish around the lock in case she had left any fingerprints. By this time, we had usually missed half of the plot of the show we were watching.

I was working at Littlewoods Pools on Walton Hall Avenue at the time and Thursdays were my days off, when Mum and I would usually go into town on a little shopping spree. On every trip I'd buy a little gift for Mrs. Gray, which she happily accepted. That is, until, the one time when I overstepped my bounds.

Mrs. Gray's kitchen taps were very old fashioned and would only trickle water in a straight line into the sink. I bought her a couple of little green rubber add-ons, which I figured would help her to swish water around the sink when rinsing it. She was out when I got home that afternoon, so I opened the package and fitted the little gadgets on to the taps.

When she got home her reaction was not what I had expected. For some reason, she was terribly offended. Mrs. Gray was eerily reminiscent of Joan Crawford in *Mommie Dearest* and instead of ripping out the wire hangers, she was tearing off the sink strips in equally dramatic fashion.

"You can pack your stuff and get out now!" she screamed. Apparently, she had never been so insulted in her life and despite my protests she would not let me get a word in.

When Eddie got home from his job at Concrete Utilities, I shushed him upstairs to the bedroom and explained my predicament. Mrs. Gray had been introduced to us by her son, who worked with my sister Joan. Eddie and I jumped in the car and went to see sister Joan and husband Peter who lived a couple of miles away.

Without hesitation they invited us into their home. We made several trips to their house at 26 Malmesbury Road, and moved in as quickly as we could. Fortunately, as we were living in furnished rooms, we didn't have much stuff other than our clothes, a few pots and pans, bedding and dishes, so it was a fairly easy move.

We would later learn that Mrs. Gray was of the opinion that Eddie was a perfect gentleman, but "She...she is another matter."

Now that's what I call eviction with conviction.

Yates' Wine Lodge

On my Thursdays off, Mum and I would take the 14 tram down to town and rummage around Blackler's store for the latest fashions, then usually go to Yates' Wine Lodge on Great Charlotte Street.

In those days you could get out of your tree for 80 pence – and when I say pence, this was pre-decimal days when there were 240 pence to a pound, so were talking about less than 20p a drink in new money. They served something called a dock of Australian White (affectionately known as Aussie White) for 40 pence, and two of those were enough to put you beyond the limits of pain. The characters in there were always amazing. Some of the old biddies would buy just one drink, then replenish their glass from a mysterious brown paper bag deftly hidden under the table.

There were several Yateses at that time but I fear that they have dwindled. The one in Queen Square now has a really upbeat menu, wine list and even champagne. My, my, now that's progress. It's even called a Wine Bar!

Some years ago one of their branches across town had a visit from a very inebriated but happy Everton supporter. He brought in his donkey, painted in blue and white stripes, in celebration of a football match his team had won that day.

Another time someone tried to get a grand piano in through the doors, amid much support from the customers, until the barman called the "bizzies" (local slang for policemen) to dissuade him.

I remember visiting another one in Norwich when we were on the road. There was a gallery up above where the drunks were sometimes known to hurl down on the crowd below after a little too much Aussie White. You would be standing with a drink in your hand and wondering how it came to be filling up when you were not looking!

You could always be certain of being entertained at good old Yateseys.

Payday Peter

After Eddie and I moved into Malmesbury Road, with Joan and Peter, Thursday nights were boys' night out, payday, and a time for celebration. This made for more than a few hilarious occasions.

Joan would make sure that we were all settled down for the night before her celebratory husband came home from their trip to the wrestling matches at The Stadium. There were a variety of events, such as...

The night he came banging on the front door. Joan opened it to find Peter standing, accompanied by a huge horse with a piece of rope around his neck. "This is my friend," he drunkenly declared. "I found him all by himself in a field on East Lancashire Road." "Take that bloody thing away," yelled Joan, and quickly slammed the door. He and his friend, Frankie Flynn, had trudged all the way to Malmesbury Road with the poor horse, only to have to take it back from whence it came.

Peter had tried the back door into the kitchen after a drunken night out on the town. He finally put his shoulder to burst it wide open. He flew in across the washing machine, which was on wheels, and promptly made a swift progress across the kitchen into the hall, breaking dishes and rattling pans as he went.

On another of the famed Thursdays, Joan had locked all the doors, front and back, knowing what to expect after the boys had had a night out at The Stadium watching Jackie Pye wrestling and stirring them all.

After banging and pleading to be let in, Peter finally climbed into the huge dog kennels, which housed their two red setters, Pal and Ricky. All this while wearing his best new overcoat, which was a sight to behold in the morning.

I quickly learned that Thursdays at Joan and Peter's were about celebration; Fridays were about forgiveness.

Butlins Holiday Camps

I decided on the wild scheme of hiring a motor coach to transport a bunch of us to Butlins Holiday Camp in Pwllheli (jokingly called Peely Weely by the folks who couldn't wrap their tongues around the Welsh pronunciation).

Butlins Holiday Camps were a great idea. Just after the war Canadian-born Billy Butlin bought up old abandoned military camps, slapped a coat of paint on the chalets, and set up an on-site variety of entertainment features, such as ballrooms, kiddies playgrounds, swimming pools, and theatres. The prices were so low, even the peasants (like me) could afford a holiday there. They were more or less a rite of passage for generations of Brits, and are still popular to this day. They are now international and have come a long way since the early days. Naturally, they are much more sophisticated, with various price levels and posh categories like Silver and Gold.

But no matter how much money you throw at it, I'll bet nobody could have more fun than we had in this early days. Our expectations were not very high, and we became devotees in no time, proudly sporting our badges, which you had to display at all times to get in and out of the various events. They allowed day visitors too, but they were not as privileged as we hard-liners.

For the all-in price of £5 a week, you could have three meals a day and take part in any number of activities. They included all sorts of contests – for knobbly knees, Miss Holiday Princess or Tarzan – to talent spotting or kiddies' races. They even had babysitters who would patrol the chalet lines in the evening while the parents were off carousing. I was never sure how that worked as they didn't have a key to the chalets, but just listened outside of the door and then reported to the Tannoy operator their findings, which were then broadcast live to the bars, ballrooms, and theatres.

I polled a bunch of friends and before we knew it there were nineteen of us, all gung ho and ready to go camping. We booked the chalets, paid our deposits, then looked in the classified ads in the *Liverpool Echo* for a coach company.

The appointed meeting place was Broadway, Norris Green, just the other side of the railway bridge. We all duly assembled, with packed lunches and luggage, and off we set with great excitement. The men were all told to bring the mandatory white hankie knotted at four corners for headgear!

All was going great, sing-a-longs in progress, until somewhere around St. Asaph in North Wales the bus shuddered to a stop. The driver, not the sharpest knife in the drawer, got out and asked a few of the male passengers if they had ideas as to why the bus was no longer running. It seemed that the radiator was dry. We waited for ages until a passing motorist ran one of them to the nearest village pub (oh yes... there was a delay in the return, by which time the coach driver was distinctly merry), armed with bottles of water. He topped off the radiator and off we set again.

We eventually arrived, much to the relief of my sister Joan, who had baby Geraldine with her. We must have been mad to embark on such a ridiculous scheme.

My brother-in-law Peter Archer entered the knobbly knees competition and placed third. This was a hilarious event where the contestants rolled up their trouser legs and stood behind a curtain, which covered their top half. There was a serious panel of judges who, aided and abetted by cries from the crowd, held up cards with numbers, much like they do today in the popular TV contests. The winners won beer vouchers.

It was at Butlins on another occasion when I met Liz (Bette) Danher. We shared a chalet when we were both in the finals of the Holiday Lovelies competition. She went on to the London finals, and I did not. During that holiday she met Mike Robbins, the debonair and charming Redcoat whom she was later to marry. The Redcoats were the entertainments staff and the Bluecoats were the catering and administration folks who kept everything running smoothly.

Bette was a cousin to Paul and Mike McCartney, whom I didn't know at that stage. Many years later, how that all changed, and it changed my life forever.

On the day we returned to Merseyside, Bette cried all the way home on the train. She was so in love with Mike. They later married and went back to work at Butlins the following season, Mike once again as a Redcoat and Liz as an announcer on the Tannoy system, which would regularly blurt out messages to the happy campers.

The first morning call went like a little something like this:

Roll out of bed in the morning
With a Great Big Smile and a good good morning
You'll find it's worthwhile
If you roll out of bed with a smile

Do your singing in the Chalet

Just before you start the day
While you're singing in the Chalet
Think of all the fun you're gonna have
The Butlins way...

We gradually lost touch. Bette and Mike moved to the Isle of Wight where they ran a pub. But I'm sure, like me, they never forgot our first adventure at Butlins.

Pillow Talk

My sister Mae spent some time in hospital after problems with ulcers. Her roommate's son used to visit his mother quite often. They were on nodding terms as it were.

Months later she was on the number 14 tram from Carr Lane to Liverpool, when this same young man got on and sat opposite her. She leaned over and introduced herself.

"Hello... I don't think you remember me?" Mae said. When she got a blank look, she tried a different approach. "Er, I don't think you have seen me with my clothes on before." Shock, horror! She tried to salvage the conversation but only ended up in the junkyard. "I mean, I have always been in bed when we have met before."

With that, he jumped up and swiftly left the tram at the next traffic light. She finished out the journey in fits of laughter being observed by the other passengers.

Oh, well. Innuendo is sometimes wasted.

The Birth of Ruth Ann McCartney: February 15 1960

In the late stages of my pregnancy, I had left my permanent job at Pure Chemicals and was working part time, mainly from home, for an Insulation firm on the Kirkby Trading Estate, GB Insulations. I had been having a few blood pressure problems, and my general practitioner figured it would be safest if I was admitted to Walton Hospital early to avoid complications. On the morning I was to be admitted, I trundled my large frame into the office to take care of the payroll before I embarking on my next adventure.

I remember, Ron, the manager in the office, being very nervous every time he heard my chair creek, and was hovering anxiously in case the action started prematurely. But it all turned out OK. That was in the days when people were paid in cash in little brown envelopes with holes in the back so that you could see the contents, even sometimes including pennies!

So then off I trotted with my trusty little brown fibre suitcase, (from a Littlewoods catalogue), and was admitted into a nice two bedded room, with a companion named Nancy, who had a hilarious, typically Liverpool sense of humour, which certainly helped.

The lovely people there tried all the usual things to coax little Ruth to make her appearance, but as that didn't seem to be working, they waved their magic wand (or was it a catheter?) and set me on the road to being induced.

As a formality, they told me that, in the event that I died in childbirth, (charming!), I must complete a form nominating a religion, and a name for the unborn child. I chose Catholic, although by that time I was a somewhat lapsed Catholic. I still had a basic Christian faith in things as I understood them, but was a bit hazy about the specifics. So I chose the name of Ruth, who was at that time a friend of mine, and who I thought might possibly become responsible, at least in part, for my little one if I didn't make it through the upcoming adventures. The Ann part of her name came when she was christened later at St. Teresa's Church on Utting Avenue East in Norris Green. My sister Joan was (and still is) her Godmother and is responsible for her immortal soul. Now *there's* a job description for you!

And so the real adventure began. I believe I was some twenty hours or more in the process of delivering this little person who would become the most important human being in my life. (Ahhh, mustn't get too soppy now). I have a woozy recollection of them finally taking her from me, slapping her (they wouldn't dare do that now), wiping her down (it would take a hosepipe now) and putting her into my arms. I know it sounds crazy, but I can still remember the final moments of her being born, an incredible moment, and her little cry as she blinked her way into the world. I even dream about it sometimes. (She'll probably smite me when she reads this.)

When I had held her for a few minutes, all snuggled up in a variety of blankies, I unwrapped my Ruth and was astonished to see that her legs were like little Michelin Man legs, with lots of folds. I didn't realise at the time that this was an indication that her bones would grow to use up all the folds, and that she would be tall. I am only four feet, eleven and a half inches! I felt that I had to hide this from people, as I thought it was a defect. But it was too late to send her back! She is now five feet nine inches and towers over me with great effect.

Then they took her away from me to the Nursery lined with cots, with a big glass panel so that visitors could see their new-borns through the window before visiting their Mums.

I was trundled off to a waiting area, a passage-way with several other "victims" to await the stitching services of a rather groovy young Dr. Kirkland. We were all left on gurneys with our ankles up in stirrups (not a pretty sight), with a loose sheet over us, in a drafty area which has loads of foot traffic, for hours. I can't imagine how this would go down today, but that was on February 15, 1960, so I know that things have improved drastically since then. And you know, we weren't as germ conscious then as we are now. Why, we even let kids ride bicycles without shin guards, helmets, gum guards and all the paraphernalia that goes with playtime these days. Ahhh... halcyon days of kids with no fear, and just maybe a few scabby knees.

When Eddie came in to visit me that night, he made all the usual clucking sounds. He already knew that he was not the biological father of this little mite, and we had dealt with that in advance. It is to his credit that he was not hostile towards her, but took to her with real affection, and was a good, if stern father. We made the best of our lives. I was not very happy when he would make Ruth stand in the corner if she didn't finish her meals, as I figured that might harm her emotionally. Knowing what we all know now, I figured that, considering her childhood, she has turned out to be a remarkably strong, caring, considerate and compassionate person. I am very proud of my little product.

The day after she was born, Ruth's biological father, Frank Clark, came to see her. He was tearful, loving, and very proud. Then he went to live in Australia! When my room-mate Nancy's husband came to visit her the first night, bearing a bunch of flowers, she grabbed it off him and battered him about the head with it, and let forth a torrent of lovely swear words and accusations about what she had just gone through, and it was all his fault. A fun packed end to a memorable day.

Frank Clark

I first met Frank in North Wales, when my marriage to Eddie Williams was going south. Eddie was involved with someone else and had asked me to move out so that he could move in his new squeeze and her little girl. Not much later he was tragically killed in a car crash in a snowstorm on his way back from a football match in Manchester. Eddie knew that Ruth was not his child and our life together was becoming precarious. He chose not to do anything about it, but fate stepped in and brought his life to an end.

As I mentioned, Frank went to visit his brother Lionel in Australia and stayed for a number of years. I married Jim McCartney, and was later widowed once more. Then I heard from Frank, who was back in the UK and was staying with his sister in Rhyl. We hooked up and decided to go on a trip with his sister and brother-in-law to Majorca. I had never found the nerve to tell Ruth the real truth. I did tell the man she was involved with, however, and he eventually spilled the beans and told Ruth.

During our trip to Majorca with Frank's sister and her husband, I called Ruth on the phone from our holiday hotel. Frank wanted to speak to her. She said to the man in her life, "Frank wants to speak to me." He said, "Frank? Why don't you call him Dad? You know he's your father, don't you." Ruth burst into tears, took the phone, and said softly, "Dad..." He immediately keeled over and had a mild heart attack. Oh boy, do we know how to handle the men in our lives!

He was OK after a trip to a local hospital and a little rest. We eventually made it back safe and sound to Speke Airport (now John Lennon Airport), where Ruth picked us up, and a wonderful reunion was had by all.

She and I headed home to our place, and he went with his folks back to Rhyl. We hooked up a few more times, and on one of the occasions we all went to the Traveller's Rest pub with Bette and Mike Robbins and their clan. But then Frank blew it and began flirting with Bette. I got mad and went home. He went back to Rhyl, then back to Australia, and I never heard from him until after we had been on television in Sydney. He wrote to me via the TV station, and Ruth and I eventually took a bus trip from Sydney to Adelaide to meet with him. We went to the Immigration Department to see if, by marrying him, Ruth and I could stay in Australia, but they would not allow Ruth to stay and said she must go back to England and re-apply. So we took one look at one another and broke into a quick chorus of "On the road again..."

Frank later had two lovely sons, Andrew and David, with his Aussie wife Heather, and they keep in touch with Ruth. In fact, they all met up when Ruth went to Melbourne a few years ago to give a speech at a big advertising convention. They got on wonderfully well. And of course, there's always jolly old Facebook, so the three of them keep in touch regularly.

But as for Frank, Ruth and I becoming one little happy family... some things are just not meant to be.

Bessie Braddock, MP

There was a famous Labour Party Member of Parliament who hailed from Liverpool. Her name was Bessie Braddock. She was a champion of the poor people and would fight tooth and nail to protect their rights.

When Eddie died in 1962, I was about to be evicted from the house at 3 Spinney Close on the Kirkby Trading Estate, which belonged to his employers, Concrete Utilities.

After I had trudged all over trying to find a place to rent (by my last count, it was forty-six places in all), unbeknown to me, my Mum wrote to Mrs. Braddock and told her of my plight. She even told Mrs. Braddock that I did not in fact support the Labour Party; nevertheless, this didn't deter her from helping me. She wrote back to Mum saying that if I would like to present her letter to the Liverpool Corporation Housing Department, she would see to it that I was suitably housed.

This I duly did, along with little Ruth, and we were eventually ushered into a little cubicle where the man who handed me a key to 1 Quernmore Walk, Kirkby, a one bedroomed flat. Before he did so he actually leaned over the desk and tried to kiss me. I was so terrified of losing the opportunity of a new place to live that I didn't smack him in the gob, but just backed out of the cubicle as fast as I could. His last words were, "I will be coming to see you..."

As soon as I moved in I had my brother-in-law, Peter Archer, change the locks. For the first several weeks, I lived in mortal terror that this creep was going to turn up and put the moves on me.

Women sure didn't have as much standing in the community in those days but Bessie Braddock stood up and stood tall for a lot of us. Liverpool has erected a statue to her memory: she was a true champion of the underprivileged.

Mind Over Matter

A few days before Eddie Williams died in February 1962, Ruth and I were shopping at Littlewoods store in Liverpool city centre.

She was just a toddler, and as we approached the escalator, I lifted her onto it, then stepped on to the next step myself. Just as it was opening up, she lost her balance, slipped and fell backwards. I did the same. I had long hair in a ponytail, and was wearing a hand-knitted dress. Ruth landed flat on her back on top of me, and I got my ponytail and my dress caught in the metal stairs as they were opening up.

There was a degree of panic from people around about, and someone had the presence of mind to press the emergency button to stop the escalator. Little Ruth was crying, people were yelling and screaming, and someone lifted me up and carried me into an office. An employee dispatched a doctor to attend to me. I was pretty badly cut up. Fortunately, apart from the shock, Ruth didn't seem to have sustained any injuries.

They called Eddie at work at Concrete Utilities and suggested he go right home, and they sent me home with a driver. That night I was in a really bad state. Eddie took me to our doctor's office, and Dr. Levy cleaned the wounds and bound me up in three places on my right side. This was on a Friday. The following Monday was the night that Eddie was killed.

Although I had been crawling around in pain all weekend, I can honestly say I don't remember what happened to my wounds after Eddie's death. I don't recall when I took off the bandages, and when I thought about it days later, after the funeral, on examining myself, I couldn't find any trace of a scar or a scratch. That was positive proof to me of mind over matter. As it turned out, I had much bigger things on my mind.

Andy Pandy's Dandy Shoes

When Ruth was a tot while living on the Kirkby Trading Estate, she loved watching *Andy Pandy* on British telly.

She was absolutely besotted with the little character. One day I bought her a pair of blue Andy Pandy shoes in a Woolworths store for five shillings, which was a bit of an extravagance in those days. My heart bled for the dear little thing, who was so serious and quiet in those days. My, what a difference a decade can make.

Anyway, she would ritually don the shoes to watch the TV show. When the end credits played the voice over music would announce: "Andy is saying good-bye, good-bye, good-bye ..." Ruth would start to sob and plead, "Don't go, Andy Pandy."

Aahhh, tear out my heart will ya?

When the shoes finally bit the dust and fell to pieces (what did you expect for five bob?) and I threw them in the bin. Ruth was mortified. She looked up at me with those big brown eyes that expressed in so many words, "You don't love me any more?"

To this day, I comb eBay and all sorts of other places to try to find a pair in a costume shop or similar.

She is in her fifties now but she will still chide me from time to time: "You threw my Andy Pandy shoes away." And a pang of guilt will come over me, but then it washes over very quickly!

Being Widowed for the First Time

Through our attendance at the Kirkby Trading Estate Social Club, where I sometimes played the piano, we met a lot of locals including a few detectives with whom Eddie became very friendly.

After Eddie's sudden death, a couple of these guys were very solicitous and used to pop by to see if little Ruth and I were OK.

On the day that I admitted Ruth to Alder Hey Hospital in May 1964, to have her right kidney removed, one of them was kind enough to drive us there and see us safely installed. Such kindnesses I will never forget.

Another man, who shall be nameless for obvious reasons, phoned me one Friday night, and asked "Are you still up?" "Yes, why?" I replied. "I have something for you. I'll ring your bell in a few minutes."

Moments later he was at my front door in Spinney Close. When I opened it, he stepped inside and went through to the kitchen carrying a big box. He said, "Put these away somewhere safe and don't tell anyone. I have just collared a guy with a van load of stolen property and thought I would find a good home for some of it." In a trice he was gone. Told me to lock up, put the lights out, and not tell anyone I had seen him.

I opened the box, hoping it wasn't livestock. Much to my delight it was about two dozen tins of salmon. I put them in the back of the pantry cupboard which was off the kitchen, and lived off them for months. Thank you dear you-know-who-you-are!

Eddie used to sometimes buy a few bottle of Newcastle Brown Ale. Although I have never really been a beer drinker (except for Oktoberfest in Munich), I rather liked this strange dark brew.

On Friday nights when Eddie would go out with his buddies, I would have one bottle of "Newkie Brown". When it kicked in, I would go through the house like a dose of salts, cleaning, polishing, changing beds, cleaning windows like a mad woman. I don't know what they put in it, but it certainly packed a punch.

After Eddie's death and all the subsequent fuss died down I was pretty low in spirits, and was inclined to let the housework go swinging. I was working full time at Pure Chemicals and my Mum was taking care of two-year-old Ruth.

One day I got a call from my friend, Mavis Golden, who said, "Why don't I come up tonight and stay the night?" I thought this was a great idea and thought we would sit and have a gossipy girls evening. However, when she arrived, she was in old clothes and had rubber gloves in her bag.

"I thought I might help you with the housework," she said. This was a gentle but tactful way of letting me know that I was letting things slide. I appreciated her thoughtfulness and in particular, the way she handled it without lecturing me. It made me pull myself together through a very tough time.

Ruth and God

On the day in late June 1964 that Ruth was discharged from Alder Hey Hospital in Liverpool after having a kidney removed, we visited my Mum on the way home to our little one-bedroom flat on the Kirkby Trading Estate.

I will never forget the day. A few days earlier, when Ruth began awakening from the anaesthetic after her surgery, I was sitting beside the bed, and she opened her eyes, put her little hand up to my face, and began singing "I love you because you understand me." It was a popular Jim Reeves ballad of the time. She sang it from start to finish, then drifted off into semi-consciousness again, whilst the nurses and I were in floods of tears. I swear that, to this day, I can't hear that song without it setting me off again.

She was still very frail, pale, and her hair was coming out by the handful every time I brushed it. But she was very alert and excited to be going home, tightly clutching her beloved Teddy Bear.

As we were about to leave Mum's house, her loving Nanny said to her: "Now don't forget, tonight, when you say your prayers, to thank God for making you better."

She pondered for a few moments, then piped up: "But why Nanny, when I didn't shout at Him when He made me sick."

"Out of the mouths of babes and sucklings hast thou ordained strength." [Psalms 8:2 Bible]

"Out of the unconscious lips of babes and sucklings are we satirised." (Mark Twain)

(Take your pick!)

Mike Robbins

I first met comedian Mike Robbins at Butlins Camp when I was a teen. He was a remarkably talented young man with great charisma and personality. He was just right for that sphere, mixing easily with the happy campers, putting people at their ease and making everyone feel comfortable.

I recall that one night when he had a particularly unruly crowd to entertain in one of the bars. He called out to an audience member, "Madam, please, please, don't smack that dear little child in here. Take him outside and smash his head against the wall." That was in the days when people still had a sense of humour.

During one of his spells between seasons, he took a job as a vacuum cleaner salesman. He once recalled going to a house where the lady said she was really broke, and was harassed with a pile of kids milling around. After some small chit-chat, he went into his usual routine by taking a piece of cardboard, scraping some soot from inside of the chimney, and scattered it on the rug in front of the fireplace. When he asked her where he could plug in the power. She said, "That's what I was trying to tell you. I'm skint and the electricity has been cut off." Oops!

On another occasion, in a house with a few snotty-nosed little toddlers running around, he persuaded the housewife that she would really benefit from buying one of his handy dandy vacuum cleaners. He had plonked his upright leather briefcase on the floor before he began his demonstration. He reached into the case to get the paperwork out only to find that one of the little darlings had already squatted down on it and left him a nice steaming deposit of poop!

"Oh, that's our Dominic, he's always doing that, isn't he hysterical?" the mother said. Au contraire, it was Mike who was nearly hysterical.

Little did I realise then that he would play such a part in my future life. We kept in touch sporadically, and after my first husband Eddie died, I lost track of many of my friends from the past.

Until, that is, he ran into my sister Joan whilst asking for directions to a funeral in Norris Green. This put us back in touch and led to my meeting and marrying Jim McCartney.

After Jim died, Ruth aspired to becoming a dancer. She formed a trio called

Talent with Meta Stewart and Janet Williams, two Wallasey girls that she met through the North West Stage School. Mike was helpful in giving them advice about how to present themselves. One of his mottos was "A good act is like a W. It begins at the top, gradually slows down, lifts a little in the middle, rests gain, and finishes with a bang." It was a good strategy. The girls had met with some local success in clubs and fashion shows. They even did a stint at The Embassy Club in London when we hired a bodyguard for the night just to give their arrival some substance.

Talent had a momentous night at Fagin's Club in Manchester on the night that Elvis died in 1977. They were just about to go on when the Master of Ceremonies got on stage, tapped the mike (like they do), and said "Ladies and gentlemen, before we carry on, I have some terrible news for you – Elvis is dead." Gasps, shock, horror... Then: "And now, ladies and gentlemen, I give you (drum roll) Ruth McCartney and Talent!"

The poor girls saw the curtain rise and a sea of open-mouthed punters sitting in front of them, absolutely stunned. Not their best performance night, as I recall. They got on and off as quickly as they could, then I drove them home to Merseyside, very silently.

I don't know if even Mike Robbins could have offered any showbiz tips on that night.

Beatles, Freemen of the City of Liverpool

After the Beatles conquered the world in 1964, Liverpool's favourite sons were honoured with a special celebration to let them know their hometown was mighty proud of their accomplishments.

The four lads landed at Speke Airport on July 10, 1964, and had their triumphant ride through the streets to the Liverpool Town Hall to receive the Freedom of the City Award. I was in the crowd on Castle Street, looking up at them on the balcony, not knowing I'd be "family" just months later. I had gone there with a young man that I worked with at Pure Chemicals. After the event we walked over to have a drink at the Eagle pub where we met Paul and Michael McCartney's uncle, Bill Mohin, and his lovely wife, Aunty Dil. Dil was to become one of my champions further down the line when I was integrating into the McCartney clan.

The pub was packed to capacity and when closing time came, Bill boomed his famous speech: "I've had your money, now sup up and sod off." He clanged the bell, and then ushered the excited crowds out of the bar.

The Eagle was for a long time a mecca for tourists, and is now a Sony Store.

As I stepped out of the door that night, my life would forever be changed because soon after was when my sister Joan ran into Mike Robbins. Realising she was my sister from the old Butlins days, he got my number. Bette called me, we got together, and she arranged for us to visit her lonely Uncle Jim at his home, Rembrandt. We travelled there together, and as Jim opened the front door to greet us, it was like a flash of lightning. I know it sounds corny, but I immediately thought, "I'm going to marry him." And indeed I did, on November 24, 1964.

Into Beatles World: 1964 to 1976

Meeting Jim McCartney opened the door to a new and exciting life. I was still picking up the threads of life since Ruth had had a kidney removed earlier that year. I was struggling to keep a job and pay our way when the earnings rule was £5 a week. If I earned more than that, I had to go to the Social Security people, declare it, and have my Widow's Pension reduced accordingly.

Then, meeting Jim, and us deciding to make a life together seemed like the dawning of a new day – and indeed it was. He was kind, considerate, patient, and ever "gentleman Jim", taking little Ruth to his heart and legally adopting her, giving her his name, and freeing us from the anxiety of our financially tricky times.

That period in our lives taught us so many things and took us to so many places around the world that we had previously only dreamed of ever visiting. This enabled us to make lasting friendships and experience other cultures, and exposure to the entertainment business. Truly an experience that money couldn't buy.

When Paul and Linda would stay with us, I would take Heather, Mary and Stella to the local Heswall shops. Stella used to beg for "fokkits" which were chocolates, and "peggins" which were gloves or mittens. She obviously had an eye for fashion even in those days. Heather lived for horses and drew me a picture captioned "Horses, horses, where would we be without horses?" Mary used to follow her Mum around when she was taking photographs, looking up intently at what she was doing. That yearning certainly stayed with her through life and she's obviously inherited her Mum's talent in that regard. Young James had not yet made an appearance.

Jim's Birthday, July 1964.

On the eve of Jim's birthday (July 7th), The Beatles were all at a celebratory after party following the Premiere of *A Hard Day's Night* attended by Princess Margaret and Lord Snowdon and Jim said he had the opportunity to be presented to Her Royal Highness, but he lost his bottle at the last minute and turned down the offer as he didn't know what he would say to her.

Just before midnight, Paul presented his Dad with a big square brown paper parcel, and said, "Go on, open it Dad, Happy Birthday." Jim opened it to find a painting of a beautiful brown gelding, a horse to be admired.

"Thank you son," he said, a little bewildered, "it's a very nice picture."

Paul laughed and said "It's not just a picture Dad, I've bought you the bloody horse and it's running at Aintree Races on Saturday." Imagine Jim's shock and delight. He who had loved horses and horse racing all his life, finding himself in the elevated ranks of horse owners. And so he welcomed Drake's Drum into his life. One of the kindest things Paul could ever have done to make his Dad a happy horse owner.

Horsey, Keep Your Tail Up

Early in our marriage, my late husband Jim would often tell me tales of his teenage years when he was a piano player in the pit of the local cinema in Clubmoor, Liverpool.

The cinema held two performances a day (or "houses") as they called them. After the first house, Jim would go around the floor and pick up the programmes that people had discarded. He'd then bicycle home to Scargreen Avenue and iron them with his mother's flat iron, take them back in time for them to be resold for the second house.

He recalled laughingly that as the music was not planned, the pianist was expected to be able to play something that suited the scene. He blanked one time when there was the funeral of the Queen of Sheba up on the screen. The only thing he could think of playing was "Horsey, Keep your Tail Up." It was an old music hall song of the day.

Paul was not the first gifted musician in the family.

The Proposal and Meeting My First Beatle

My first meeting with Paul McCartney was on the night that Jim had proposed to me.

Ruth was tucked up in bed at Rembrandt, the house in Heswall on the Wirral Peninsula that Paul had bought under the advice of his accountants in London for a fraction of the price it's worth today.

It was a modest four-bedroomed house – with incredibly only one bathroom – but in a very nice neighbourhood and certainly more "posh" than I was used to.

Jim and I had sat on the long black "pleather" couch in the lounge room, with its long burgundy velvet curtains, dark green carpet and central fireplace, and we talked for hours about what we wanted to do with the rest of our lives. Mine had been somewhat difficult since Eddie's untimely car-crash death. Jim had also been widowed eight years earlier when he lost his beloved wife, the boys' mother Mary, from breast cancer. He was pretty isolated, living in this lovely but lonely house with views of the River Dee and North Wales. It also had a half-acre back garden where Jim could grow vegetables and flowers, and a greenhouse with vines for making wine. But a house is not a home.

However, the constant trail of fans made it difficult for him to go out of the front of the house, and he relied on his sisters, Milly and Ginnie, to come every Monday to do his laundry, change the beds, cook, and generally look after him, as he had not had the confidence to hire a housekeeper. He had never learned to drive, so daily routines like grocery shopping, visits to the post office etc., and the onset of arthritis hindered him from being as active as he would have liked.

We talked a lot about our lives, our loneliness, our need to take the next steps, and eventually, while I was playing the piano, Jim came behind me, put his hands on my shoulders and said: "I want to ask you something." I looked up at him and said, "The answer's yes," and he laughed and said, "I haven't even asked you the bloody question yet." I guess that was as close to a romantic proposal as I was going to get. So we toddled back over to the couch, and Jim said, "We both know we need to do something, but what would you like to do?

Do you want to be my housekeeper, do you want us to live together, or do you want to get married?" I said I would only want to consider getting married, as I was concerned about little Ruth growing up with a mother who was living with a man that she wasn't married to. I was pretty old fashioned in those days. This sat fine with Jim, who, of course, said he would need to let Paul know, as Paul provided for him with his lovely home, Rembrandt.

But I digress. Back to that evening…the phone rang. It was in a little cubbyhole under the stairs, and I heard Jim say, "Hello son. Yes, she is. Yes, I have. Yes, we are. Just a minute son, I'll put her on the phone." My knees were knocking. Paul was checking up on a) whether I was there, b) if his Dad had asked me to marry him, and c) if we were going to get married.

I'm not sure who was the most nervous on the phone. I said a timid "hello" and he countered with, "Hello, this is Paul" (as if I didn't know). Then he said, to break the ice, "You sound nice," or something equally fatuous. He said he was going to jump in the car and drive up. In 1964 it usually took a good three hours to drive from London to Merseyside. So drive he did and when Jim heard the Aston Martin coming up the noisy gravel driveway, he nipped through the kitchen to open the garage doors so he could drive straight in, douse the lights, and come into the house through the back kitchen. Mind you, by then, it was the wee small hours of the morning when there weren't any fans lurking.

I was washing teacups when he came in, and we exchanged fumbling greetings, and of course, put the kettle on again. We chatted and then he asked me to get Ruth out of bed. She was in her little pink flannelette pyjamas. I sat her on his knee, she was rubbing her eyes, and when the penny dropped, she said, "I know who you are! You're on my cousin's wallpaper." I was mortified. My niece, Geraldine, had a little Wendy house at the bottom of their garden in Malmesbury Road, Norris Green, with Beatles wallpaper. That sure broke the ice! Then Ruth lifted up her pyjama top and showed him her scar where she had had her kidney removed just five months earlier. Paul told her that Ringo had appendix scars too, and in no time, it was like we had all known each other forever. It was a surreal moment in time to watch my four-year old chatting away with a world-famous person as if she somehow knew we all just put our pants on one leg at a time. She's still the same to this day.

Jim and I planned our nuptials promptly, and the next day, Jim sent a car through the Mersey Tunnel for my Mum to come and stay with us as a chaperone for a while. Paul had to get back to London for recording commitments, and while we were finishing his laundry and he was packing his things, my Mum made him some sandwiches – aka butties – (and the ubiquitous flask of tea) for the journey. A couple of hours after he left, he called from a payphone in Brownhills in the West Midlands, in the days before the M6 and the M1 used to actually connect, and asked to speak to my Mum. He thanked her – for the *marzipan* butties! She didn't have her glasses on when she'd whipped them up, and had thought it was cream cheese.

On our wedding day a few weeks later, he sent us a telegram which read: "Wishing you long life and happiness...and lots of marzipan butties."

The Bells were Ringing...

Jim and I were married on November 24, 1964 after taking a taxi from Rembrandt to a little chapel in Carrog, North Wales, where the Reverend Buddy Bevan performed the ceremony.

Jim had phoned ahead and set up the ceremony with Buddy, and we first drove to St. Asaph Cathedral to pick up the licence. On the way we asked the taxi driver if he would be willing to be our best man. He was thrown for a loop. However, when we arrived at The Rectory in Carrog, it was suggested that Grif Jones, the local gravedigger (affectionately known as 'Grif The Grave') be our best man, and Mary Bevan, wife of the rector, be my matron of honour. Grif was dispatched home to clean up, and duly returned in his best Sunday suit. I will always remember his long hands dangling from the sleeves of his navy blue suit.

To my chagrin, no photographs were taken of the ceremony. Buddy's wife Mary served as the organist. As we walked down the aisle, in true Beatle fan style, she played one of their songs, as she was too excited to play something more traditional. We did at least get "The Wedding March" on the way out. Mary was the sister of Mike Robbins, who figured in our lives monumentally.

After the ceremony, we had libations across the road at The Rectory and returned to Rembrandt in the taxi. When we got back to Rembrandt, my Mum (Edie) along with Jim's sisters, Milly, Ginnie and Edie were all ready and waiting, (yes, two Edies for the price of one). Ruth was dolled up in her party frock, which I had bought from the local dress shop the day before, and Bette Robbins, Jim's niece who introduced us, was also there.

They had conjured up a wedding cake and some champagne from The Victoria Hotel in Heswall, just down the road from Rembrandt. After the famous "marzipan" telegram arrived from Paul, we were also touched to receive a nice congratulatory telegram from Beatles manager Brian Epstein, wishing us both a great future together. Where was a scanner when you needed one?

A small celebration ensued and the guests left early in the evening. We put Ruth to bed and sat in the lounge awkwardly finishing off the last of the champagne.

When Jim and I retired to bed it wasn't long before we were aware of lights flashing up at the bedroom window. The back garden at Rembrandt at that time led on to an empty plot of land, and the journalists and fans had got wind of the event. For some reason they were flashing their lights at the house. Fortunately, Ruth was sleeping at the front of the house so she was not aware of the activity. I did then, and for a long time after, try to keep her shielded from the circus that would become Beatlemania.

A *Daily Mail* journalist, whom Jim had dealt with before, got through on the phone and arranged to come by next morning to do an interview. This was all a little bewildering to me and a little exciting, but I had no idea how it would develop as time went on.

I was horrified to find the next day that when the press boys arrived, one of them actually followed me out to the kitchen and tried to hit on me! Today I would have smacked him in the chops and given him a few choice words. At that stage I was so afraid to put a foot wrong that I shrugged it off, loaded up a fresh tray of refreshments and took it through to the lounge.

I found that when it came to all things Beatles, it was wise to keep your best foot forward.

Christmas 1964

It was with great excitement that Jim, Ruth and I travelled by train from Lime Street, Liverpool, to Euston Station in London to spend our first married

Christmas with Paul and the Asher family.

Paul picked us up in his Aston Martin and drove us to our hotel in Russell Square. I remember that as we were cruising along, Paul and his Dad were chatting. We were in a traffic jam as he slowly glided into the car in front of him. He touched the bumper. It wasn't a big collision, but the lady driver jumped out in a great state of wrath and stormed towards the car.

She banged on the window, which Paul slowly lowered. It was amazing to see how quickly her demeanour went from "What the hell?" to "Can I have your autograph, please?" He quickly complied and she tottered back to her car in amazement. As the traffic moved away, she kept looking back over her shoulder. She just couldn't believe her luck, both good and bad.

On Christmas morning Ruth and I took a taxi to Mass while Jim relaxed at the hotel. Whilst we were stopped in traffic, a very inebriated man opened the door of the taxi and staggered inside. Ruth clung to me in fear. The driver immediately got out and slung the guy out onto the street.

When we got to our destination I proffered the driver what I thought was an adequate tip. It evidently was not, as he threw it on the pavement.

"Here lady, you keep it!" he said. "Obviously you need it more than I do." Oops. My first real taste of the big city.

Christmas lunch was being served at the home of Dr. Richard and Margaret Asher, the household where Paul was living at the time. The house was a dream. I had never seen such a massive Christmas tree. The fireplace was roaring, lots of presents were under the tree, and a long table was magnificently laid with crystal glass, beautiful place settings, decorations, Christmas crackers, candles and all. Margaret Asher carried in the turkey, Richard carved it ceremoniously, and all the trimmings were laid on the table. After that we had brandy soaked, lighted Christmas pudding with sixpenny pieces and little trinkets buried inside. It was like a true Dickensian Christmas.

In addition to Dr. and Mrs. Asher and their daughters, Jane and Clare, was their son, Peter, with his musical partner Gordon Waller, who sadly passed away in 2009. At the time Peter was dating a young lady called Betsy Doster, who was the publicist for Sam the Sham, whom I had never heard of at that time. It all seemed very exotic to me.

Ruth's face was a sight to behold. This was like a fairy tale to her. We sang carols, ate, drank, and were merry. They had presents for us all under the tree, and even the wrappings with beautiful paper, golden ribbons and tinkly bells were something to remember. After the meal was over we all traipsed down to the basement to burn the Christmas paper in the boiler. This was to be the place where, on a later date, Dr. Asher was found dead.

Jim had a great affection for Richard Asher, who spent time with him at Rembrandt. They used to go for walks together in Heswall Lower Village, and sit in the back garden and do crossword puzzles. As a memento of his visit, Dr. Asher sent Jim an Oxford English dictionary, which I still have. It was one of Jim's most treasured possessions.

As a sparsely formally educated man (although very gentlemanly and worldly wise), Jim was extremely flattered to have the attention of a man of such great intellect and good standing both in his community and the medical research field.

Jane's father Richard was a physician at the Central Middlesex Hospital. He'd combined clarity of thought, deep understanding of the everyday problems of medicine and possessed a sparkling wit. It was he who gave Munchausen's Syndrome its name in 1951, after the famous baron who travelled widely and told tales that were both dramatic and untrue. In 1947 he was among the earliest to identify the dangers of institutionalisation and too much bed rest.

Her mother Margaret was a professor of the oboe at The London Guildhall School of Music, and taught George Martin to play the instrument. She also taught Paul to play the recorder whilst he was living on the top floor of their house in Wimpole Street.

We were indeed privileged to be so hospitably received in their magnificent home. I remember that as I walked in, thinking I had never seen so many books in my entire life.

On Boxing Day, Paul picked up Ruth from our hotel, and took her to visit Alma Cogan, the very popular musical star, whose name was linked with Brian Epstein at one time. Ruth recalls that it was a like a palace out of a picture book. Alma's apartment was the scene of many parties around that time. I believe she was England's highest paid female singer in the Fifties and Sixties. She played host to such diverse people as Noel Coward, Tommy Steele, Danny Kaye, Princess Margaret, Michael Caine, Roger Moore, Lionel Bart, Bruce Forsyth, Cary Grant, Sammy Davis Jr. and countless other stars.

There was even a little buzz that John Lennon may have had a little something going for a time, which even Cynthia Lennon thought might have been true. It has been said that Paul first played "Yesterday" on Alma's piano. It is written that he told her that it had come to him in a dream. Alma was only thirty-four when she died in 1966.

While all good things must come to an end, London in the Sixties was a magical time, and Ruth and I were privileged to have experienced a taste of it.

The Scaffold

My dear stepson, Mike McGear/McCartney, was a member of the highly successful and oft controversial group called The Scaffold. They performed poetry, satire, music, and everything in between. They reached quite a peak of fame with their ditties "Thank U Very Much" and "Lily The Pink".

Perusing through his book, *Mike McGear's Thank U Very Much: A Family Album*, I was surprised to find that The Scaffold had played at the first marriage of Sir Richard Branson in the very early days of Richard's Virgin enterprises. I reminded Richard of this in a recent email when I was pursuing my bombardment of the various Virgin Airlines to carry my organic teas, and he did remember, of course, and sent his best regards to Mike.

I was always happy when The Scaffold played locally and enjoyed going to see them at places like the Everyman Theatre in Liverpool. I still follow all of their careers and enterprises and they have remained very socially conscious, but always full of humour – an essential ingredient of life on Merseyside.

Roger McGough is now the proud owner of a CBE Award and is a very prominent poet, broadcaster, author, playwright, and voice over artist. I find it hard to believe he is in his seventies! He lives down south but I believe his spiritual home is still Liverpool.

In all the years of being asked for his autograph, Mike has resolutely signed "Mike McGear". He has always been very modest about his musical talents, playing them down in favour of his big brother. Hence the name change. In Liverpool, "gear" translates to smashing, splendid, or great. In a supreme effort not to ride on the coat tails of his brother's fame, he made the distinction of being Mike McGear when his theatrical endeavours began to bring him fame, but not necessarily fortune.

He remains an avid photographer, patron of the arts and all things Merseyside. He is a much-loved figure and still lives in Heswall with his wife Rowena (his first wife Angie is sadly no longer with us) and their brood.

Michael (McGear) McCartney

Mike is one of the gentlest, kindest, most talented people on the planet. Yet, being born as the second son to Mary and Jim McCartney, he has never been fully recognised for his many facets and God-given talents.

When Jim and I decided to get married, at very short notice, Mike was away on tour with The Scaffold. I didn't realise until later that Jim never really put him in the picture as to what was happening. So it must have been an awful shock for him to find he was getting a new stepmother and stepsister, and we would all be living together at Rembrandt. Much to Mike's credit, he never showed his shock, dismay or whatever he was feeling at the time, to me. He arrived home late one Saturday evening with fellow group members, and their then lady manager. The house was crowded with aunts, cousins, my Mum etc., all there to celebrate Jim's engagement and impending nuptials. Mike took it all in his stride, but I would have been horrified if I had known that this was his first knowledge of the plan. I still don't know what transpired between Jim and Mike on the subject of our marriage.

Anyway, a couple of days later, he had to go to on the road again and was not around on our wedding day when we finally tied the knot.

I never quite knew at first what exactly it was that Mike did. One Saturday morning when he was having his first pot of tea with us at the kitchen table, he told us he had met a young lady, also named Angela, the previous night at a local club, and would be bringing her to meet us that afternoon. Angela Fishwick was a local girl and we got on splendidly. Her parents, Edith and Frank, formed a great bond with Jim and I and in no time, the family was just automatically extended. Frank played the piano, as did I, and we had many fantastic raucous evenings at our house, their house, and Frank's golf club in Leasowe.

When Mike and Angie arranged their wedding, it was at the same church where Jim and I tied the knot. Paul and Jane Asher stood for them as Best Man and Maid of Honour. They bought Ruth a pageboy outfit (yes, why would they do anything as conventional as a bridesmaid's dress?) and she attended them, carrying Angie's favourite stuffed toy, Piglet, to be a part of the celebration.

We held the reception at Rembrandt with a cast of thousands including Tony Barrow, the PR man for The Beatles, and lots and lots of colourful celebrities. I recently found a photograph that one of the family took in the back garden, which I have included in this tome.

They moved just a few blocks away to their own dear little place called Sunset, in the Lower Village of Heswall, where Angie proved to be a wonderful cook and homemaker. They had three lovely daughters, Benna, Theran and Abbi, who, through the wonders of the Internet, I can now communicate with across the pond. Angie and I both had accounts at the local grocers, the local wine store and petrol station, which would lead to some amusing mix-ups with deliveries when the locals couldn't fathom out which Angie McCartney was which!

Sadly, their marriage didn't stand the test of time, and they both moved on to other partners, other lives, and other pursuits. But I will always remember those times with Mike as happy ones, his delicious sense of humour and whimsy. I remember Tim Rice (then partnering with Andrew Lloyd Webber) telling me that he thought Mike's talent even surpassed that of Paul's, but of course, with his older brother's monumental success having come first, the world would never learn this fact.

Paul produced an album for Mike called *McGear*, and they enjoyed their collaboration. Paul had also given Mike a camera for his twenty-first birthday, which began his love of photography which has continued on, leading to many successful books, exhibitions and tours right through to this time. Long may he reign!

Angie has left this mortal coil but her spirit lives on through my grandchildren. He is again happily married to a sweet lady, Rowena, and they have three beautiful and talented sons, Josh, Max and Sonny, so the circle of life continues. Ruth and I always call him on his birthday in January and he is finally getting "with it" on the cyber front, so we can follow his activities on his website. He even Tweets now! Clever boy.

Peter Asher

My earliest recollections of Peter (Jane's brother) are of my first Christmas in London, 1964, when we celebrated Christmas Day at the Asher family home on Wimpole Street.

As time went by and we all scattered around the globe, I didn't see Peter again until about 2007 when we became fellow Committee members on various events relating to the California-based Britweek functions, founded by Nigel Lythgoe, and promoted to forge business relationships between the Brits in California and trade at home and abroad.

These events usually take place at the private residence of the British Consul; firstly it was Rt. Hon. Bob Peirce and his lovely wife Sharon, and later Dame Barbara Hay. Although it still retains its official title of Britweek, in fact it now extends to at least two weeks, sometimes more, with many events in and around Los Angeles, Orange County, San Francisco and San Diego. Seems the Brits are popping up all over the place.

Peter has continued his vast interest and experience in the music business, both as a performer, mentor and manager. It doesn't seem like almost fifty years since we first met, and he, for one, has stood the test of time brilliantly. He still delights audiences at the Fests for The Beatles and fans love to not only hear his music but also listen to his stories, which span so many decades.

Cynthia & Julian Lennon

I met Cynthia Lennon briefly at various Beatles-related events over the years. Though I got a very warm vibe from her, we never had much opportunity to really connect. Not until later, that is.

After Cyn and John had parted, she married Roberto Bassanini and lived in Wimbledon. We met up briefly during one of our stays in the south of England. I recall visiting her home where Roberto was upstairs in bed and calling down for various refreshments.

We hooked up again when she lived in Ruthin, North Wales, and we were invited to her wedding to John Twist in 1967. My only lasting recollection of that day is of little Julian, in a suit that was a mite too big for him, looking bewildered and anxious.

Later when she was single once more, she moved back to live on the Wirral, she and Julian would often visit Jim and I at Rembrandt. Ruth always used to say, "Do I *have* to play with him?" He was a hyper lad, and she was by then springing up into a tall kid. She was less than patient with a younger boy racing her for the backyard swing, the bouncy ball, etc.

It was Cynthia who suggested to Jim one time that Ruth and I get away for a little holiday and a break from his much needed, round-the-clock arthritis care. She offered to come by Rembrandt frequently to keep Jim company or to run any errands he might need, and to back up Jim's sister Milly who was to stay with him. So off we went on a fourteen-day Mediterranean cruise for some rest and relaxation.

It was around this time that John began renewing his interest in Julian. He sent him a motorcycle for a present, along with an invitation to visit with him and Yoko in America. With some misgivings, Cynthia went along with the plan, as she didn't want to be the one to come between Julian and his dad. There can be no doubt of Julian's love for his father, and it is too sad that they never had enough time together.

We had a happy time at Julian's twenty-first birthday party at Stringfellows Club in London, where I briefly met lots of celebs, including the young but very beautiful Rob Lowe. Julian rode into the party on a white horse!

I have known Julian Lennon since he was little 'un way back from the Sixties. He and Cynthia were on their own by the time I really got to know them. They have a similar bond that Ruth and I share. That age-old adage is true: that what doesn't kill you only makes you stronger.

In grown-up years, Ruth was a choreography contestant and Julian a judge at a Claim to Fame contest held at the Embassy Club in London in 1981, and for no apparent reason (other than the obvious one of their surnames), the press linked them as a romantic item. Not so. Truly, just good friends. And besides, Ruth was a lofty three years older than him and obviously not his type!

We went our various ways and then met up again in Los Angeles in 1984 when Julian was launching his first album, *Valotte*. Nothing ever changes with either Cynthia or Julian; you just take up where you left off like nothing had happened. I believe that's a true sign of friendship.

During a later period when she lived in England and we lived in Nashville, Cynthia permitted Ruth and Ken Barker to video her for a documentary which still has not seen the light of day. Maybe one day...

Cynthia and I chat regularly on the phone and she speaks to Julian every day. They are as close as Ruth and I are.

I was so happy when Julian recently sent me a copy of his beautiful coffee table book, *Beatles Memorabilia*, documenting all of his father's belongings that he has managed to gradually retrieve. It must mean so much to him. His venture into the world of photography is now being valued, as it should be.

He paid a visit to the set of *Dancing With The Stars* recently in Hollywood, and spent some time recording with Steven Tyler. I'd like to have been a fly on the wall at those recording sessions. Whenever any Lennon enters a recording studio, magic is guaranteed to happen. Julian's own new album, *Everything Changes*, is due out in early 2013 – as always, it's well worth your while.

Fanz, Fan mail and Fanaticz

In the early days of my marriage to Jim, through opening Paul's fan mail, I discovered a long-time fan of Paul's named Cristy Trembly. She is still in touch today and works in television, mainly with CBS. She is involved in production on several of the popular series, including the highly popular *Dancing With the Stars*.

In the early Sixties, she would write to Paul at the Heswall address, and after a time, I began to recognise many of the recurring addresses. (Americans put their sender's address on the outside of the envelope, but often not on the actual letter). So one of Ruth's tasks in order to earn her pocket money was to open letters, paper clip the envelopes to them, sort them into countries, and file them in shoe boxes which were all over and underneath our long dining table at Rembrandt. (There was nothing as grand as a stapling machine in those days).

The boxes roughly represented geographical locations. For example, Australian mail went on the floor (down under!), Asian and Pacific mail on the window ledge (far East). This was a geography lesson for her as well as the beginnings of her awareness of the fan culture. This guided her in forming our current service, www.ifanz.com, which caters to over five million people who want to circulate their information to 'Fanz' and 'customerz'.

When I personally responded to Cristy she sent Ruth a lovely little rag doll with a porcelain face, which she treasured.

Many years later, when Ruth and I were speaking at a Beatlefest in Los Angeles, Cristy was in the audience and we made personal contact for the first time. She is one heck of a girl and has travelled the world.

Another memorable connection was with two Japanese girls, Tomoko and Katuko. They once sent Ruth an enormous Japanese doll on a wooden plinth. It was magnificent. Unfortunately, it became a casualty during one of our many house moves after Jim died when we had to move from place to place during our 'survival' period.

Another interesting and somewhat alarming thread of fan mail was from a young lady whose postal addresses kept getting closer and closer. This culminated in a phone call one night from the Dockside Police in Liverpool. She had been discovered as a stowaway on a freighter, which had just arrived. She said she was invited to the home of Paul McCartney. Paul was home at the time and spoke to her on the phone. I can't quite remember the chain of events, but it ended up with her arrival at Rembrandt. We fed her, made tea (of course), called her a taxi and booked her a room at a small Mount Pleasant hotel. However, it did take a little negotiating to get her to leave.

Years later I remember Linda telling me that this girl was a constant visitor to their house in Cavendish Avenue, and even took the kids to the local park. Linda had met her in a grocery store and I guess she didn't feel as if she were a threat. We were all just a little more innocent then. She sent me several pictures of Heather, Mary and Stella taken on the swings and roundabouts at a park in St. Johns Wood with this young lady. After I told Linda about her turning up in Liverpool, I guess she became a little more wary.

The Beatles truly did have worldwide appeal and to several cross sections of people.

Freda Kelly

Freda was originally Brian's assistant at the North End Music Store. When the whole Beatles thing came into being, she became their Fan Club Secretary after the original lady passed it on, due to her other commitments.

Freda was the most loyal and devoted person one could wish for, discreet, trustworthy, and until 2011, never considered even doing an interview about her time with them.

I used to take her shoeboxes full of mail that Paul had received at Rembrandt, and our friendship goes back to the early Sixties, just after I was married to Jim.

Later, of course, I began the Wings Fan Club for Paul after his split from the Beatles, and gradually, Freda and I lost touch.

In early 2012, Pete Price ran into Freda in the street in Liverpool, and we got back in contact. My, have we got a lot of catching up to do.

As she is now a grandmother, she has finally decided to put some stories down for the record, and is in the process of completing a documentary to be called *Good Ol' Freda*. This is a self-funded entrepreneurial effort, and fortunately, a lot of fans have rallied around to help with the finances. (Good Ol' Freda was the affectionate name the boys used to call her). You can visit this link to find out more: fredakelly.wordpress.com/

She came over to the States in 2011 to appear at The Fest for the Beatles and planned to do the same in 2012. A great girl, and I am so glad to be back in contact. I'm looking forward to the completion of the film, and I'm sure she'll have some great stories that haven't been heard before.

Help! I Need a Honeymoon!

In January 1965, two months after Jim and I were married, Jim asked Alistair Taylor, Brian Epstein's General Manager, to book us a trip for a honeymoon.
He arranged for us to go to Nassau, Bahamas, where the boys were filming *Help!* It all seemed very exotic to me. At that time, Ruth was a co-member of my British Passport, under our then name of Williams.

We flew from Liverpool on BOAC to London and then transferred to our international flight. We were very distressed to find that Ruth didn't appear to be on the passenger list. It seems that I was listed as Mrs. Angie McCartney and she as Ruth Williams. Somehow, this had slipped through the cracks. After some explanations, it was remedied, but Jim muttered, "This is bullshit!" He then vowed to legally adopt Ruth when we returned home and put McCartney at the end of her name. This he did with all haste.

We were well taken care of at the wonderful Balmoral Club, where Ruth celebrated her fifth birthday. The chef, a German lad whose English was not exactly on the ball, made her a cake which read: "Happy Birthday Ruth, Jah, Jah, Jah!" This was one of many occasions which, on reflection, should have been recorded on camera. But at least we still have our memories.

Ruth was befriended by a lovely little American girl, Robyn. I can't remember her last name, but she took Ruth under her wing and guided her through the delights of the swimming pool. I wonder if she will ever read this and check us out. She was very lithe and had lovely long blonde hair.

Whilst at the Balmoral Club, we witnessed the arrival of Senator Ted Kennedy, complete with neck brace, after he had been involved in a plane crash a few months earlier. Being a greenhorn from England, I was not too aware of who he was. There was a flurry of his "people" making the arrangements for luggage.

We were sitting in the lobby at the time, waiting to be picked up by one of Brian Epstein's drivers to take us to the filming location. The manager of the resort served tea to everyone. I remember us making small talk with the dear departed Senator and his wife, Joan. Wow, if only I had known about my future plans for Mrs. McCartney's Teas, I could have really done a bang up PR job on him. But that was yesterday...

Brian was most solicitous during our stay, despite the many duties he had regarding the production of the movie. One night, as we dined under the stars and palm trees, the local wandering musicians came to our table and played "Yellow Bird (Up High in Banana Tree)." Jim gave them a more than ample tip. From that point on, any time they saw us, they made a beeline in our direction, even following me to the ladies room one evening. I distinctly remember them playing that flaming song outside of the window while I relieved myself. I still laugh to this day when I hear it.

Brian would send a car for us each morning to go to the location where the boys were filming, and it was fascinating. There was one particular scene where they were on bicycles riding around in a circle. Paul had the line, "A man's gotta do what a man's gotta do." For some reason, the sound was not being captured to director Richard Lester's liking. I was flabbergasted at how many takes they had to go through in the blazing hot sun until Lester was satisfied.

Filmmaking is not as easy as most people think. So much of it is "hurry up and wait" time, sitting around in the trailers or whatever other shelter they have, often in makeup, costumes and wigs. Makeup artists also had to stick around to do touch-ups to keep the film's continuity. In those days they had to take Polaroids to keep track of how everyone looked, and to ensure everything was as exactly as before.

It appeared to me that there was no real rapport between the boys and Eleanor Bron, who was the female lead in the movie. While they were nice to her, she was more middle-class and well educated than they were. I remember seeing her shoot a scene where she and Ringo had to dive into the water. She was wearing a cloak, which spread out in the water and covered her head. Ringo seemed to just flail about, and later told Dick Lester, that he couldn't really swim. But he was certainly game enough to go for it.

We didn't ever see Eleanor in the evenings, either in the restaurant, or the bar, so I guess she must have retired to her room early, probably to prepare for the next day.

I recollect that the boys were pretty laced on something most afternoons. I think it's been well documented they were smoking a lot of pot, even whilst working, which seemed fairly acceptable. Poor Dick Lester would have to do take after take while the lads were giggling their silly heads off. But he was very patient with them although I can't imagine how much footage was wasted (like the lead actors).

Dick had his wife and little son with him. The boy was very hyper, forever running around on the set, and I remember that Jim, the strict disciplinarian, was horrified at how little control the parents had over his behaviour.

We had some great evenings in the bar with fun people like Roy Kinnear and Victor Spinetti, who was an absolute hoot. After a couple of refreshing adult beverages his Welsh accent would become more and more pronounced, causing great hilarity. Journalist Donald Zec was often on the scene, and he too, had lots of funny anecdotes to add to the mix.

British actor Leo McKern (the baddie) would regale us with stories of his many adventures in stage and films. Because of his persona in the movie, the boys would always hiss and boo when he came into the bar. A real Bahamian Pantomime scene. He was a very jovial man and such an experienced actor; everyone was a little in awe of him. He was an Aussie by birth but had come to prominence on the London stage, appearing in all the classics from *Uncle Vanya* to *A Man For All Seasons*, and later in the television series, *Rumpole of the Bailey*. He made no bones about having a glass eye. He had lost it in an accident when he was fifteen, and come to terms with it, even finding it a distinct advantage in many cases as it singled him out from many other performers. He didn't seem to be one bit embarrassed to talk about the loss, even threatening to take it out one night in the bar for a bet. I left before that line of chatter got any more out of hand.

Many happy memories of that memorable trip. Certainly a honeymoon to remember.

George Harrison

George was an occasional visitor at Rembrandt and was quite fond of his "Uncle Jim" as he called him. His first greeting would always be "Hello Ange, put the kettle on." It seems that in every phase of my life, tea has always been centre stage.

He also loved Jim's custard, and whenever he popped in, that was another order of the day. He always wanted to know the secret of how Jim could make custard without it forming a skin on the top. The funny thing is, Jim would never tell him. He did, however, tell me, and whenever I make custard or trifle I always do it Jimmy Mac's way.

Ruth was going through piano lessons (which she hated) and one afternoon I picked her up from her music teacher's house. She was grumpy on the way home but she lightened up when she saw that George was in the lounge. She plonked her music case down and he asked how she was getting on. Sensing her lack of delight for her music lessons he sat her down at the piano, took a seat on the bench beside her and taught her a Raga, explaining the rudiments of Indian music. That got her attention.

I remember we had a nice afternoon at Kinfauns in Esher, the home where he and Pattie lived, on one of our trips to London. It was a bungalow with psychedelic paintings on the outside. Pattie was very sweet and made us most welcome.

After our paths went different ways over the years. I didn't see much of George or Pattie until his Mum Louise Harrison's funeral in July 1970. Then, years later, Ruth and I were at an Indian restaurant on Ventura Boulevard in Sherman Oaks and ran into Pattie with her then husband, Eric Clapton. When I think back over the years, we have all put a lot of miles on our clocks.

She has published a couple of books, including one of her photography, which have been very well received. She did a book signing at the Ingleside Inn in Palm Springs not long ago, but unfortunately, due to clients keeping me busy, I wasn't able to go. Then a little later, there was another one at Catalina Island, which is just a hop, skip and a hydrofoil ride away from here, which friends of mine attended and really enjoyed. Her personality is still very warm and engaging.

Hunter Davies

In the early years of my marriage to Jim, biographer Hunter Davies spent a few days with us at Rembrandt to work on the book he was planning. It was the first ever authorised biography of the group called *The Beatles*.

He was a very engaging young man and we spent some enjoyable hours around the kitchen table with Jim giving him some family background. He wrote about how happy Jim was when Paul told him he could give up his job and bought him a house called Rembrandt on the Wirral Peninsula. He documented how Jim and I met, married, and then adopted little Ruth and gave her his name. In the telling of the story Jim realised how happy we all were.

Hunter painted a very fair and accurate snapshot of Jim at that time in his life. He intimated that Jim was comfortably settled in his new home with his new wife, who would drive him everywhere (Jim had never had the financial means to learn to drive when he was young), and how he now appeared to be in his second youth.

We had a great time together and Ruth and I even got silly enough to make him an apple pie bed. We had very happy memories of our time together, and his book was, and still is, a true depiction of the lives of the Beatles and their families and friends up to that time.

The original copyright was way back in 1968, and it's been reprinted several times since. I had lost track of my original copy and I bought a new version in paperback in early 2012. It was an interesting experience to re-read it after so many years. It brought back many memories.

I discovered a postcard which he sent me dated February 7, 2003, saying he has happy memories of dancing around to "When I'm 64" and goes on to say "I'm now 67 – and still no email." Oh c'mon Hunter, get with the programme!

I figure that by now he has been forced to join we cyber slaves, as I note that he has published over thirty books, including biographies, novels, and children's books. These include many works on the Lake District, and *Confessions of a Collector*. He is married to fellow writer, Margaret Forster, whose track record is not too shabby either... she being a prolific author and biographer "in her own write" (as John Lennon might have said).

Is The Doctor In?

Jim had weekly visits from his general practitioner to keep an eye on his general condition. Tuesday afternoon was a ritual: a pot of tea, two bottles of beer, and a drop of Scotch. The doctor would check Jim's pulse, blood pressure, and from time to time prescribe various medicines to try to assist his arthritis pain.

Jim had the old-fashioned working class respect for the medical man, and used to give him an annual Christmas gift of three hundred quid. We were quite taken aback one year when he asked Jim if he could double up on the amount because he wanted to buy a colour telly! Jim acquiesced and had me make out a cheque for £600.

In the early days of our marriage Jim and Paul had a joint Barclays Bank account, into which Paul would make regular deposits, including his substantial song writing royalties. Jim was very particularly prudent with this money.

Our yearly allowance from Paul's office at that time was £7,000 per year, payable every April (the beginning of the new tax year in England). For running the household, groceries, petrol, helping hands to cousins, taxi fares, hospital meals, Ruth's clothes, school trips etc., I was given a budget of £3,000 per year. I was required to meticulously keep a note of all our expenditures to verify how I was spending my £60 a week housekeeping budget. Often times we would go well over that amount when various relatives would ask Jim for help to avoid them having their electricity or phones cut off. I would run around the area, dropping off cheques, or cash, to take care of such matters.

I still have all my diaries from those days, and when I look through them and see how much of my time was spent taking folks to doctors, dentists, railway stations, I am amazed. Jim was so self-effacing he would not have considered ever refusing to take care of his family in this way, as he felt that he was the privileged one with an allowance from his son.

I sometimes smile when I see that I meticulously recorded every little expenditure, even shoelaces, and other minutiae. My diaries have accompanied me on my peripatetic meanderings around the globe.

Every week I would drive Jim through to Liverpool to pay his betting account with his bookmakers in cash. He always loved to have a flutter on the horses, and watched them all on telly with great interest. He would spend a considerable amount of time studying form. He only bet in a very small way, but he really loved it and soaked up all the "form" of the horses and their trainers.

That is why it was such a thrill when Paul gave him a racehorse, Drake's Drum, for a birthday present.

Jim's Gems

Jim had many funny sayings, which was usually prompted by a question from Ruth.

It went something like this: "Daddy, why does...??" He would reply, "Cos there's no hairs on a seagull's chest." Or, if Ruth would ask a particularly hard question, he would reply with "It's imposausigable."

He used to say that the two most important words were 'toler' and 'moder' – meaning toleration and moderation. It was how he thought one should live one's life.

Another ditty was, "If you can't say anything nice, don't say anything at all."

Another amusing thing he told me was that when he was a kid, and his father brought home tobacco from Cope's Tobacco Warehouse where he worked, he would send Jim to deliver some baccy to a neighbour and to say: "If my Dad asks me how much did you give me, what shall I tell him?"

He had not only a great sense of humour, but also a great sense of right and wrong. He was so humble, appreciating his financial position once Paul had reached fame. Paul bought him a house and promised to take care of him financially, which in turn made Jim generous to a fault. He was the only person I knew who would tip the cashier at the entrance to the Mersey Tunnel!

Upon reflection, I think he tried to overcompensate for his good fortune, having led such a frugal upbringing and seen so many tough times raising his two boys after Mary died, trying to be both father and mother to them. Well done, Jim. Well done.

It's good to know that Paul was a very good son and kept his promise. He took care of his Dad financially to the end of his life.

Fire! Fire!

We thought it was hilarious when Paul told us that during a meal in a posh restaurant, Rory Storm's mother panicked when the chef, preparing crepes suzette at their table, thought the place was on fire when he poured on the brandy on the dish. She promptly grabbed a syphon of soda water and doused the meal, the chef, and the nearby diners, much to their surprise and dismay.

Whenever I am in a restaurant featuring flambé dishes this always springs to mind. I manage, however, to resist the temptation to bring the proceedings to a speedy conclusion.

John Winston Lennon

What can I say about John Lennon that hasn't already been said? Having first known of him as a famous celebrity and then having him in my home as part of an extended family and houseguest was a bit surreal.

Yet, to me, he was not the big, bold, acerbic guy that the world often saw. I knew he could be sarcastic and was a very complex man with a brilliant mind, but from my perch I saw him as a frightened little boy. His fame had created an invisible wall around him and nobody can ever know what their experiences may have been like unless you lived through the madness as they all did.

Jim was always a little wary of John, and even Paul, I think, was at times aware of the need to tread lightly in his presence, so great was their competitiveness. Yet they shared a bond – the bond of sharing their loss of their mothers at a young age. It was worse for John than for Paul because Paul at least the continuity of living with his dad and brother Mike. Poor John literally had his mother ripped away from him, several times throughout his life.

I have a very fond recollection the time he and Paul spent a few days with us at Rembrandt when Paul decided they should go to nearby Chester on a little shopping spree. Jim suggested that either I drive them or ring for a taxi. Paul insisted on a real adventure and wanted to take the local Crosville local bus, which they did. They also "disguised" themselves in a couple of ratty old raincoats that Jim used to keep in the greenhouse and trilby hats (fedoras), and old pairs of Jim's glasses.

They evidently had a fine old time, and when they came home late afternoon, Paul said I should be expecting some deliveries. John had bought a huge crucifix, a Bible, some candlesticks, old books and various other items from an antique shop. Paul, on the other hand, had bought a pine-framed bed, which was riddled with woodworm and threw me into a right old panic. I got one of the local handymen to come around and spray it with some foul smelling remedy, which I hoped would kill the little critters.

John was very patient with Ruth, who was a lively five-year-old girl at the time. He did silly things and pulled faces to make her laugh, and read to her at night. He had a very serious conversation with her about her teddy bear, "Mr. Ted". Good old teddy still lives in a chair in the corner of her bedroom and wears a black bowtie, which belonged to Jim.

I remember a morning when Brian Epstein called from London to say that The Beatles were numbers one, two, three, four and five in the charts. I made the inevitable pot of tea, went upstairs and wakened the boys, got them down into the kitchen to tell them the news. They were chuffed.

Cynthia once related to me how John respected me for chiding him on his manners. Once he absent-mindedly handed me his empty cup and saucer, waggling it to indicate he wanted another cup of tea. I sternly told him, "We have a word in this house – *'please'*." I wasn't going to let anyone, not even him, misbehave in front of little Ruth who was being raised in a household where manners were a top priority. I remember getting looks from Jim and Paul who were shocked that I would take the great John Lennon to task, but he evidently understood my motives.

As the years went by we didn't see very much of John, except when we went down south. Paul once took us to Kenwood, his house in St. George's Hill in Surrey. I remember there being a suit of armour in the hallway and some very ornate pieces of furniture. It seemed like a mansion to me. And of course, we would see him, along with the others, at various concerts and in the Bahamas during the filming of *Help!*

After the break up with Cynthia when Yoko came on the scene, we saw more of her and little Julian, a friendship which is as strong today as it ever was.

John's Aunty Mimi

When I first met John's Aunty Mimi I thought she would be a rather stern lady. She reminded me of Barker & Dobson's toffee – a bit brittle on the outside, but with a soft centre. She always had John's welfare at heart but really wanted him to be a lawyer or a doctor – anything other than a rocker. Of course, she was extremely proud of his success when it happened.

She would occasionally come over to Rembrandt with Louise and Harry Harrison, and we'd sit out in the back garden and have a leisurely afternoon tea. She said she didn't really like mixing very much and was a rather private person. That said, she and Jim hit it off really well and would meander off down the garden to look at his rose garden, his vegetable patch, and of course, his beloved grapevines.

But she always seemed to carry a certain sadness about her. Maybe because she had never had a child of her own, just her tenuous relationship with the gifted John.

It's funny how music and gardening can bridge any gap.

Michael Parkinson ("Parky")

I first met journalist and TV host Michael Parkinson when Paul, Jim and I went to Granada Television in Manchester, along with John Lennon. John and Paul were doing a segment for the evening show of their song "We Can Work It Out," when John played the church organ used by Ena Sharples of *Coronation Street* which I describe elsewhere in this book.

A Yorkshireman, and a friend of the equally famous British TV personality Michael Barratt, we had some things in common. I followed his progress through his talk show series, through his Australian adventures and back to the UK. In fact, it really pissed me off that I signed up on cable TV for BBC America so that I could follow his series, only to find that it was not accessible. But never mind, eh, at least I found Graham Norton and *Little Britain* that way, so it was not a completely wasted effort. Then came Netflix and Hulu, YouTube, and all manner of other gadgets, so I can usually find whomever I want to watch.

Michael still remains one of my all-time heroes, and his TV interviews are legendary. He has interviewed some of the most iconic people (and some less so) in the entertainment business. I never tire of watching him handle some of the greatest egos of our time, and taking them down a notch or two when the occasion calls for it. In mid-2012 I bought his book *Parky's People* which is a splendid read, with lots of his recollections of celebrity successes and catastrophes. That, too, brings back lots of memories of the good old British TV days.

Ray Connolly

I remember a very nervous Ray Connolly coming to Rembrandt to interview Mike shortly after Jim and I were married. As Mike was still sleeping, Ray and Jim got chatting. In fact, Jim did most of the talking as Ray suffered from a bad stammer, and Jim did his best to put him at his ease by talking about it and getting it out in the open. He was working for the *Liverpool Daily Post*, prior to moving to London to work on the *London Evening Standard*. Mike eventually emerged, and the three boys had a nice chat, while I made the mandatory pot of tea.

Ray met Paul in September 1967 during the filming of *Magical Mystery Tour*, when he'd only been at the *Standard* a short while. He'd been told by his editor to follow the coach to try to get a story. Being new, he didn't know many people then, and was feeling very unsure of himself. On the first night in Devon, when Ray was sitting at the bar, Paul came in and sat on the next barstool. Nervously, Ray said to him, "I know your Dad". "Dad" was evidently the magic word, and Paul took him under his wing after that.

The following Boxing Day, *Magical Mystery Tour* was broadcast on BBC Television, and although it was panned by the critics in the papers the next day, Ray was asked by the *Standard* to write a follow-up piece. So he tried phoning Paul at his Cavendish Avenue home where Jim, Ruth and I had been staying over Christmas. He spoke to Jim, who asked him to call back in half an hour as Paul was still asleep. (His connections to the McCartneys always seem to involve sleeping!). Ray kept repeatedly calling, and he remembers Jim saying, "I tell you what Ray, God loves a trier. I'll go and wake Paul up for you." So it turned out that Paul chatted to Ray from his bed for about twenty minutes about the disastrous reactions to *Magical Mystery Tour*. Ray got a front-page story out of it, which he says did his new career no end of good.

Ray and his wife, who he calls Plum, met up with us all at Mike and Angie's wedding reception at Rembrandt. Mike and Angie went off on honeymoon (along with Ruth and I – how romantic was that?), and Paul took Ray and Plum off to his Aunty Gin's house in Dinas Lane, Huyton.

Mike would often stay with Ray and Plum, at their Campden Hill Road house from 1969 onwards. Jim and I visited him there a couple of times as Jim would always insist on giving their little 'uns a half a crown each in that old fashioned way of his. That wouldn't go far nowadays, the little 'uns are now big 'uns: Louise, now 44, Dominic, 42 and Kieron, aged 40.

In a very recent email from Ray, he said how he has always thought how Jim's phrase "God loves a trier" shaped him. He'd never heard it before, but he still says it, and still thinks it.

He is now perhaps best known for writing the screenplays for the films *That'll Be The Day* and its sequel, *Stardust*, for which he won a Writers Guild of Great Britain best screenplay award, and for his many interviews with the Beatles.

But going back to our first meeting, it also forged a link between Ray and the McCartney family, which has continued ever since. John Lennon also had great faith and trust in Ray, as do I. As I often say, Ray is one of the only two prominent journalists in whom I have complete and utter trust. The other is Roy Greenslade, who interviewed me about Gary Glitter and kept many confidences.

In later years, some people thought Ray's honesty and loyalty were a disadvantage, when it became known that John Lennon told Ray he'd left The Beatles months before it became public knowledge, and had asked him not to divulge it. It meant he missed the scoop of his life as a journalist but he has never regretted keeping that confidence to himself.

I love reading Ray's blog. He has some fascinating pieces in there, ranging from his childhood adventures, to his regrets in life, to his gratitude for the life he has now. His books have kept me enthralled for many an hour on my iPad and Kindle (now considered an antique – the Kindle, not Ray!).

He broke the barrier for many writers when he decided to publish his novel *Sandman* online, downloadable one chapter per day, for free! It generated an amazing amount of interest, with 60,000 downloads the first day.

Ray is still married to the same dear wife, and he's currently working on a screenplay about Dusty Springfield, which I know will be a big hit when it finally reaches the screen.

There's an interesting YouTube item of him discussing the break-up of the Beatles. You should look him up: www.rayconnolly.com and you will find some great reading on his blog. Go look him up – you'll be glad you did.

Ringo Starr

I first met Ringo Starr when Paul took Jim, Ruth and I to visit him and his wife Maureen at Sunny Heights, their lovely country home in St. George's Hill, a lush Surrey suburb.

My lasting recollection is of a tree house, a go-kart track in the grounds, and my special favourite, a beautiful dishwasher in the kitchen. Zack was just a toddler then – now he is a world famous drummer in his own right, including touring with his Dad's All Starr Band.

At that time I had been trying to wheedle Jim into letting me have a dishwasher. Technological advancements be damned! Jim said the invention was "stuff and nonsense" and that we'd always washed our dishes the old-fashioned way, by hand. Or rather, by my hand. I quietly told Ritchie (Ringo) this, and when he took us on a tour of the house, he included the kitchen, and did a pitch to Jim about the dishwasher! I was eternally grateful to him for that.

Soon after we got back home, Jim said softly, "I suppose we should get one of those new-fangled things." Until he saw Mo and Ritchie's, he had always assumed that the dishes went round and round, much like a clothes washing machine!

So I got my wish, and boy, was I glad, considering the amount of entertaining that followed over the years. It came in handy when Paul came home and invited lots of family, or Mike was in town and brought home many of his fellow performers and their various companions.

Elsie and Harry Graves

In the early days of my marriage to Jim, I had the pleasure of meeting Elsie and Harry Graves, Ringo's Mum and stepfather. Talk about two lovely people. They would sometimes come over to Rembrandt where we would all sup tea (of course!), and chew the fat about the old days in Liverpool before it was turned on its ear by these four mop topped lads.

Ringo bought his Mum a lovely bungalow in Gateacre, on the outskirts of Liverpool, and we would sometimes go over and visit them. Harry loved working in his garden, and they both lived a very simple life. He and Jim liked to talk about plants and gardening while we women and little Ruth always found plenty to chat about. We were not such slaves to TV then as people tend to be now.

She told us of her early struggles as a single mum, before she married Harry Graves, a dear sweet and kind man. She would sometime be afraid to open the front door in case it was the rent man. So she'd tell Richie (Ringo) to bend down and look under the gap at the bottom of the door to see if it was a pair of boots, in which case, it might be the Dreaded Rent Man.

Elsie told me that since the Beatles' success, Richie gave her an allowance. Every time she received it, she would put £10 into a Post Office savings account for Richie "in case it all ever went away and he needed the money." Bless her heart, if she only knew. She was very proud of him and never failed to cut out clippings from the papers and magazines and keep them in scrapbooks.

Then again, as parents and stepparents, we were all proud of our Beatle Boys.

Dick James Honours Luncheon

In the brand new year of 1965 when Jim, Ruth and I were spending time in London, we were invited to a luncheon honouring Dick James, the Beatles' music publisher, at the Café Royal on Regent Street.

We were picked up in a limo from Cavendish Avenue and there was a fellow guest already in the car. He took an immediate shine to little Ruth as she told him a very corny joke on the way there. It was about a rich man from the Middle East who had a thick accent. He came to England and wanted a big house built with lots of gardens, a lake, swans, chandeliers, and, as he put it "a statue in every room". When the big day arrived and the builders were putting on the final touches, he arrived in his chauffeur-driven Rolls Royce. He inspected the staff on the steps, then entered the house to be shown around by the chief designer. He seemed very pleased with everything except that he was a bit puzzled with the big alabaster and marble statues of nymphs, angels, gargoyles, and all manner of massive pieces. When he asked the designer "But vot are deese?" He was informed, "But sir, you asked for statues in every room." "No, no," he replied, making a mime of speaking into a telephone, saying, "I meant, Hello, Stat You?"

Jim and I had heard this a dozen times and shrugged it off, but our fellow traveller was tickled to pieces. He was the Master of Ceremonies at this celebrity and press-laden event, which had already had a spot of excitement before he took the stage. Paul, recovering from a heavy duty New Year's party season, asked for cornflakes and milk for his breakfast and not the smoked salmon, champagne and other high-falutin' stuff that the guests were being served. Of course, a runner was promptly dispatched to get the necessary breakfast staples for Paul, and later, when things got under way, it was announced from the stage that a little guest (Ruth), had something to tell them. So he got Ruth to stand up on her chair and present her little story. I guess that was her first public appearance. No doubt it gave her a taste for the limelight.

When we left the hotel that day, there was a mob of fans outside. Word had somehow spread about the star guests, and it was the first scary experience we had of them rocking the limo from side-to-side. I remember security pushing Ruth down on to the floor to keep her away from the screaming girls who were clawing at the windows as our brave driver negotiated a way out of there. A baptism of fire for sure.

Rembrandt Rocks

You could truly say that from 1964 to 1976, our house Rembrandt rocked! From time to time, Mike would come home to Rembrandt with various friends and hangers-on. Let's just say those moments never failed to entertain.

I remember one night when Jim was away in Mexico at his nephew Keith McCartney's wedding and my Mum, Edie, was staying with me. We were awoken in the middle of the night by loud music and the distinct smell of bacon. Mum and I donned our dressing gowns and went downstairs to investigate. Imagine our surprise and horror to find two very tipsy young girls with frying pans on the stove burning the heck out of bacon while sloshing down glasses of wine. We offered to take over before the house was burned down.

That was the night that we found the hilarious Freddie Starr in the lounge, making an appearance from behind the long maroon velvet curtains which shielded the bay window area from the main room. He was doing a very unseemly impression of Marlene Dietrich singing "Falling in Love Again". Trinity member Brian Auger was there, playing the piano in a masterful manner.

The following day was Ruth's seventh birthday. When she came home from school in the afternoon to prepare a tea party with her chums, she went upstairs to find a supine Rod Stewart fast asleep in her bed! She has oft been heard to make comments to the effect of, "When Rod Stewart was in my bed..." Of course, always failing to mention that she was a seven-year-old child at the time.

Another one of Mike's memorable houseguests was Billy Connolly. That was after Mike had married Angie Fishwick and moved into the Heswall Lower Village. It was a Christmas party at Rembrandt, and the house was overflowing with guests. At one point Billy decided to jump out of the upstairs landing window at Rembrandt with a little plastic Batman parachute from a cereal packet. How he managed to land on the gravel without hurting himself I will never know.

The next morning, Boxing Day, Angie McGear asked me if she could borrow some items for their breakfast, so Ruth and I headed over to dispense a few goodies. As we drove up the driveway there was Billy in red boxer shorts, attempting to vacuum up the snow on the front porch! Ah, those were the days.

Mike was friendly with Paul Jones of Manfred Mann. They and The Scaffold were doing a gig at the Liverpool Playhouse and Ruth and I went to the show. The next day Paul (Jones) visited us and it was the first time he ever met Ruth. He obviously took a shine to her as he used to send her the odd postcard from London from time to time. She was very impressed. We also had a lovely evening with Paul and Barry Ryan (The Ryan Twins) who were very popular at the time, and were charming house guests.

Mike also brought Dusty Springfield and Madeleine Bell to Rembrandt one night. I distinctly remember it was the first time I had ever tasted vodka, and certainly not the last. Mike asked me to be sure to get some vodka for Dusty. When they arrived, for some unknown reason, they both sat under the grand piano in the living room. I remember being appalled when the supremely glamorous Dusty whipped off her wig to reveal a flattened down and plain head of hair. That was a fun night.

The Rt. Hon. Tara Brown

One night, Mike brought home a gaggle of friends from some late night event, and as usual, hearing the noise downstairs at Rembrandt, I decided to investigate.

I know, dear reader, you are thinking "nosey old beezum," and you would be right. But, given Mike's track record for bringing home rowdy revellers, I was always anxious that this lot didn't set fire to the house.

Amongst them was a very correct and well-mannered blond young man. He was introduced to me as "Tara". He and his wife stayed overnight. The next morning as I was getting breakfast for the mob, a telegram was delivered to the house. It was addressed to The Right Honourable Tara Brown.

I signed for it and laughingly said, "Someone is obviously playing a joke on you, Tara." Imagine my surprise and embarrassment when he said, "Oh no, Angie, that is my title."

It turns out that he was heir to the Guinness family fortune. Yes, those "beverage" people from Ireland.

His wife said at one point in the conversation something about their children. When I asked about their kids (ages, sexes, names and so forth) she replied, "Oh, one of them is called Julian and the other is..." Then she tailed off absentmindedly and turned to her husband and asked, "What's the other one's name, darling?"

I was a bit taken aback. Being from such a basic working class family I was stunned that a mother couldn't actually remember the name of one of their offspring. I suspect the servants knew the children's names more readily.

Tara was immortalised by John Lennon in "A Day in the Life", but it was his wife's comment that "blew my mind".

Christmas Cakes

In October 1965, Jim announced that he thought he and I should start a new tradition, that of making Christmas cakes for the family. Evidently, he and Mary had made them in the past. It was a pretty daunting task for me, stepping into a void left by his beloved Mary, the boys' mother, and as we sat down to make a list of family members who should receive them, I'm sure Jim wasn't aware of my trepidation treading on this hallowed ground. The first year the recipients numbered seventeen in all.

Jim had an old recipe, a newspaper cutting as I recall. So we set to work with a list of ingredients, ordered them from our local grocer, Cartmills, and set to work.

We had to buy a massive bowl, lots of utensils, sieves, greaseproof paper, and baking tins to fit each cake. It became a very time consuming deal, to make the mix, dried fruits, candied peel, raisins, brandy, dried currants, butter, brown sugar, flour, eggs, salt, nutmeg, allspice, nuts, and the grated zest of lemons and oranges. And of course the brandy.

I was very nervous about the process originally, but with Jim's help, I became an expert at this and over the years, it became as easy as falling off a log. Ruth loved being a part of the process, despite being so young, and I realise now she always had the cooking bug.

As each one was made, cooled, and prepped to be frozen in the big chest freezer we had in our garage, I got to be an expert, knowing how much further down the line to get them out, pierce holes in them and inject the said brandy (or what was left of it with a full day of kitchen duty behind us) using a syringe obtained from a local pharmacy. I can only imagine the pharmacist's reaction when I said the syringes were for injecting booze into Christmas cakes. Oh yeah, in the McCartney household! Christmas cakes. Riiiiiiight.

Then at the appropriate time, they were all hauled back into the kitchen at Rembrandt, defrosted, topped with marzipan, wrapped and frozen again until it was time for icing. Oh boy, what a lot I learned about cake making that first year.

Icing was a real learning curve for me, but Jim seemed to have it down pat. Then finally, we would put the little Christmassy decorations on top, sleds, Santas, silver balls etc., and wrap them up with coloured cellophane paper and tie them with ribbon, ready for me to make the rounds and deliver them to Aunty Mill, Aunty Gin, Bette and Mike, Ian and Jackie, Diane, Joe and Joan, their kids, Edie, Jean and Ted Merry, Kath and Reg, etc.

Knowing now how people scoff and mock fruitcakes, I wonder whether our gifts were a blessing or a curse, but of course, because they came from Uncle Jim, I guess I would never know.

The only thing I do know for certain, it was a happy family occasion for Jim, Ruth and I starting and continuing this process, and one that lives on in my memory, and that she and I still carry on to this day. Hmmm... maybe I should make Mrs. McCartney's Christmas Cakes to go with the Mrs. McCartneys Teas?

Thumbs Up in The Philippines

I remember Paul coming home to Rembrandt in August 1966 after their disastrous exit from the Philippines where First Lady Imelda Marcos was outraged because they did not attend a function at her invitation.

Paul sat at the kitchen table and described the trip, which seemed cursed from the get-go. He said when they first arrived, they were driven around in an open-topped vehicle and Paul was doing his usual "thumbs up" sign to the cheering crowds. Wondering why they suddenly stopped cheering and seeing their faces change from expressions of delight to hostility, Paul later learned that the thumbs up in that country is the equivalent of the "up yours" middle digit in our part of the world. Oops!

I know it is sometimes hard to recall all the details of every story that Paul told us, but my memory is refreshed by Tony Barrow in his excellent book: *John, Paul, George, Ringo and Me*, when he gives his first-hand account of what went down.

Due to a variety of mis-communications, the Beatles and their party were not present at a special luncheon hosted by Imelda Marcos. It was suggested that The Beatles might "call in" on the First Lady at 3 p.m. on the Monday afternoon, before proceeding on from the Malacanang Palace directly to the concert for the first performance. The story goes that the local concert promoter had made it sound more like a casual proposal than a command from the President's office. Only later when Brian read the Manila *Sunday Times* did he realise that this was in fact a serious invitation. It also indicated that the invitation was for early in the morning, and not 3 o'clock in the afternoon, and so forth.

None of this was on their official itinerary, and a lot of confusion ensued. The newspaper quote I have says: "President Marcos, the First Lady and the three young Beatles fans in the family have been invited as guests of honor at the concerts. The Beatles plan to personally follow up the invitation during a courtesy call on Mrs. Imelda Marcos at Malacanang Palace tomorrow (Monday) morning at eleven o'clock".

Quite early on Monday morning some military officers came to the Manila Hotel and announced that they were the reception committee to escort The Beatles to the palace. They also stated the luncheon would be attended by hundreds of "children of the aristocracy."

Epstein wasn't going to allow anyone to intrude on the Beatles down time. The President's Men left, and shortly after, Brian received a phone call from the British Ambassador's office on the subject. The Beatles were not even aware of the invitation until later.

A television news item said that the children had begun arriving at 10 a.m. and waited until after 2 p.m. Not the best PR in the world for the boys. There were allegedly death threats floating around. Brian gave television people an interview, explaining that neither he nor the boys had been handed any invitation. This transmission was mysteriously blotted by unexplained interference during the broadcast so that nobody heard his explanation. After the concert that night, the police escort was withdrawn, and a very scary situation faced the boys and their crew.

Their exit from Manila was fraught with difficulties, baggage handlers wouldn't help, the police moved them on while they were trying to unload their baggage and gear. It was evidently "all hands to the pump" including Tony Barrow himself, to get their gear into the airport, and even the escalators were shut down as they tried to progress to board their flight.

I remember hearing that the roadies got the worst of it, trusty Mal Evans was thrown to the ground and kicked, Brian Epstein was hit in the face, all in all, a horrible end to a very confusing visit. They didn't get their passports back until the very last minute. At least KLM was willing to delay take-off until everyone was settled aboard. Paul, as usual, was the perfect diplomat, and did a radio interview apologising for their failure to meet Imelda Marcos, saying that they knew nothing of her lunch party. Good old Paul, always the one to pour oil on troubled waters.

I would like to mention that Tony Barrow recently sent me another copy of his book, in which all of the above is referred to, and he kindly gave me permission to use it. It's a collectible for any self-respecting Beatles fan for sure.

Thank you Tony. Always a gent! Want to be my PR agent?

Viv Stanshall

On one of the many occasions when Mike McGear brought home a bunch of musical gypsies, Viv Stanshall of The Bonzo Dog Doo Dah Band was one who clearly stood out.

Angie McGear's Mum, Edith Fishwick, was sitting next to him on the couch in the lounge at Rembrandt, and he mistakenly thought it would be fun to try to slip his hand down the front of her blouse.

No doubt he had been partaking of some libations before that sophomoric prank. Poor Edith was mortified. She was a very dignified lady in her fifties, and not only were her daughter and son-in-law in the room, but her grandchildren as well. Plus Jim, who was the perfect gentleman, and was not at all amused. But booze and medications put a different slant on behaviour for many people.

I didn't have as much bottle in those days as I have now. I would have given him short shrift and asked him to leave, but in former times, I was afraid to put a foot wrong. Today, that foot would be deeply planted up his rear end!

Waterproof Reporter

Jim and I tried to keep a low profile. We did this particularly for the sake of little Ruth, who was a tad bewildered at the need for secrecy about her new brothers and their whereabouts.

One day in 1966 I answered the doorbell at Rembrandt and found a soaking wet journalist on the front porch, asking if he could speak to Mr. or Mrs. McCartney.

My first instinct was, of course, to invite him in, sit him down in the lounge, get him a towel to dry himself, and make the mandatory pot of tea. Jim, on the other hand, plied him with a few questions before noticing that it wasn't even raining that day!

This enterprising scribe was particularly crafty. Evidently he had visited the Gayton Garage Service Station up at the traffic roundabout on Telegraph Road, got them to lend him a hosepipe, doused himself with water, and ran down Baskervyle Road to our house to try to get a scoop. As it happened Paul was home at the time, so this wily fellow got his mark when Paul came downstairs into the lounge. I give him top marks for imagination. But not an umbrella.

Yoko Ono

I first learned about Yoko from Paul when he came home to Rembrandt for a little R and R. He described her as "this avant-garde Japanese artist that John is interested in". It all seemed a little odd to Jim and me. We learned of her Indica Gallery showing in 1966 where she invited John to climb a ladder and write the word "yes" on the ceiling. Indica was run by the Beatles' friend John Dunbar, who at that time was married to Marianne Faithfull.

The relationship was rather fluid at that time but I believe that as the months progressed, Yoko became more prominent in everyone's lives. Various stories abound about some of the stunts she pulled to get John's attention.

She was born in Tokyo in February 1933, the eldest of three children. Her parents, Eisue and Isoko were wealthy aristocrats. Her father was evidently a frustrated pianist but worked in mathematics and economics, and became the head of a Japanese bank in San Francisco in 1935. Yoko stayed behind in Tokyo with her mother and didn't really begin to know him until she was two years old. It is said that her father was a direct descendant of an Emperor of Japan.

I remember Paul telling us that when she was a child, she would have to ask for an appointment to speak with her father. If he was displeased with her, she was made to kneel on rice. How about that for child cruelty?

She later moved to America and attended school, at which time she became very bohemian, much to the chagrin of her parents. She hung out with writers, artists, musicians and the like, and hence developed her artistic bent.

I have only met her once, very briefly in an L.A. restaurant with her PR man, Elliot Mintz. He introduced us and I recall having a warm feeling as we shook hands. Shortly after that, she sent Ruth a recipe for a celebrity cookbook she was working on to raise funds for charity.

Hopefully, she and Julian have mended their relationship somewhat now, as life really is too short to hold grudges. Forgiveness is a great healer. Sometimes it takes a little working on, but if you persevere, you really can get there in the end. At least, that's my theory, although I will admit there are a couple of people from my past and not so distant past that I am having to work on forgiving. But I am working on it.

Beirut

In June 1967 Jim, Mike, Ruth and I went on a vacation to Beirut. Alistair Taylor, the Beatles' 'Mr. Fix- It', suggested the location.

We stayed in the magnificent Phoenician Hotel, which at the time was marred by construction. Despite that, we still managed to have a good time.

One day we took a trip into the local countryside, and the limo driver took us to his brother's restaurant up in the mountains. We were seated at long outdoor tables under the trees where they placed before us jugs of ouzo, a flavoured liquor, and many small pewter platters containing delicacies. We took our cue from our host and duly delved in with our fingers, tasting the many concoctions. Some were palatable, some decidedly dodgy.

At one point Mike had just put something in his mouth and (more to be polite than anything else), asked the driver, "This is interesting; what is it?" He wished he hadn't asked. The reply came back, "Sir, this is a rare delicacy for our honoured guests... It is the eyeball of a yak." A lovely looking creature to be sure, but I don't really fancy snacking on one of his eyeballs.

The driver managed to down sufficient quantities of ouzo to make him almost incapable of driving back down the hairpin bends, subjecting us to a ride of terror on the way back to the city. That was a white-knuckle drive if ever I had one. But there was more to come.

On the way down we passed a parked car with a very distressed looking man beside it. We stopped and Mike got out and went back to find out if his car had broken down. It was not that, but the poor man had just completely lost his nerve looking down into the chasms over the side. Give Mike his due, he offered to run the man and his lady passenger down to the flatlands, which he did very gingerly. I give him ten points for that.

At sundown one evening Jim and I were taking in the view from our balcony when we heard gunfire. Sure enough, the cops were detaining a truck driver who had been speeding. In an effort to stop him, they shot at his tires!

The Lebanon police did, however, have one very wise traffic regulation: no trucks or heavy vehicles could use the roads during normal daylight hours. This certainly helped relieve traffic problems.

Another interesting little episode was when Ruth was playing with her slinky toy on the stairway outside our room. She came back in and said, "I have just seen a daddy and his little boy with no clothes on, tickling each other on the bed in the next room." We quickly moved her playtime to the inside of our suite. Hmmm. Talk your way out of that one.

We also took a side trip to the Holy Land. Unfortunately I was suffering from 'Delhi belly' and had spent the entire previous night on the bog. The short plane ride was very turbulent and two nuns didn't help our peace of mind across the aisle, feverishly thrashing through their rosaries and praying loudly (in their own tongue of course).

We visited the Wailing Wall, the birthplace of Jesus Christ, where we were accosted by a man selling cans of Coca Cola (which quite destroyed the sanctity of the occasion), and the Gardens of Gethsemane.

During that trip the Six-Day War between Israel, Egypt, Syria and Jordan broke out. We nervously made our way to the airport, where hours later we caught a flight home, and were relieved when our plane safely touched down in Jolly Old England.

Despite all good intentions, I don't believe we ever allowed Alistair Taylor to plan another trip for us!

Brian Epstein

The Beatles' manager Brian Epstein was exceptional in almost every way. He was a great businessman and a very courteous and mannerly young man.

Brian had taken all the right steps in getting Jim to sign Paul's contract when the Beatles' negotiations first began. Jim was very impressed with him and his parents. Queenie and Harry.

When we spent time in the Bahamas on our honeymoon, Brian was constant in his regard for our comfort, transportation, and lodging. He even took us out one evening to a nightclub, which all seemed a little weird to me, with people smoking huge joints, and fire eaters and limbo dancers on the scene. Nevertheless, Brian did everything in his power to take care of us.

We were so shocked when he died on August 27, 1967. Jim, Ruth and I had spent the day at Bangor University in North Wales, where the Beatles and "the other George Harrison", a journalist with the *Liverpool Echo* (I know, I know. Two George Harrisons. What are the odds, right?), were attending a seminar with the Maharishi Mahesh Yogi.

We all had lunch in a canteen-like area at long wooden tables, where simple fare was served: salads, water, bread, and fruit.

As we got in our car to drive back to Heswall, Paul came out and stuck his head in the window to bid us farewell. While we were talking, George Harrison (the journalist) shouted from the steps, "Paul, Brian's on the phone, he wants to speak to you about tomorrow." So Paul left to take that call. It must have been about 2.30pm so we know Brian was alive and well then.

It was the Bank Holiday weekend and traffic was heavy. We stopped on the road for a bite of lunch and to let Hamish, our little Scotty dog, have a run and a wee wee.

As we got in the front door at Rembrandt, the phone was ringing. It was Louise Harrison, George's Mum. She said that Brian had committed suicide, or that it might have even been murder. She had heard something on Radio Caroline, the pirate radio station, and at that stage the news was very garbled. We were in complete shock. We'd just heard Paul called to the phone to talk to Brian! It was many hours before we could reach any substantial conclusion to the situation.

It had to have been an accidental overdose. He had just spoken to Paul to say he would join them the next day.

What a void his death left in so many lives.

The Beatles didn't attend the actual Liverpool funeral, in deference to the parents, as their presence would have made it into a media circus.

The service at the graveside was held by Rabbi Dr Norman Solomon, who said, disparagingly, that Epstein was "a symbol of the malaise of our generation". The comment shocked and saddened many in attendance for it was completely out of line and very uncharitable.

A few weeks later, on October 17, all four Beatles attended a memorial service for Epstein at the New London Synagogue in St John's Wood (near Abbey Road Studios), which was officiated by Rabbi Louis Jacobs. I still have the programme as a memento of a very sad day.

The service was attended by many of Brian's friends, family and clients. The mourners included Cilla Black, Gerry Marsden, The Fourmost and Billy J. Kramer, and The Beatles and their ladies. I also remember touching base with Lulu that day. She wore hot pants with suspenders holding them up!

History seems to have downplayed Brian's role in The Beatles' success but to those of us who were there and in the know, none of it would have been remotely possible without Brian Epstein's participation. A play about his life will open in Liverpool in late 2012. A movie is also said to be in the works, and there have been rumours that film actor Jude Law has bought Brian's diary, in preparation for possibly playing the part of Brian. This is unconfirmed however.

Godspeed Brian ... Godspeed. And *Mazel tov*!

Come Back Milly

When the Beatles performed on the BBC's *Our World*, which transmitted literally around the globe on June 25, 1967, Ruth made a big sign on a piece of cardboard which said "COME BACK MILLY." The BBC estimated that the broadcast reached 400 million people. That was quite something in those days. You can see it to this day on YouTube in the beginning of the video clip.

Paul and Mike's Aunt Milly had just departed for Australia to visit her son Jim Kendall and family in Adelaide. She was badly missed by us all.

Mike took the sign to the studios and held it up to the cameras. Believe it or not, Milly told us she had not long arrived and was tired and exhausted from her journey, but they had the telly on in the next room, and were sort of half-watching the screen, when suddenly this placard came up. They were all flabbergasted, as at that stage we were not as tech saturated as now, but it was a real link between our two hemispheres.

I guess you could say it was the first email.

Subsequently, an annual event has been dedicated: Global Beatles Day on every June 25. The fans play Beatles music all day and celebrate in various ways. Their music now spans several generations and will no doubt continue in the years to come.

Needless to say, Milly didn't really stay long down under and turned around and came back to the UK.

Gilbert Becaud

In 1967, Jim, Ruth and I took a trip to Paris. It was one of those occasions when Jim asked Alistair Taylor to fix us a little holiday. Little holiday? He booked us a suite at the Plaza Athenée in France, the likes of which I had never seen in my life. I thought we were staying in a museum, it was so palatial. They probably had gourmet urinal cakes.

When we got settled in, we got a call from a young man at EMI-Pathe Marconi, whom Alistair had evidently contacted and asked to be our guide. He was very solicitous and would regularly pick us up in a limo and take us to all the sights:

the Eiffel Tower, the Louvre, a trip along the Seine and the Champs Elysees. One day he asked if we would like to visit Gilbert Becaud in the recording studio. Of course, we were delighted to accept the invitation. We thought it would be exciting to see this French megastar in action.

He duly picked us up the following morning and we were ushered into the studios. We sat in the control room and watched the great man making a recording. Little Ruth was urged to be very quiet, which she was, and as this was one of her first forays into the recording world. Naturally, she was wide-eyed and fascinated by the whole process.

When there was a short break in production, Becaud came into the control room and asked the engineer who we were. He explained in French that the gentleman was the father of an artist on the EMI label. He came over to him and asked, in his delightful accent: "So, you are related to someone? Who are you?" Jim replied, "I am Paul McCartney's father." That didn't seem to fly and we were astonished to hear him say, "I don't care whose family you are, get out of my studio."

You can't imagine how crushed Jim was, and I was not far behind him. We scuttled out, into our waiting limo, and rode very silently back to our hotel. For such a self-effacing man as Jim, it was utterly humiliating.

Recently I found on Google that Monsieur Becaud's birth name was François Silly. And there you have it.

The Magical Mystery Tour Fancy Dress Launch Party

On December 21, 1967, Mike was already in London prior to this event at the Westbourne Suite in the Royal Lancaster Hotel, and as Jim didn't feel well enough to travel, Angie McGear and I took the train from Lime Street to Euston, where Mike picked us up and took us to our hotel. It was a costume party and he had rented outfits for us both. Mine was an Eastern Princess, complete with lots of veil-y things, voluminous pants, beaded headdress and curly slippers. The top half was a little snug on me, so I wore it back to front with a blouse underneath and left it open.

On arrival we saw various incarnations of Charlie Chaplin; Ringo was an

Regency Gent, Maureen an Indian Princess; John was an Elvis-styled teddy boy with Cynthia as a "Quality Street Chocolate Box" crinoline lady; Paul and Jane Asher were a matched pair of Pearly King and Pearly Queen; George showed up as an Errol Flynn type character with Pattie as an Eastern Princess too! Cilla Black's husband Bobby Willis was a nun in full habit, and the hit of the night was Derek Taylor as Adolf Hitler. He had rented a perfect SS uniform, right down to the jackboots, and had dyed his hair jet black and slicked it down in the appropriate style. He had, of course, shaved his moustache to the regulation square.

As the night wore on and we all became increasingly hammered, Derek sent over a note inviting me to his room, saying, "I know I ain't no Robert Taylor, but then you're no f***ing Claudette Colbert, but do you want to get together later?" I resolutely declined his invitation, but later he wandered over and said "Sorry about that. I'll buy you breakfast on the train back tomorrow morning." Angie and I gingerly climbed into a cab and caught an early train back to Liverpool, both feeling very much the worse for wear. It was in the days when the waiters would walk up and down the carriages carrying trays of bacon and sausages sliding around in pungent grease. We both refused breakfast and made for the bar carriage to order a hair of the dog that bit us.

I further confused the poor British Rail staff by asking "Have you seen a man dressed as Adolf Hitler?" They just gave me a puzzled look and said, "No madam, not this morning." Derek never did make that journey. A fun evening indeed, for which we all paid in the next twenty-four hours. Thank heavens for Alka Seltzer and Bloody Marys!

To Malta with Milly

When she returned from Australia in 1968, Jim decided we should take Aunty Milly on a little holiday as a thank you for all the times she had looked after him domestically at Rembrandt. After she lost her husband Bertie, she let her house on Upton Road go for sale, and took over a smaller place on Village Road in Bebington, right across the road from Bette and Mike Robbins.

She was such a game girl, our Milly. She had a wealth of comic songs, old songs from the variety theatres, and at parties, we would always make sure she burst into song with such gems as "The Cheese Song" and other ditties in her repertoire.

One this occasion, we all flew out from Liverpool to Malta. We hadn't realised that as it was Easter, and Malta being a devout Catholic country, we would be arriving on Good Friday, a sombre day, with everything closed, and even the maids in the hotel bowing their heads and praying under their breaths as they dusted the banister rails at the Sheraton Hotel.

On our journey, our hostess plied us with far too many cocktails, and before we landed, poor Aunty Milly was feeling icky and reached for the little bag in the pouch in front of her and used it copiously.

It was only later, when the message came over the loudspeaker that we were approaching our destination, and should prepare for landing accordingly, that Milly realised she was minus dentures. We rang for the hostess, who obligingly retrieved the missing choppers from one of her trash load. What a lovely task that must have been. But she was as cheerful as could be as she brought them back to a very embarrassed Milly, assuring her that they had been sanitised and were all ready for action again. If only she'd used Fix-o-dent!

Fred Astaire and Ginger Rogers

Although I personally never met the legendary Fred Astaire, I was a huge fan of his films, especially the ones where he paired up with the great Ginger Rogers.

When supermodel Twiggy was visiting with us at Rembrandt one time, she told us that when she was at the zenith of her fame, she was entertained by Fred at his Bel Air home. She said she was mesmerised to be in the company of this charming man. She said it was a memory she would revisit forever when, as she said her goodbyes and left, he not only accompanied her to the front door, but also danced her down the steps to her waiting limo.

Many years later Ruth found herself stopped at a traffic light in Beverly Hills alongside Fred who was driving his brown Rolls Royce. She made a gesture of bowing to him, and he responded by doffing his Fedora in her direction with a gracious smile. She too was bowled over and said she drove home about six inches above the ground.

Why don't we have any stars like this any more? I recently watched a lovely documentary on Turner Classic Movies narrated by Nigel Lythgoe about Ginger Rogers, which of course had several fabulous clips of her stints with Fred Astaire as well as many other roles in dramatic movies. She made seventy-three movies in all, and yet remains in people's memories mostly for the ten she made with Fred Astaire.

On one of my first visits to Palm Springs some years back, I went on a tour of the stars' homes, included in which was the lovely but simple home of Ginger Rogers in Rancho Mirage. She spent her retirement there and became a prolific painter. She belonged to the Church of Latter Day Saints and lived quietly after two strokes had left her wheelchair bound. But, according to her assistant, she still liked to have friends over for movie nights.

The famous quote about the two entertainers was that Ginger did everything Fred did, except backwards – and in high heels! She has stars on the Hollywood Walk of Fame as well as the Palm Springs Walk of fame and I know is remembered worldwide

Liverpool Echoes

Coronation Street is still running on TV in England, and I suspect, many other parts of the world. It is officially the longest running TV soap opera.

I remember, not long after Jim and I were married, Paul invited us to tag along with him to Granada TV in Manchester to do a show with Michael Parkinson. We drove there, where we met up the other Beatles. They were going to perform "We Can Work it Out", and John thought it would be a good idea if he played the keyboards on Ena Sharples' harmonium, which was regularly used in the series. It sounded great.

That was also the day that we ran into Kenny Lynch, one of the few black singers on the British pop scene in the Sixties, in the cafeteria. He astounded the woman behind the counter when he asked her: "Do you serve niggers?" She was so taken aback she couldn't speak. So Kenny followed up with, "OK then luv, give me an egg buttie and a nigger for me crocodile."

Tommy Cooper, the much loved bumbling magician was appearing at The

Shakespeare Theatre Club, which was mc'd by the equally loved Pete Price. On Sunday afternoon, at the "get in", his crew arrived with a huge truck containing all his props, and proceeded to set up for the evening show. Sound check came and went, and Tommy ran through his stuff with no reference whatsoever to a huge red telephone at the back of the stage. Pete would recall that throughout the week, Tommy never made any use of the phone prop. When closing night came around and Pete went onstage to thank Tommy, he couldn't resist asking "So what is the red phone about?" Tommy beamed at him with that half mad stare and said "I dunno, I haven't thought of a gag to go with it yet." Of course, Tommy Cooper was renowned for his famous box of hats, and the sketch where he would recite a long poem, rapidly donning the hats to be in character for every voice.

He died on stage – what a great way to go.

Hamish and Fred - The Other Odd Couple

Ruth was seven years old when she broke her leg. It was the day before she was due to appear in a dancing school presentation. She was out with a school friend and her mother at West Kirby beach, climbed a wall and fell.

The mother had her taken by ambulance to Birkenhead Children's Hospital. Ruth had been instructed never to tell anyone her phone number, so when the nurse asked her for the vital information she was rebuffed.

"I'm not allowed to say," Ruth said. It turned out that one of the nurses thought she recognised her and figured out it might be that "McCartney kid from Heswall". So the hospital called the local police station who sent Mr. Plod, a policeman, to Rembrandt. He duly alerted us and Jim and I set off post haste for the hospital. She was allowed home by nightfall.

Paul came up from London and seeing this forlorn little figure lying on the couch, wrote on the back of a ciggy packet, "Can I buy her a puppy?" I deferred to Jim, who said yes. The two of them set off to a local kennel and came home with Hamish, a darling but feisty black scottie. He used to snag spiders and keep them warm under his chin until he was ready to eat them.

Another of his favourite pastimes was torturing Fred, our tortoise, who lived in the back garden. He didn't actually want to eat Fred, but just enjoyed toying with him. He'd turn him over on his back, watching his little legs, paws, claws or whatever flailing in the air.

Fred tended to be a bit of a runaway, (or crawlaway) and was constantly being returned to us by concerned neighbours. We eventually painted his name on his shell to make sure he was identified properly. None of your high falutin' microchips in those days!

Who would have thought a dog and a tortoise would provide so many hours of entertainment?

How I Won The War Premiere

In 1967, Jim and I attended the London Premiere of *How I Won the War*, starring John Lennon, and directed by Dick Lester. It was a hilarious fun poke at war, and starred Michael Crawford (before his career as a serious singer), comedic actor Roy Kinnear, and even Neil Aspinall had a small part (uncredited) as a dead soldier.

After the performance, we were all invited back to Cilla Black and Bobby Willis' apartment in Portland Place.

That was the night that, as we trooped out of the limos to enter the building, a very tipsy gent in top hat, white tie and tails (no, it wasn't Fred Astaire), staggered up to John Lennon and asked in a very plummy accent: "I say, aren't you one of those Beatle chappies?" John nodded in agreement, then the man thrust a notebook and pen in John's hand and said, "Then give me your autograph, it's for my daughter, I can't stand you myself." To which John adroitly responded, "Well f*** off then!"

As we all crowded into the lift to go up to Cilla and Bobby's flat, Mama Cass was in there too. She had recently been apprehended at Heathrow Airport and accused of taking a blanket from her hotel. Paul stunned us all by saying, "Hi there, blanket thief." Fortunately she took it in good part and laughed it off, but my dear husband, Gentleman Jim, was mortified.

Cilla and Bobby were wonderful hosts and entertained us beautifully. I know from my dear friend Pete Price that Cilla continues to be very warm and hospitable and he spends many happy hours of his precious leisure time with her.

Louise Harrison

I first met Louise ("Lou") Harrison at one of the Beatles' premieres, and we took to one another pronto. Same sense of humour, same background, upbringing, work ethic, etc.

She had lived in the States for many years and had always been a champion of the Beatles way before they hit it big in America. She was a radio show host and worked away at introducing the boys' music to local stations. She contacted Brian Epstein and urged him to send her some copies of their records to spread the word. She has remained incredibly loyal to her brother George and to his memory and his music.

For more than forty years people have been urging her to write a book. Finally at the age of eighty, she began. She said she was so tired of people writing unfounded rubbish, when they had maybe sat next to George on a plane for a couple of hours. She keeps busy with the tribute band that she formed, Liverpool Legends, but is finally setting aside time to get her thoughts and experiences down on paper.

She is a great environmentalist, too, and used to record public service announcements for radio about being Green long before it became fashionable.

When I lived in Nashville she called me to say she was driving through on her way to South Carolina to do a cable TV show with Ken Barker, and picked me up to accompany her. I remember that we nearly missed our call time. We'd forgotten we were entering another time zone, but managed to bound into the studio just in time for the red light to go on.

She recently hosted a CD called *Fab Fan Memories*, mainly comprised of contributions from fans, with their memories not only of George, but also of all of the Beatles. It was nominated for a Grammy in 2012 but was up against the legendary Betty White and didn't make it, but it was a great compliment to Louise's tenacity in getting it that far.

She also launched Louise Harrison's Help Keep Music Alive, Inc., a new non-profit organisation dedicated to bringing the music and message of the Beatles to kids. Liverpool Legends tours around the States to raise money to help keep music programs active in the schools.

We were all on a Q & A panel at a Beatlefest some years ago, along with Neil

Innes and Gerry Marsden, and a rollicking good time was had by all. Neil said something that tickled her fancy, and she absolutely lost it. I remember the session being held up for heaven knows how long while she tried to compose herself. Every time we would get started again, she'd suddenly splutter into laughter until she had all of us in the same state. Pity the poor moderator. It's like when you're a kid and start laughing in church.

Lou moved from Branson, Missouri, to Sarasota, Florida in 2012, and has made the fatal mistake of telling me she has a spare bed. So look out Sarasota!

Baron David Puttnam

I met David Putnam when he was just David – no titles, just a regular nice guy, a friend of Mike McCartney's. We had all been to a Scaffold show in London, and a gang of us went to a restaurant for supper, including Ray Connolly, Polly James and all the members of The Scaffold.

At that time David was involved in the advertising business and was managing a couple of photographers, including the talented and famous David Bailey. It happened to be the first time Ray Connolly and David Putnam met, and formed a writing relationship that would go on to involve them both in screenplays and production of a couple of hugely popular movies, *That'll Be The Day* and *Stardust*.

David was very active in political affairs and later became involved in the movie business. Of course, he crossed the pond and even spent a couple of years as CEO of Columbia Pictures in Hollywood.

His films have included Academy Award-winning *Chariots of Fire*, *The Killing Fields*, *Midnight Express*, *Local Hero*, and many more memorable movies. His interests also range from education to social awareness to philanthropy; indeed he is a man of incredible talent and remarkable tenacity. He has certainly come a long way since the early days of hanging out with arty types such as our Mike and his satirical buddies.

I even tried to get a job working for him at Universal Studios, but he had already brought with him his trusty secretary from England, so that was a no no. But, as they say, God loves a trier.

Blackbird (Singing in the Dead of Night)

My Mum Edie was staying with us at Rembrandt in early 1968, recovering from an illness. Paul came home late one night and sat on the end of her bed and asked her, "Can you sleep OK, Edie?" And she said, "Well, on and off, but when I'm awake I always love listening to the blackbird that sings just outside of my bedroom window."

So Paul went downstairs and got brother Mike's big old tape recorder, I think it was a Grundig, and he brought it up and sat with Mum quietly until the bird started his nightly concert.

Paul captured the sound, took the tape away and edited it. A little later he went into the studio and recorded "Blackbird". Before he started to sing, he said "This next one's called 'Blackbird,' dedicated to Edie." I still have a copy of the original tape where Paul starts out by saying, "This one's dedicated to Edie", and whenever I hear the song, I feel very proud that it was dedicated to my Mum. I know there have been other stories over the years, where people have tried to say that the "black" in the title was about an African American, and the "bird" was referring to a woman – Liverpool slang – and that it was related to the Civil Rights movement, but it was in our little back bedroom that he originally recorded the sweet singing blackbird (in the dead of night). It is one of the special flowers in my garden of memories.

Ruth was in a Beverly Hills lawyer's office years later and became aware of some legal activities going on between Apple and the band Mr. Mister (whom this lawyer handled), involving the phrase "take these broken wings and learn to fly". She went downstairs to a bookstore on the ground floor of the building and bought a book by Lebanese author Kahlil Gibran called *The Broken Wings*. Soon after, the legal wranglings went away.

"Blackbird" finished up on the Beatles' *White Album* later in 1968.

Lady Jane

Before Linda Louise Eastman, whom I adored, there was the lovely Jane Asher.

One day when Paul and Jane were spending time at Rembrandt, they were all gathered around the kitchen table, and I was opening a tin of Nestle's cream to pour over the desert I was about to serve. I was so engrossed, listening to Jane's stories from times at the BBC that I absent-mindedly forgot to shake the tin until *after* I had removed the lid. The cream flew up the wall, in my hair, in my glasses and all over the dog. See, you don't have to wait until you get old to be absent-minded!

Jane was such a wonderful influence on everyone. Her elegance, beauty, and genuine high class captivated us all. Yet she was completely adaptable in our more down-to-earth household. She was always happy to cook and taught Ruth many fun things such as knitting, crocheting, cutting out strings of paper teddy bears, and making a toy theatre from a cardboard box and pipe cleaners. She was extremely artistic and inventive and gave Ruth a real role model to whom she could look up. She also influenced Ruth with early aspirations to become a good cook. Thank you Jane.

She fitted in perfectly at the family parties, mixing freely with all the rowdies and drinkers who would carouse either at Rembrandt for the traditional family New Year's Eve party, or at Bette and Mike's, Aunty Milly's or Aunty Ginny's houses, and also cousins Ian and Jackie's home in New Brighton.

She had me knit her a full-length jacket one time, which I was happy to do. Shortly thereafter when she was touring the United States in a Shakespearean play, she sent me a thank you gift of some fabulous Stevens of Utica towels. I kept them for years until they became threadbare.

When Jane and Paul returned from Rishikesh after their sojourn with the Maharishi in 1968, they visited me in Clatterbridge Hospital. I was recovering from an asthma attack. Jane was very gracious with all the patients and nurses, who were thrilled to meet her. She brought me a beautiful black velvet embroidered evening bag from her trip, which I still use to this day. More recently I watched her in a hilarious movie called *Death by Accident*, and she still looked radiant and magnificent.

Jane now runs a catering business, specialising in high-end custom-made cakes. She counts Prince Charles as one of her many clients.

What I love about Jane the most was that although her background was very different from ours, she never let it show. I will always have the greatest admiration for her and the many things she taught us all.

I follow her activities online, in her catering business, her acting career and her philanthropic and charity based interests. In late 2012 I read that she is once again appearing on stage in *Charley's Aunt*, reverting to her original love, the theatre.

Lady Jane will forever have a special place in my heart.

President Nixon

I distinctly remember sitting in our living room at Rembrandt watching the inauguration of President Nixon in January 1969. Linda was not too happy about the choice of her country's new leader.

As Brits we were fairly ignorant of the whole political game in America at that time. But Linda said her father didn't think this was going to be a good move for the country. As things turned out, how right he was.

The whole Watergate debacle was underplayed in the British media, and until I came to live in the States, I never really had much of a handle on its significance.

The first eye-opener I had was when I watched *All The President's Men*, the classic 1976 movie starring Robert Redford and Dustin Hoffman, which I watched in London after Jim had passed away.

I was absolutely transfixed by the plot – the reality show to end all reality shows. And now, as I write this in 2012, there are still debates about how it was all handled, and the part the media played in it all. Nixon insisted that he did not know anything about the tapes, but time has proved him wrong. Much of this information has now been leaked. I remember there being a lot of dismay when President Ford pardoned him. Upon delving deeper into this, I believe that Ford did what he thought was best for the history books, and felt it was time for Americans to put this behind them and move on.

Ladies and Gentlemen... (drum roll)... Pete Price!

I met the incomparable Pete Price back in the late Sixties when a neighbour brought him to our home at Rembrandt. He and Jim hit it off immediately, although Jim was very self-effacing and Pete was very flamboyant. We shared many a cup of tea as well as a lot of laughs.

Pete was a stand-up comedian of some note at that stage. He was known for his elaborate wardrobe, which included a newspaper suit, gold lame knickerbockers, and a full-length fox fur coat.

Years later when I was managing Gary Glitter and arranging a tour of nightclubs in England, we hired Pete to be the opening act of the show. That decision led to many gut-busting moments on the road, which never fails to bring a smile to my face. None more so than a leather rhinoceros that resided in the lobby of a local hotel, near the famed Batley Variety Club in Yorkshire. It's now called the Frontier and was the brainchild of Mr. Peter Fleming and his partner in Kory Entertainment, Mr. James Corrigan.

The rhinoceros was a fixture at the hotel until our gang checked out, taking it with them. They shoved it into Glitter's suite one night after the show where he was "entertaining" a couple of young ladies (not too young I will point out). They got a passkey, opened the door and threw this thing in the door. It frightened the beejeezus out of Glitter and put him off his stride.

At Batley Variety Club, a revolutionary 1600-seat cabaret dinner theatre in West Yorkshire, Pete was pouring his heart out singing "My Way" and became very confused when the audience started roaring with laughter. Poor Pete was unaware that the crew had toted this ugly leather animal on a dolly and propelled it across the stage behind him. That animal provided as many laughs as Pete did.

Pete relished the absurd and loved it when I wrote him a cheque for his services on the back of a big cardboard cut-out of himself, which he duly took to the bank amid much consternation of the tellers. In those days you could legally write a cheque on anything at all provided all the details were made clear and it bore the appropriate signature. Imagine trying to deposit one of those in an ATM.

Some forty years on Pete and I remain close friends. In fact, we speak every

Tuesday night live on his show at www.citytalk.fm. It's a way for me to stay in touch with what's going on back in Liverpool and keeps me from getting homesick.

Like the Paul Simon song, Pete's still crazy after all these years.

The Beatles Break Up

It was a very sad time when The Beatles broke up. Surprisingly, we were somewhat out of the loop up on Merseyside, and I tried to keep as much of the news away from Jim as possible. Not only were his rheumatoid and osteoarthritis becoming more distressing and painful, but also he was suffering from shingles, and his nerves were in a terrible state. But no matter how we tried to cushion the blow, the awful awareness was hard to avoid, with massive television, radio and newspaper coverage on the subject. It was like a messy divorce. Publicly, they had split in April 1970, but the legal stuff dragged on for years.

Paul was greatly concerned that the other three boys wanted to appoint Allen Klein as their manager whilst Paul wanted his father-in-law Lee Eastman to take over. This was cause for dissent amongst them all and didn't help matters. So on New Year's Eve 1970, he filed a lawsuit against his fellow band members.

Paul had put on weight, grown a beard, and imbibed a little more than usual. He seemed to cling to Linda more than ever for support. They were hounded by the press when they made their appearance in the High Court in London, and it was obviously a very sad and stressful time for them both.

The judge finally agreed his case on March 12, 1971. How ironic that The Beatles won a Grammy for *Let it Be* only four days later. Paul and Linda accepted the award from John Wayne; both were dressed very casually at what is normally a black tie occasion. When they took the stage, took hold of the three Grammy statues, Paul merely said "Thank you" and left the stage.

The Beatles were finally dissolved legally in January 1975. A lot of public slanging matches went on, which I know they all regretted much later. But words were said in the heat of the moment, which caused even more anguish to each of them. Everyone handled it in different ways, but in the end, they all were friends again.

We didn't see much of them around the time of the final split, although Jim and Paul had a couple of phone conversations. Jim never imparted to me what Paul said on the subject, but Jim was always a bit tearful when he hung up the phone. He felt so deeply for his beloved son and what he was going through at the time.

Paul and Linda spent some time at the farm in Scotland to reflect on their lives, their future, and his musical career. He decided he didn't want to become a solo artist, and thus, the idea of forming Wings began. The rest, as they say...

Four Lads Who Shook the World

In the early Seventies Pete Price was working as a D.J. in the Seychelles when he hit upon the idea of Liverpool erecting a monument to the Beatles. He wrote to the City Council and various other bodies who didn't really fancy the idea. Go figure. They only made the city world famous and made England untold millions, if not billions, and continue to do so in tourism.

The more Pete thought about it, the more their refusal rankled him. So he did what any good instigator does, and wrote to *The Liverpool Echo* about his idea. By the time he got back home from his working trip, the story had exploded, and was being featured on the radio shows and in the newspapers. It was literally the talk of the town. But still there was no concrete plan to officially do anything about it. In fact, he still has some of the letters and flyers from those far off days.

Pete contacted famous Liverpool sculptor Arthur Dooley, and in 1974 together they hatched a plan. They were thinking of having a Madonna-like mother figure with the babes in her arms, and this eventually evolved in the statue that still stands in Mathew Street adjacent to the Cavern: the famous: "Four Lads Who Shook The World."

It wasn't an easy road, as there was a lot of opposition as well as support for the idea.

Peter took over the Shakespeare Theatre Club and held a fundraiser. The much-loved Frankie Vaughan performed, Pete hosted the show, and there was lots of local support from musical acts and comedians. Pete didn't seek any glory for doing this, but was just happy to get it all moving.

Jim and I bid on and won a picture in a silent auction, and felt we had at least contributed to the event.

Pete raised about £1,500 that night. He asked Arthur Dooley how much he wanted for creating the sculpture and he asked for £1,000, which Peter happily paid him. Pete gave what was left over to Frankie Vaughan for the Boys Clubs Charity, which he supported. That created another memorable event in West Kirkby, when the streets were blocked off from there to Caldy, as a crowd excitedly awaited the arrival of Frankie, who was a hugely popular star in those days.

Then Pete had a scroll made to commemorate the occasion, and gave it to the city. The statue has greeted thousands of people from all over the world and is a proud fixture of the city. You can thank Mr. Pete Price next time you see him.

Elton John

When Paul would come home to Rembrandt, he'd always ask me what music I was listening to on the radio. One time I told him about Elton John, the new guy who sang a great track called "Your Song". Paul hadn't heard of him at that point, but obviously looked into who he was. The next party he hosted in London included Elton on the guest list.

It was the launch for Wings' *Red Rose Speedway* on November 8, 1971. The list of invitees was an interesting bunch. They ran the gamut from Lulu to David Essex and Keith Moon, Terence Stamp to Ronnie Wood, and many more.

I remember Elton walking in, sporting a plum coloured velvet jacket, black shirt and a silver-topped walking cane. It seems that he had sprained his ankle that day. At the time Elton had a lovely head of fair hair, reaching down to his shoulders. He was rather shy and sat alone against a wall in London's Empire Ballroom where the party was being held. I sensed his loneliness and asked various guests to go and talk to him so he wouldn't feel left out.

I wonder if he ever remembers that far-off occasion, and like to think I was instrumental in bringing him to Paul's attention.

He wouldn't need anyone's help in that direction now.

Wings Fun Club

When Paul first had the idea of starting a new post-Beatles band he came up with the idea of me running a fan club. He eventually decided to call the band Wings, and his fan club was called The Wings Fun Club.

As my middle name is Lucia, we took the name "Lucy" and made her the secretary. We opened a post office box at Heswall Village Post Office (now no longer in business I hear), and we were off to the races!

It didn't take much time before the word was out and the mail started pouring in. The devoted mailman faithfully delivered the mail, and I would correspond with the fans from my trusty portable Underwood typewriter. I had bought this for £20, which Jim gave me to put on a horse one day at Chester races. Not being a gambler, I pocketed the money and instead sent off for a typewriter, which duly arrived in a lovely little red zippered case.

Following my earlier grooming of Ruth to work with the Beatles fan mail, I once again roped her in to open the mail, paper clip the envelopes to the letters, check for enclosures, such as postage stamps, membership fees, international reply coupons, and items fans wanted to have autographed and returned. It wasn't anything like the volume of the Beatles-related stuff, but still became quite a steady job.

As time went by, and Jim's poor health became more of an issue in our lives, Paul suggested we move the operation to his MPL offices in London. The magazine format later changed to a newspaper type of publication. The Fun Club remained active until just after Linda's passing, and people still search on Google trying to find copies. They can usually get them on eBay from time to time. Because they're a collectors' item, they evidently fetch a pretty penny.

It is fun to look back and see yet another venture which began on our dining room table become a much bigger publication, just as it gave Ruth the experience that eventually led her to form our www.iFanz.com site. She will say that her childhood experience with fan mail sowed the seeds of her realisation that it is so important to "know thy customers", to quote her.

The Lovely Linda

Sometime in the early Seventies the doorbell rang at Rembrandt. I opened the door and, much to my surprise, there stood my daughter-in-law Linda with her daughter Heather sleeping in her arms, dogs around her feet, and not one, but two taxis in the driveway.

Paul had been called away and she was fed up being alone up at High Park Farm near Campbeltown, Scotland. So – *as you do* – she called a local taxi firm to drive her about three hundred miles to Heswall to hang out with Jim and us and the family until they could be together again.

The plan for two taxis was to carry the luggage, the animals, and the humans, so that if one should break down on this long, arduous journey, there would be back up.

My instincts kicked in and I went into the kitchen to put the kettle on to brew a pot of tea. I saw Linda pay these guys from a roll of money in her little multi-coloured "rag" bag, which she always carried. They didn't even want to stop for a cuppa, and we recommended them to the local pub, where I'm sure, as Scotsmen, they wanted to go for something a little stronger before freshening up for their return journey of eight or nine hours. I can't even imagine how much that must have cost. But I'm sure it was worth every penny for Linda to be in the bosom of loving family (albeit the in-laws), instead of watching the mists rolling in on the Mull of Kintyre whilst her man was on the road, although it always seemed inevitable that Linda would be drawn to a life in music – Linda's father was Lee Eastman, a powerful New York lawyer for many famous musicians, performers and songwriters.

She would often tell the story of when she was about one year old, her father commissioned writer Jack Lawrence to write a song for her, simply titled "Linda". It was published in 1946 and recorded by Buddy Clark in 1947. She said that because Jack was going through a difficult time financially, her dad said he could barter for his legal bill with a song.

Then in 1970, Paul wrote her another song called "The Lovely Linda". And lovely she was. In the light of criticism from the fans she held her head high. In the light of criticism from the music establishment, she held her tuneful voice. Ruth often reminds us when she's taking pictures, that Linda's own photography taught her to "look up" when taking photographs. "There's always another point of view if you just change yours," she would say. How right she was.

Walking in the Park with Eloise

One afternoon in June 1974 the phone rang at our Beverly Drive bungalow in Heswall. It was Paul, calling from Nashville. I handed Jim the phone. Paul said he and Linda were in a recording studio with Chet Atkins, the famed guitarist, whom Jim had long admired, and Floyd Kramer. Paul and Chet had been chatting about their dads, when suddenly Paul came up with the idea of recording a tune that he had heard Jim play on the piano when he was a lad.

Paul couldn't remember the middle eight bars, hence the phone call. Jim went over to the piano in our living room to play him the tune. His hands were badly affected by rheumatoid arthritis by this time, and he rarely touched the keys. But I held the phone to the piano while Jim played the song. That was it.

Some time after that call Paul visited Rembrandt with a copy of the record in hand, distributed on the Apple label. It was called, "Walking in the Park with Eloise" by The Country Hams. The B-side was a Paul and Linda composition called "Bridge On The River Suite". Jim was more delighted than you can imagine, being a part of this production and actually holding a vinyl copy in his hands. I still have that record. It has been around the world with me on my various travels.

At that time the public was not aware that it was Paul's recording. I believe he played washboard on it too, like the skifflers used to do. When I was at a Beatlefest years later, I was asked about it, and if I wanted to sell my copy. The answer was a firm "no" as it is one of the few possessions I treasure from happier times.

Cut to several years on. We were running Cloth Cap Management in Birkenhead, when one of our people, Chris Mellor, thought that maybe I should be receiving publishing royalties on that song, as the sole beneficiary of Jim's Will. So after a lot of digging and delving, this finally came to fruition, the result being that the Performing Rights Society, on seeing a copy of Jim's Will, began allocating a percentage of the royalties to me, via MPL Publishing. They are not very big payments, but always most welcome. I believe Paul performs it occasionally onstage, thus generating performance royalties. These trickle through to me twice a year, now, of course, done electronically, thanks to all these new-fangled computer systems.

McCartney Family Outing

On one of the occasions when we stayed with Paul, Linda and Heather at Cavendish Avenue in St. John's Wood, Paul got a wild impulse. He suddenly said, "Let's go out for afternoon tea." This sounded like a splendid idea, and we all quickly spruced up. Little Heather put on a blue organza frilly party frock, but insisted on wearing her blue wellies with it. Not best sartorial choice, I will admit, but she was so excited about the whole thing.

We duly drove to the Savoy hotel and were ushered in by an obsequious staff member who was overjoyed to see one of England's most famous faces arriving, together with a posse of people.

We were seated in this hushed restaurant, where the waiters seemed as though they were on castors, so smooth were their movements. We were treated to all the usual afternoon tea delights, with white gloved service, cake tongs, three-tier cake stands, cucumber finger sandwiches, strawberries and clotted cream, and of course, ceremonial pots of tea, served to us as though we were royalty.

Little Ruth was just beginning to become aware of her surroundings and was very impressed, as were Jim and I, although we grown-ups tried to appear more laid back about it. At one point Heather insisted on standing up on her chair and causing a bit of a ruckus, much to the consternation of our fellow diners. A nervous maître-d came over and asked if we might tone it down, and he was not very well received. Poor Jim was mortified. He was very much from the old school: "don't make a fuss", "don't draw attention to yourself" etc., while Paul and Linda were far more liberated and used to having things their own way.

It was another instance of the difference in attitudes between the older and younger generation. An example of Linda's self-confidence, as opposed to

Jim's diffidence. I first noticed it when, as we went out of the front door at Rembrandt to get into the car, Linda automatically sat in the front with Paul, leaving Jim somewhat nonplussed, and having to ride in the back with Ruth and I. Whereas, in other circumstances, he as the older man of the family, would normally expect to sit upfront, and have the women ride in the back of the car. How times have changed since then.

The Carpenters

Like millions of others, I was fascinated by the music of The Carpenters in the early Seventies. So when I heard they were going to appear at the Liverpool Empire, it became my life's mission to get tickets to the show. In those days, when a big American act was announced, people stood in lines around the block on the opening day of ticket sales. There was no Ticketmaster back then and patience was definitely a virtue.

Around that time Paul came home to Rembrandt for a couple of days. His cousin (on his father's side), Ian Harris, was visiting, and was also a huge Carpenters fan. Upon learning of our keen interest in the group, Paul called Alistair Taylor in London to wave his magic wand, and scored some tickets for Ian, his daughter, Liz, Ruth and myself.

We were so thrilled, not only with the fantastic concert, but to meet them backstage after the show. Karen, who was drumming in those days, was fairly exhausted but she and Richard received us very graciously. We exchanged pleasantries and they sent their best regards to Paul, who they held in high esteem. But who didn't?

Ruth was too shy to ask for an autograph but treasured the evening's printed programme, which she kept in her little trove of keepsakes for a very long time until it finally disintegrated.

We didn't have the luxury of scanners in those days, either. Time has taught us to digitise lots of stuff since then – photos, autographs, programmes, tickets, etc. – and what a world of difference that has made.

As for the Carpenters, the memories of that night don't need to be digitised. Like many others, they shall forever remain in my head.

RIP Jimmy Mac

Jim's health deteriorated over a period of several years, from the onset of arthritis just before we met in 1964 to his sad passing on March 18, 1976.

Bless him, he was willing to try anything that was suggested. Treatments included hot hand wax to footbaths, acupuncture to calcium injections, and many oils and medicines.

When we first met he was still pretty active and loved to potter about in his garden and greenhouse, and go for walks every day down to Heswall Lower Village with maybe a stop off at the Victoria Hotel for a whiskey and water. Then when Paul bought him a cottage in Carrog, North Wales, he loved to go on fishing trips on the River Dee.

But as the illness progressed and he became less able to do these things, he retreated to his armchair and watched a lot of television. He loved American programmes like *Rowan and Martin's Laugh In* and *Dallas*, but was happiest watching afternoon racing from the various English tracks. This still gave him the opportunity to have a "flutter", (a bet on the races) which would precipitate a phone call to his bookie in Liverpool. Then periodically I would drive him through the Mersey Tunnel to either collect his winnings or pay his debts.

After he had knee replacement surgery, it took Jim a long time to rehabilitate. We had a lovely man named Ken Kessie come to the house to help him with physical therapy. There was also another man named Roger Waterworth, who was blind, whose wife used to drive him around. They both did wonderful work to try to help Jim but we couldn't stop the progress of the painful disease. Of course, the weather in England didn't help with so much rain, fog and dampness. If we had only known what we know now, maybe he could have asked Paul to buy him a little place in Arizona or Palm Springs where the dry desert air would have been beneficial. It was so sad to watch him deteriorate and to lose his independence.

There was a lot of difference of opinion in the family as to how his final time should be handled. Jim always told me that he wanted to die in his own bed and not in some hospital. I could understand that some of the older generation of the Mac family thought I should be asking Paul to pay for a nursing home. I tried to explain to them that we were doing what Jim wanted, and in their grief they just couldn't accept that. It resulted in some unfortunate attitudes. We did have a night nurse for about the last week of Jim's life, mainly so that I could at least get a few hours' sleep. But at distressing times like that, sleep seems to evade one.

Mike's first wife Angie was with Ruth and I sitting at Jim's bedside when he finally left us, along with her youngest daughter Abbi. As he exhaled his last breath, and finally stopped, little Abbi said, "Oh look, Poppy's stopped." Out of the mouths of babes...

I had never actually seen anyone die before, and no matter how prepared you are for it, it comes as a terrible shock. We all kissed him and said a little prayer, hugged one another and wept. The cycle of life had finally ended, but Jim was surrounded by many of his loved ones. And that's how I want to go, too. (Or maybe to be shot by a jealous lover!).

RIP John Lennon

Like countless other people around the world, I vividly remember December 9, 1980, the day we heard that John Lennon had been murdered the night before.

We were living in King's Lynn, and had gone into the office early to decorate the reception office. Ruth was up a ladder, wielding a roll of wallpaper and I was on the upper floor doing manual bookkeeping in big blue ledgers for the artists that we managed at that time, the biggest one being Gary Glitter.

One of our young assistants came into the office and asked, "Have you heard the news?" We switched on the radio, and there it was. Unfathomable, unbelievable.

Ray Connolly, our dear friend and journalist had been planning to fly from London to New York that day to interview John. After lots of negotiations, he had finally clinched a date with Yoko over the phone.

Ray had a long time connection with John, as indeed he had with all of the Beatles, and held many of John's confidences. Does anyone remember when we could trust the media and believe what they told us? Now, the only certainties in a publication are the date and price on the front page.

We were visited that day by Geoff White, of the band Paris 9, and his companion, Carty, who had driven from Liverpool to King's Lynn to spend some time with us. I remember we all went to eat in a local Chinese restaurant that night (or was it a Greek restaurant?) and we were all stunned. Although I had never been very close to John, I felt he was like family, because of his closeness with Paul.

Ruth was prompted to write the piece at the beginning of this book about this, reflecting her feelings about the shattering effect on Paul of the sad ending to their amazing musical and emotional partnership.

Even though more than three decades have passed, John's death is still felt in the McCartney household.

Michael Jackson

I recall a time when Paul told us he had been advising Michael Jackson to get into publishing, i.e. buying up other people's catalogues, just as Paul himself had done with many things ranging from "The Canadian National Anthem" to the works of John Philip Sousa etc.

As things turned out, it was advice he may have regretted offering, when the battle for Paul and John's early compositions eventually ended up in the hands of Michael's people, and then became the central point of a long legal wrangle, ending with Paul not even owning the publishing on his masterpiece: "Yesterday". I won't subject my readers to the well-documented history of their publishing, which can be found online, but suffice it to say, in their early days, they were not as aware of the ramifications of music publishing as they eventually became, to their cost.

Paul's MPL formed a publishing company in 1971, and the business has been marked by considered acquisitions and sensitive, honest handling of copyrights. Among the writers for whom MPL administers are Frank Loesser, Carl Perkins, Buddy Holly, Jerry Herman, Harold Arlen, Jelly Roll Morton, Meredith Willson, Louis Jordan, Bessie Smith, Jule Styne, and Hoagy Carmichael. The company also administers the songs from many Broadway shows including *Hello, Dolly!*, *Annie, Grease, Peter Pan, Guys and Dolls, Hans Christian Andersen, Mame, A Chorus Line, The Music Man, La Cage Aux Folles* and others. Their catalogue of standards is unsurpassed, containing classics such as "Ac-Cent-Tchu-Ate The Positive", "Autumn Leaves", "Baby, It's Cold Outside", "Big Girls Don't Cry", "The Christmas Song", "Unchained Melody", "One For My Baby", "It's So Easy", "Blue Suede Shoes", "Sentimental Journey", "Tenderly", and "Till There Was You".

So, not only did Michael heed Paul's advice, but extended his reach to the Beatles' catalogue, which eventually finished up being owned by Sony. Talk about a long and winding road.

Here There and Everywhere: a Beatles Documentary

In early 1996, Ruth and Ken Barker sallied forth to England to capture some documentary footage for a piece about Beatles-related folks, which has still not yet seen the light of day. We were living in Nashville at the time, and Ruth set off to visit such folks as Cynthia Lennon and Jim Christie, Neil Innes, Bob Wooler, Billy Hatton, and various historical sites related with our heroes. I still have the tapes squirrelled away in a safe place. Who knows, there may yet be even another Beatles documentary to be launched on an unsuspecting public!

On their trip by EMI in London, Ruth had a few words with Linda, who was in a limo in the courtyard, waiting for Paul to join her and zoom off to we-know-not-where. Linda was very warm and acknowledged a letter I had sent her from Nashville, and asked how we were all getting along. Of course, just as Paul was about to join her, they were swept away by the various security and minders who were looking out for his safety.

Ken and Ruth did the usual spots: The Cavern, The Casbah Coffee Club, the old Bold Street haunts, staying with my sister Joan in Norris Green as a base while they were on their guerrilla-style shoot.

Whilst in the south of England, they visited the site at West Malling where "I am The Walrus" was shot for the infamous *Magical Mystery Tour*. It so happened that day that wrecking crews were smashing up the wall, and Ruth and Ken came away with a few historic pieces of that edifice, which, again, I have safely squirreled away to this day. I could never quite decide what do with them, but maybe once this majestic tome of mine hits the bookshelves, someone will come up with a good idea. Till then, they are just pieces of concrete at an undisclosed location.

When I read about some of the weird things that fans collect, I am prompted to think that they may even like to have a lump of concrete! After all, I, along with many others, treasure my pieces of the Berlin Wall, although that was a far more historical occasion than the filming of a drop of music for a TV film. But one never knows.

RIP Linda

On a sunny Sunday afternoon in April 1998, the phone rang at our home in Playa del Rey. It was Lyle Gregory, a radio producer who wanted me to go live on the air in a few minutes to talk about Linda McCartney's passing. At that stage, I didn't know anything about it and came as a terrible shock. I called Ruth, tried to gather my thoughts, and within seconds, Lyle was back on the air, connecting me with radio host Michael Jackson.

Paul and the children had obviously wanted to keep it all as quiet as possible. The first story out was incorrect, saying Linda had died in Santa Barbara, California, when in fact it was at their ranch in Tucson, Arizona. As so often happens when shocking news breaks, either of a plane crash, an earthquake, or some other catastrophic event, the rumour mill goes crazy without accurate background checks.

Apart from our sadness and shock, I just didn't know what to say and I was totally unprepared. Being live on the radio was not an easy way to grieve. I don't remember what I said, and I can only hope that I treated the news with the respect that it deserved.

Now that I've had more than a decade to think about what to say, Linda was a devoted wife, a wonderful mother and one of the greatest advocates for the ethical treatment of animals.

As a single Mum, before she met Paul, she had a good relationship with her daughter Heather, and times had not always been easy for them. Whilst living in the States, she would get various trusted people to sit with Heather while she went out on photographic assignments. In fact, as is well documented, it was through one of these assignments that she met Paul.

She loved to cook, ride horses, and be beside her loving husband. She was always happiest with animals around her. I can remember waking up in the middle of the night one time at Rembrandt, when they arrived from the farm in Scotland, and in addition to the usual gaggle of dogs, I could hear clucking sounds. Yes, they had stopped somewhere on the journey and bought some hens. She shut them in the downstairs cloakroom until morning, when she and I attacked cleaning up chicken poop. She had lined the floor with newspapers and put down dry food and bowls of water for them, but they still managed to make the place look like Oliver Stone had just shot a war movie in there. When daylight came around, she wrangled them back inside their newly-bought cages, and prepared to carry on driving back down to London where heaven only knows what adventures awaited them.

It had never been her ambition to be an onstage performer, but when Paul wanted her in the band Wings, she did exactly what he wanted, although she had to suffer a lot of grief from both fans and the press. But she battled on, and then established her vegetarian line of frozen foods and cookbooks. In fact, I understand she was working on another one when she passed away. But there were plans to have someone else carry on her legacy and I have a couple of beautiful books, which she signed and sent to me.

The saddest part of all is that, even with Paul's success and fortunes, in the end there was nothing he could do to prolong her life. He was at her bedside with the kids when she finally closed her eyes and was out of her suffering.

Her name and memory live on in Liverpool where the Linda McCartney Cancer Centre is a dedicated organisation working towards not only a cure, but to comfort the victims and their families while they are undergoing treatment. I donate a portion on the profits from my little tea company to these good folks. Help if you can: www.rlbuht.nhs.uk

Martin Lewis

Over the years, we have frequently come into contact with the engaging, witty and humorous Martin Lewis, a Brit who has been in the States for many moons and an expert on all things Beatles related.

His website describes him as P/Resident of the United States - with the "P" scored through in red. I urge you to take a look at www.martinlewis.com/

He frequently presides over various Beatles' seminars, festivals, (Fests For The Beatles, formerly known as Beatlefests), and celebrations. He is a welcome addition to many events. We often meet up with him at the British Consulate dos.

OK Martin, that's a fiver you owe me for free PR!

May Pang

I met May Pang some years ago at a Beatlefest in Chicago, which also included Cynthia Lennon. Cynthia and I were on a panel together, answering questions from the fans, when the moderator said he had a surprise for us. We turned around and there was May.

At first I was shocked, wondering how Cynthia would receive her, as May and John were together for some time, as has been well documented over the years. Fortunately May and Cynthia had a history as well – a good history. They embraced and were very warm and friendly with each other. They continue to keep in contact.

May was originally personal assistant to John and Yoko. She has emerged as another great photographer and her book *Instamatic Karma* contains many wonderful pictures. She was quoted as saying: "There were times I was a bit reticent in taking out my camera, like when some old friends stopped by to hang out. I didn't want to intrude on these moments but John insisted. He felt that I captured him in ways that no one else did because of his comfort level with me... For years, only my closest friends got to see these photos – which were literally tucked away in a shoebox in my closet. They were surprised that these images did not convey the John that was portrayed in the press during our time together. In fact, they saw a side of John seldom seen." She lovingly portrays pictures of John sailing with young Julian, and even one of John signing the legal papers that officially ended the Beatles partnership.

She is a very active lady, a single Mum with two grown children from her former marriage to producer Tony Visconti. She now has a popular radio podcast show and a line of feng shui jewellery. Like a lot of the Beatles' ladies, she has emerged from the shadows and is thriving.

Beatlefest aka The Fest for Beatles' Fans

I caught up with old friends and fans at the Fest for Beatles at The Mirage in Las Vegas in 2007.

Ruth and I strolled through the Bellagio on our way to the Mirage, taking in some of the wonderful plants, mosaics, and other wonders at Steve Wynn's magnificent hotel. Then on to the Mirage where Pauline Sutcliffe was overseeing the auction of some of her brother Stuart's art. The Mirage also features the Beatles' musical *Love* produced by Sir George Martin, a Cirque du Soleil production including the music of the fab four. The one-year anniversary of the show's opening had occurred a couple of days earlier, attended by Paul, Ringo, Yoko, and Olivia Harrison. In fact, *The Larry King Show* was aired from there. Quite a week for the Mirage and all things Beatles.

Ruth and I had fun walking through the various exhibit rooms, displaying scads of memorabilia, record albums, from buttons to Beatles jackets. I enjoyed chatting with the owner of "www.beatwear.com" a Beatles clothing store located on Matthew Street in Liverpool. Thanks to the Internet, he is able to ship all around the world.

A bar inside the Mirage called The Revolution Lounge holds a prominent place in the hotel, with the most amazing light show and projections on the walls and ceiling, accompanied by Beatles music.

Martin Lewis introduced a stellar line up including Denny Laine, Pete Best, Denny Seiwell and Lawrence Juber. Denny and Lawrence were members of Wings (at different times) with Paul and Linda. This session was held in a concert room where the musicians broke into impromptu versions of several old hits. Also part of the talented line-up was producer Mark Hudson, who has produced many of Ringo's albums.

It was great catching up with Denny Laine and Denny Seiwell, and we all shared recollections of times past on Merseyside. As always, I saw several generations of fans, from folks my age to little tots all singing along to their favourite songs. The Beatles seemed to touch just about everyone.

Scenes From My Life

Me, pushing a pram at about 18 months old, in Liverpool. *Photo: Mae Stopforth*

Me, Mum and sister Joan on the sea wall at Hoylake when the tide was out. *Photo: Bob Stopforth*

Enjoying the gourmet delights of egg,
chips and beans at Butlins, circa 1962.
Photo: Bette Robbins

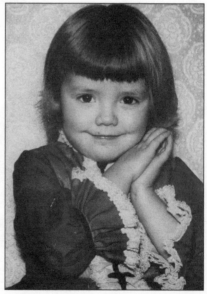

Ruth – before she was officially a "poser"!
Photo: Angie McCartney

Me with little Ruth and new husband Jim in the lounge at our Rembrandt home, shortly after our wedding.
Photo: Peter Archer Snr.

Ruth and Paul in front of Rembrandt 1966. *Photo: Angie McCartney*

Me and Ruth on the way to London from Lime Street Station, Liverpool in 1967.
Photo: Jim McCartney

Me, Jim, Jane Asher and Paul in the garden at Rembrandt after Mike McGear's wedding to Angela Fishwick in June 1968. *Photo: Edith Stopforth*

Ruth and Paul in the garden at Cavendish Avenue, summer of 1968.
Photo: Angie McCartney

Jim and his beloved horse Drake's Drum, at Colonel Lyde's stables in 1969.
Photo: Angie McCartney

Paul, Linda Ruth and Heather on
the stairs at Rembrandt in 1970.
Photo: Angie McCartney

February/Daily Expenditure · *Rembrandt*

Date	£	p	Date	£	p
2nd			Tv aerial	7	00
	2	00			
	2	00			
		65	Laundry	5	11½
	1	81½	Piano Tuner	3	00
		58	Laundry	6	21
		40			
	1	18			
	1	80			
	2	00			
	3	00			
		40			
6th	1	00			
	3	00			
	1	40			
		65			
	8	57			
	2	69			
	2	05			
	10	00			
	2	00			
	3	00			
	1	50			
	2	65			
		50			
		12			
	3	45			
	4	00			
	8	00			
		75			
		25		1	85
	1	50		2	00
		57		8	50
	1	17		2	00
		40		2	00
	2	00			
	6	20			153

My daily diary. I tracked all expenses by hand – now I use Excel! *Photo: Angie McCartney*

Heather, Ruth Paul with Mary aloft, Linda carrying Stella and Jim at High Park Farm, Mull of Kintyre, Scotland, summer of 1971. *Photo: Angie McCartney*

Linda, Stella, Mary, Paul, Heather and Jim at Rembrandt, summer of 1972. *Photo: Angie McCartney*

Jim and Ruth playing silly buggers in the back garden at Rembrandt, circa 1972. *Photo: Angie McCartney*

Cousin Geraldine Archer, Ruth in her David Cassidy T-Shirt, Julian and Cynthia Lennon in the garden at Rembrandt, circa 1972. *Photo: Angie McCartney*

Paul, Linda and baby Stella saying hello to Jim at Rembrandt, 1972. *Photo: Angie McCartney*

Ruth, Mary, Heather, Stella and Paul goofing around at
Rembrandt in 1972. *Photo: Angie McCartney*

Me and Jim in the back garden at Rembrandt, having a
smooch. *Photo: Ruth McCartney*

Beatlefest, 2004: Mark Lapidos of The Fest for Beatle Fans, Lou Harrison, Me, Alistair Taylor, Ruth and half of Pauline Sutcliffe.
Photo: Martin Nethercutt

Me, Ruth and 42nd US President William Jefferson Clinton at a private party for his book tour in Los Angeles, 2004. *Photo: Martin Nethercutt*

Celebrating Roseanne Barr's birthday with the late, great Phyllis Diller. I thought it was a pyjama party! *Photo: Ruth McCartney*

Me and Sir Richard Branson reminiscing about the good old days at the
Britweek.org Gala in Beverly Hills, 2010. *Photo: Ruth McCartney*

Me and the second man on the moon, Buzz Aldrin, at Britweek 2010.
Photo: Ruth McCartney

Ruth, me and Martin at the launch party of JPSelects.com where my Organic Teas were selected as the first brand by John Paul Dejoria. Beverly Hills, 2011.
Photo: Anna Griffin

Eloise Dejoria, me and my new hero John Paul Dejoria at the White Party evening at The Gathering @ Aria in Las Vegas, 2011. *Photo: Ruth McCartney*

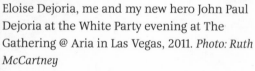

Me and the Reverend Jesse Jackson at his 2012 Birthday Celebration. *Ruth McCartney*

Leaving Liverpool: King's Lynn,
Norfolk, London, Sydney, etc.

After Jim passed away and our circumstances immediately changed, we moved into a different phase in our lives, I made a decision that was not my wisest. It was a bad business decision and I lost everything, including the little flat we moved into after Jim died. Like Rod Stewart once sang, "I wish that I knew then what I know now."

We moved to King's Lynn in Norfolk, then on to London, took a variety of jobs, learned who our real friends were, and picked up the pieces. Through a stroke of luck we were able to buy a pair of tickets to Australia where we begin a whole new life courtesy of our lifelong friends The Crawfords who gave us a home in their newly constructed extension. Life is a series of unexpected events, new connections, new relationships and new adventures. Boy, were there a lot of adventures...

A Piece of Cheese for The Cat

In 1980 after we had lost our Merseyside home to the bank, we moved to King's Lynn in Norfolk. It was a sleepy little town, but oh so full of characters.

We lived in rented flats, one being in Tilney All Saints. It was out in the boonies with wild bats that would fly around up in the rafters after dark. Then we found a flat close to our High Street offices, which was above a Bowling & Social Club on the Queen's land at Sandringham. It was across from the Village Church where the Royals would sometimes visit, and we would be besieged by the press, wanting to come and take photographs from our upstairs windows. We got one or two photos of our own that way, too.

We would be amused to see the Queen Mother driving her green Ford Fairmont around the area. She would go into the local sweet shop to buy treats for her grandchildren. We would see her "detail" (private detective) sitting in the front passenger seat, white-knuckled, looking very pale, as the dear old lady would drive in her inimitable manner. She was very petite and could barely see over the top of the steering wheel. And you never saw her without one of her large floppy hats.

Ruth planned to buy a property from the five thousand pounds remaining from a small trust fund that Jim had left for her to put a roof over our heads. She found a delightful old property, which was part of a group of mill houses, overlooking a courtyard.

We were one floor up and much to our dismay we had a cranky elderly lady living downstairs who used to rant quite a bit. The previous owners of Ruth's flat were brother and sister. This old girl got the idea there was something improper going on, and used to bang on her ceiling and yell about. One of her favourite middle of the night rants was "And she who sleeps with her brother!" I wonder what she thought about Ruth and me.

Then she took to breaking the windscreens of every car parked outside her front door. She would often shout about coming up to visit us and bringing a piece of cheese for the cat. We didn't have a cat.

One evening as we sat in the window seat and looked down the courtyard, we saw an old lady in a white nightgown. She sported long white hair and carried a lit candle in an old-fashioned candleholder. She appeared first in one window, then seemed to walk to the next one, then the next one. When we talked to a neighbour about this sighting, she said, "Oh, that would be the ghost of a lady who lived there who is still waiting for her husband to return home from sea." She also told us that the three windows we saw her pass through were all separated by walls and were different apartments. It puts shivers down me spine just thinking about it.

On another occasion we had a friend staying with us, and she slept in the same room as me. She woke me up in the middle of the night to say she had just seen the original exposed beams of the house, yet when she turned the light on, the newly refurbished surface was securely in place.

We would frequently find windows open when we returned from work at night, windows that we know were securely closed when we left. Then there were the lights and even the stove warm on a couple of occasions. So we knew we were not alone.

We had moved there with our little business, Cloth Cap Management, when all else had failed, and we were forced to leave our flat in Brancote Walk in Oxton. They do say that whatever doesn't kill you makes you stronger. I'll not dispute that statement.

UFO

Sometime in the early Eighties I was driving back home in King's Lynn in the middle of the night after a gig. I was on a lonely road near Royal Sandringham when I suddenly saw to my right a sight that chilled me to the bone. It was dome-shaped object with a series of lights beaming down from underneath.

I pulled the car over, switched off the engine and the lights, checked that the doors were locked, and sat there with my heart pounding. I don't know how much time elapsed – it was like living through a nightmare - when suddenly it stopped hovering. It took off with a "swooshing" sound going back up in the direction from whence it came.

After I composed myself, I switched the car back on and drove the rest of the way home. I let myself into the flat and sat up all night with all the lights on.

Say what you will, but there's no doubt in my mind there's other "intelligent" life out there. In more recent times, NASA's Mars *Curiosity* explorer is delving more and more into that aspect.

Even our own dear Martin Nethercutt is officially a Martian, as Ruth had his name inscribed on a plaque that is attached to the rover that landed in 2012. Maybe that accounts for some of his odd behaviour!

Gary Glitter

I wondered long and hard whether to even write this passage as a lot of the stardust from Gary Glitter's name has faded over the years due to deficits in his character, and if truth be told, he was an odd duck when I knew him. There was something just off about the man.

You see, I was his co-manager back in the Seventies when he still had some sparkle. Glitter, along with T. Rex, Slade and Sweet were part of the glam rock movement, which sprung up in the United Kingdom in the early part of that decade. The entertainers wore campy and androgynous clothes, make-up and hairstyles. Glitter was perhaps the most outrageous and pushed the limits of bad taste by sporting a notoriously bad wig. We used to call it Barney (a play on Barnet, Brit rhyming slang for Barnet Fair/hair). One night in Edinburgh when Barney flew off and went surfing into the audience, a quick thinking roadie tossed a bottle of Coca Cola into the three-phase power system and caused an immediate black-out until the offending hair piece was found and reapplied to the star of our show.

The massively elaborate stage gear was a big part of Glitter's act. After the shows we used to take his clothes back to the hotel and dry out the sweat with a hair dryer. Ughh! He had one particular white sequined tailcoat that was becoming the worse for wear, so Ruth took it to pieces, made a paper pattern, and created a new one. This flaming project took over the entire floor space of our little apartment on the Royal Sandringham Estate, and she lovingly sewed it together on a small Singer sewing machine.

Glitter hired a very talented musician, who unfortunately, didn't look as good as he sounded. The poor guy was miked up to a lengthy extension cable and had to play his instrument offstage, behind a curtain. You just had to be glam in those days.

The groupie scene was alive and well/sick in those days. Some of these brazen skeezers would work their way from the truck drivers to the roadies, to the drum roadies, to the band, with the hope of getting to Glitter. If they only knew.

Mickey May, Glitter's head roadie, usually took care of Glitter's needs, including selecting "talent" for after the show backstage visitations. I used to ferret out the younger ones and would either take them home or put them in taxis to keep them from the fate that might have been worse than death, although we didn't know the full extent of his proclivities in those days.

Always the ham, Glitter would end each concert with the song "Remember Me This Way". He'd always sign off, "I love you!" and then would name the city. One night in the Midlands, he was so stoked and had no idea of his whereabouts. As he sank to his knees he shouted, "The Potteries – I love you!"

I got on much better with the roadies and backing musicians, who were a rowdy and playful bunch. The boys would get into some fun stuff to break the monotony of touring and cheap hotels – like super-gluing the keyboard keys down, or the piano player's glasses to the top of the piano. I recall a gig in St. Albans, where our overnight accommodation was in a chintzy country hotel. It was there where Brian "Saxophone" Jones (also still going strong on Merseyside), marched into the breakfast room and plonked down his Liverpool FC backpack and loudly requested: "Can I have two poached eggs on beans on toast and a mug of tea with five sugars please, luv?" The standard menu was made up of such delicacies as kedgeree, herb omelettes and French toast. "This isn't a Little Chef, sir," she icily replied.

In a Belfast hotel, one of our crew startled room service by calling down for "two soft boiled eggs and some soldiers please." This was at the height of the IRA's activities and the word "soldiers" set off an immediate alarm response. Everyone was immediately evacuated to the car park in the wee small hours until it became abundantly clear that "soldiers" was the term for fingers of buttered toast to dip into the boiled eggs.

I remember another occasion when I was the rotten egg. I was watching them chatting up girls at the bar after the show, and one of them, whom I knew to be recently married to a lovely girl, was doing his spiel. He was not too happy when I tugged on his sleeve and said loudly, "Sorry to interrupt, but I wanted to remind you it's time to take your syphilis pills."

That was long ago and far away, but Glitter still remained the same, if not weirder. I remember watching the telly and seeing a story about him finishing a period of incarceration in Thailand for nefarious activities with under-age girls. He was clearly uncomfortable with this newfound attention, which shone a spotlight on his strange peccadilloes.

Despite all of his activities and the recent revelations, there are still a number of Gary Glitter appreciation Facebook pages out there. Some girls will never learn.

Spike Milligan vs. Gary Glitter

One day while I was managing Gary Glitter at Cloth Cap Management in Birkenhead, Merseyside, I received a phone call from Spike Milligan. I was excited to be speaking to him, having been an admirer since my youth. He was demanding to speak to Glitter. I explained to him that our office was in Birkenhead, and that Glitter lived in the south of England. I politely offered to take a message, but he insisted that he wanted to speak to him personally, as he had discovered that "this man has sullied my woman." Wow, pretty scandalous stuff for those days. I managed to placate him to a degree, and promised to give his number to Glitter and have him call the very angry Spike. I don't know which of Spike's wives he was relating to, as I know that he had three during his lifetime.

But nevertheless, an incredible talent, who in lots of ways reminds me of John Lennon on reflection. I bought several of his humorous books and read and re-read them. In fact, writing this has prompted me to go searching on Amazon and go around one more time. It would have been wonderful to see those two brilliant minds together.

MPC Artists and Management in Soho

During our time in London I got a job working for Michael Peter Cohen, who was a prominent agent and manager of many BBC radio personalities, both in radio and television. The offices were in Soho, which at the time was the "naughty" district of London. There were peep-shows, strip clubs, seedy watering holes, lots of "ladies of the night" pounding the pavements, and even a sex shop or two.

There was a club nearby called The Office where gentlemen would go after leaving their real office, to gamble, drink, mix with "ladies". Their gimmick was that it had public telephone booths, which relayed sounds of typewriters in the background while the patrons called home to say they were delayed late at the office. Genius if you ask me.

Michael had connections to the J. Walter Thompson Ad Agency, then the biggest agency in the world. He would periodically fly over to Beverly Hills for meetings with them and, amongst others, Artie Mogul. Artie Mogul was an executive at Warner Bros. Records, Capitol Records and MCA Records in 1976, and was named president-chairman of United Artists Records, which he purchased in 1978. A true giant in the music business in those days. He died in 2004.

Michael would have me telephone the Beverly Hills Hotel and ask for him to be paged. This was in the days when pageboys would walk around the hotel and poolside with a blackboard on a stick with the name of the person they were seeking, and cry out, "Paging Michael Cohen". I don't even know if he was staying there, but it obviously sounded good to have someone paging you from England. He knew the merit of PR in those far off days. I never did get to speak to him on these occasions, so I have to assume he was not really there.

Michael's wife was from South Africa and I believe her family was associated with the diamond business. He would occasionally bring his young son Jonathan to the office. I see from their website that he is now in partnership with his father and the business has flourished tremendously since my early days there.

One of Michael's clients, Mike Read, the famed radio DJ (still going strong) employed Ruth as his wake-up caller since he had to be on air very early. She would make the calls before setting off to her first job at Roundel Productions.

Michael had good connections with the BBC, which led to us being able to go to tapings of various TV shows, including *Top of the Pops* where we first saw Rod Stewart, Electric Light Orchestra, and many other musical acts and entertainers of the day.

This is also where we first saw The Young Generation, Pan's People, The

Second Generation, and various dancing troupes, one of which included Nigel Lythgoe as a young hoofer and choreographer. Little did we know what heights of success he would achieve in later years.

Michael's son, now all grown up, is part of the team. Their highly successful firm handles not only TV personalities and entertainers, but sports personalities, books, voice-overs, and a myriad of related business ventures.

As we say in England, "Good on ya!"

More London Adventures

Ruth and I have survived several "interesting life development" patches, which has been our bond over the years. We've often had several jobs at the same time to make ends meet, sometimes sleeping on the floor in a friend's flat.

One of her jobs was at a company called Roundel Productions, an audio video promotions company.

One day she was asked if she had her passport with her since they needed someone to fly out immediately to Hamburg. The firm was launching a new IBM product nicknamed 'The Monster', and their person on the ground needed back up. She did, so, armed with some petty cash, off she popped. I was working one of my many temp jobs at the time, on a TV nightly show called "*Help!*" As always, we lived together and shared a car. She called me briefly from Heathrow airport and was pretty excited to be flying to Hamburg.

Our *Help* show went live on air every night at 6 p.m. People would call in asking for help and advice on all manner of topics. It was all hands to the pump when airtime came around, and silence on the set was mandatory.

Moments before we went live, my phone rang. It was Ruth on a line with lots of static. All I could make out was "... but I'm alright." My heart skipped a beat. Then seconds later one of the technicians said there was something coming through about an explosion at the Hamburg Convention Centre. I was beside myself.

We found out shortly after that what happened. Ruth had been standing behind the IBM product (encased in a foam-lined cabinet) and as the compere announced, "...The Monster", she had to pull a handle to release the piece of equipment out of the cage. As she pulled the lever, a spark set the whole damned thing alight. There was immediate panic, and Dennis Norden, the celebrated writer and TV celebrity, made an announcement telling everyone to keep calm, don't panic, and to leave in an orderly fashion.

Ruth's first instinct was to rush back to the dressing room area and bang on doors, alerting people, one of whom was the much loved actor Andrew Sachs from *Fawlty Towers*.They all reached the car park without injury, but there was much confusion, smoke, and emergency vehicles. It was later that night before a very unnerved Ruth arrived at Heathrow, and eventually got back safely into our little pit.

We wept and clung to one another. After going through so much together, we were frightened at the thought that it might have ended like that.

A Land Down Under

In early 1983 we moved from London to Sydney in search of a better chance and better weather. We had a wonderful experience in Australia with our dear friends the Crawfords when they took us in and gave us a home. We had so much fun and laughter come in our lives with our Antipodean connections, including our loads of nieces, nephews, and their assorted offspring who had emigrated from Wigan to the Queensland area. We worked and played, and renewed old associations, including Ruth's biological father, Frank Clark, and half-brothers Andrew and David.

After a fifty-two hour flight with horrendous stopovers, the Crawfords threw us a surprise welcome party. All the neighbours showed up… Yikes. At least they recycle!

The Crawfords of Australia

In the mid-Seventies, Mike Robbins had asked me if I could provide beds for his friends from Sydney, who were coming to Liverpool for his son Ted's twenty-first birthday party. I was happy to do so, but more than happy when I opened the front door of our little Beverly Drive Bungalow in Gayton to four of the most wonderful people ever to come into my life: Babs and Will Crawford, their daughter Shayne and son Rory. Still like family to this day.

You know how you just hit it off immediately with some people? This was one of those occasions. Mike had met them whilst working the cruise ships where Babs was an entertainer, Rory her accompanist, Will her business manager, and Shayne her general "mother's little helper" and companion.

Then in 1983, they were to play an even bigger part in our lives when we were near rock bottom in London, having lost our home, moved to the big city, and done all manner of jobs. The theft of my mink coat provided us with the insurance money to buy two one-way tickets to Sydney. One of Ruth's jobs was as a bartender at the Admiral Codrington pub behind Harrods. She happened to tell one of her customers (a travel agent), our tale of woe. He said we'd never be allowed entry into Australia on one-way tickets, but needed to either provide proof that we could support ourselves (half your luck) or show on-going travel plans. So this wonderful man (whom I had never even met) told her to get to his travel agency office the next morning where he would provide us with tickets on-going from Sydney to Auckland, New Zealand, and return to London. He made her promise that as soon as we landed she would mail back the other portions, which she did.

So in no time we were up, up and away, a journey which took us from London to Paris (where we sat on the tarmac for eleven hours due to an air traffic controller strike), Paris to Jakarta (I've no idea why), Jakarta to Darwin, and finally, Darwin to Sydney.

We were so broke that we welcomed each new flight to see what they might have to eat on board. And when we finally landed, utterly jet lagged, badly in need of a shower, and starving, we were met by a big gaggle of Crawfords and their friends, whose welcome made us forget the trials of the past three days. Willy insisted that we do a tour of the Sydney Opera House on the way home.

Upon our final entry to their beautiful home in North Curl Curl, it was marked by cries of "Surprise, surprise..." Oh yeah, we were surprised alright. We looked like a couple of homeless people (which at that time was a more than accurate description), and smelt like we had spent the night in a dumpster. Anyway, all went well. They had built a special extra room onto the back of their house for us, combined with a bar, which we all sampled with gusto.

Then came the rain! The worst they had had in sixty years, they said. The downpour managed to find the snags in the newly built extension, and water began pouring in. Rory and Will came to the rescue with stepladders, buckets, sheets of plastic, and anything that would plug holes or catch water. We were all so jaded at that point, we were laughing and crying at the same time. But eventually, blessed sleep, and a morning of sunshine, a new day, a new life beginning. (Now how many times have I heard that?)

The whole family has for a long time been involved with the Sydney Opera House in various capacities, from box office to lighting, to staging and production etc. I feel that the place almost belongs to them.

Rory also flies for Qantas, so visits us frequently on his stopovers to Los Angeles. We have made a few trips to Australia over the years. In fact, Ruth and Martin spent their honeymoon there. Truly an incredible country where nobody takes themselves too seriously, and they work to live – not live to work, like we do in other parts of the world. Friday afternoon sees a mass exodus to the beach. Not a bad idea. And I don't need to tell you about their sense of humour and the ability to take the mickey out of themselves.

When I win the lottery I might just finish up in Sydney.

Getting a Grip Down Under

As Babs and Will Crawford had many ties with the media in Australia, they suggested getting in touch with the *Sydney Morning Herald* and some local TV stations to tell them that The Fabulous McCartney Gals were in town.

Sure enough, this created a buzz, and we were invited on to a local Morning Show in early 1978 to tell them what had brought us to Australia. Naturally, we didn't want folks to know we were down on our luck (always looking on the bright side), and were a little guarded during the interview.

In the green room, we met the delightful Pammie Saunderson, who was the PR lady to Danny La Rue, the British female impersonator and personality who was making an appearance on the show promoting some gigs. He was absolutely charming, and outrageous to a degree where he took people's breath away. When he was in mufti, he was a very butch male, although never hiding his sexuality, but in costume, he was incredibly glamorous and over the top. This was long before we discovered Dame Edna.

Pammie was an ex-pat Brit who had been out there for many years, representing such people as Bill Cosby, Pam Ayres, and various other performers who would come out from England and the States. She and I formed a bond pronto which lives on today. Delightful sense of humour, of course, and a lifetime chum.

We shared the bill with Nathan Pritikin, whose revolutionary diet was hitting the headlines at that time. I was amused to find that he had brought his little packed lunch with him, not wanting to risk the catering services at the studio. He was not necessarily promoting vegetarianism, but rather reducing fat in the diet. He became remarkably successful, although the Aussies took some convincing that his way (fruits and veggies) was best. They were too entrenched in their barbies of steaks, eggs, and gloriously fatty foods. But still, he tried.

Watching the show from Adelaide in Southern Australia was Frank Clark, Ruth's biological father, who ultimately got in touch with me via the TV station, resulting in us getting together, as I mentioned earlier.

Our appearance also led to us being contacted by another Brit, Fred Williams, a journo who was working for Rupert Murdoch's *Sydney Morning Herald*, resulting in some interviews which brought us in a couple of grand (a Godsend), and invitations to various events and job opportunities. And so our Antipodean adventures began.

Overtime at the Newtown Photo Lab

Ruth and I worked for two nice men, Rick and Len, who ran a series of ColourCare Photo outlets in and around Sydney. Come Christmas time, they had the usual

Santa Claus photograph booths in all the big stores. Rick and Len helped us write a particularly colourful chapter of our lives in Australia.

We used to hoof it from North Curl Curl via the Manley Ferry and train to Newtown, outside of Sydney. We'd then pick our way carefully past the pubs when they did their early morning hosing out of the tiled bars to get rid of the puke, piss and other bodily liquids, and open up our little domain.

It was across the street from an off-licence (what the Americans call a liquor store and known to the Aussies as a "grog shop") run by two delightful Greek chappies. As soon as they saw that we were at the switch, they would toddle across with a jeroboam of champagne. Thus began the daily ritual of opening the bags of Polaroids that had come in overnight from the branches, process them to go upstairs to the lab for developing and printing. We'd then merrily chomp through the day until the photos were developed and ready for us to pack and mail out to the eagerly awaiting parents.

This went well until one day when there was a phone call from a distressed mother who said, "You've sent me a picture of this darling little boy on Santa's lap. Um, I'm not saying there's anything wrong with him but he's black, and my husband is white, and he has been away in the Army for ages. I don't know what he's going to say if he sees this."

Seemingly, in our happy afternoon phase, we'd skipped one envelope in the outgoing system, and thrown the sequence of pictures out of whack by one print. She obligingly agreed to go back in the next day for a new, free, picture of her little boy. We never heard from her again, and concluded that it must have ended well.

Another episode happened where a distressed photographer called in to say that "Santa's croaked." It seems that poor old Santa had left this mortal coil in the middle of a roll of film. When she discovered his demise, rather than waste the rest of the celluloid, she continued to plonk little kiddies down on his lap, shoot the picture, and move on to the next unsuspecting child.

Then she put up a notice at the front of the Toyland Grotto. It read: "Santa's gone to feed his Reindeer." After a few frantic telephone calls to try to locate the owners of the firm, she tracked them down, but the store manager wouldn't let the undertaker remove poor old (by this time stiffening) Santa until after closing time, several hours hence. Our only regret is that we never got a photograph of him finally being transported, still in his Santa suit and black shiny boots, sitting bolt upright in his Santa chair, via the back steps to wherever they take dead Santas.

Perhaps the worst part was that Santa was no longer around to claim his overtime.

A Really Meaty Story

During our sojourn in Sydney, Australia, we spent some time staying with a delightful man named Adrian Tondi in his lovely apartment on Lavender Bay, right across from Luna Park. He made us most welcome, although he didn't have much furniture, so we made do with sleeping on our bags of luggage.

His mother was the owner of a local racecourse and he had various business interests, so he wasn't there very much. He did give us free range of the property and its facilities, the contents of the fridge, the bar, and whatever else we could find. It looked across the bay to Luna Park, the famed amusement park adjacent to the Sydney Opera House.

One day, he asked Ruth to do him a favour: take his tuxedo to the dry cleaners as he had an event coming up. She duly dropped it off and later, got a phone call from a slightly bemused young lady who asked, "Do I take it Mr. Tondi doesn't want the steak sandwich in the breast pocket?"

Seems that Adrian, on one of his forays into the nightlife of Sydney, had stopped off on his way home at Harry's Cafe de Wheels in Wolloomoloo. He bought himself a spot of supper, had a bite and stuffed the rest in his pocket then forgot all about it. Harry's was the famed spot where all the toffs and all the drunks would stop off late at night for sustenance. By the time the sandwich reached the cleaners, it was green and furry, so of course, Ruth declined the offer of recycling.

Professor Dr. Geoffrey Edelsten

While staying on Lavender Bay, it was suggested that, to earn extra funds, Ruth might like to do some catering on a yacht belonging to Dr. Geoffrey Edelsten, then a famous surgeon who was a high flyer, moving in circles of celebrity, high finance, and 'A' listers of all kinds. He used to entertain his celebrity contacts on weekend trips around the Sydney Harbour, where the beautiful people loved to be seen. In those days, the paparazzi had not yet taken a hold, but all of the regular journos and cameramen were always on hand to see what celebs they could capture for the tabloids.

He used to dock his yacht close by Adrian Tondi's place on Sydney Harbour, which is where we would go aboard on Saturdays, and Ruth would work her culinary magic in the galley (with me as number one on the clean-up crew), and serve all manner of delicacies and cocktails to the guests.

His first wife was known for driving a pink Cadillac, and they also had a pink helicopter, in which would ferry their guests to and from the lavish social events. Why, oh why didn't we have a camera? She in fact told the press that he bought the Sydney Swans team as a gift for her. (Aged sixty-six, Dr Edelsten married his second wife in late 2009. Beforehand, he claimed he and Brynne Groden, then twenty-five, a former California fitness instructor, would wed at the Crown Casino, Melbourne, with *Seinfeld's* Jason Alexander and *The Nanny* star Fran Drescher officiating, and that Fleetwood Mac would play at the reception. I am not sure if this ever came to fruition.)

Dr. E. was actively involved in the music business for a time in Australia. His path would take him from riches to rags, culminating in a spell in prison, a brain tumour and a move to Beverly Hills where he became a famed plastic surgeon, car collector, patron of the arts: you name it, he did it. In 2001, he operated a company called "Gene E" which offered paternity testing by mail order. He was subsequently struck off the medical practitioners' lists and has since re-applied several times, without success.

He published a book in November 2011 called *Enigma*. A very interesting read. He is now back in Melbourne, I believe – yet another of the colourful characters with whom we have crossed paths on our journeys.

This spread deliberately left blank for your notes of how fantastic this book is,

and a list of the people you're going to recommend it to.

Our First American Sojourn

On our exit from Australia, we travelled Southern California. We began assimilating into the American way of life, which we found wonderful, plus the constant sunshine was warming in more ways than one. We tried to decide what do with the rest of our lives, being overwhelmed with the amount of choices and the warmth of the welcome from the Kendall family who gave us a home.

After pursuing some contacts we had learned of in Australia we went ahead and took the plunge (again!), and moved from Orange County to Hollywood. We got temping jobs again, my secretarial skills once more saving the day while Ruth made her first foray into the commercial production business, leading to many long lasting friendships and connections that we cherish to this day.

This portion of our story takes us through the USA, before we travelled on to Germany, Russia and Siberia, and back to the good old US of A in our pursuit of the American Dream.

But more of that later. If you're still with me?

Cousin Beryl Kendall

One of my McCartney in-laws who played a very special part of my life was Beryl Kendall. She was the wife of Tom (Aunty Milly's son). Tom was a seismologist, and they travelled the world to many remote places.

When Jim and I were first married, I experienced some difficulty integrating with some parts of the family. Not so with Beryl, with whom I hit it off without any reservations. Her mother still lived in a little house in Everton, and was related to the German Hess family. Her brother had a green grocery business in Wallasey and used to bring Jim sacks of potatoes from time to time.

Beryl bore three lovely children: Debbie, Lyn and Tim. She and Tom were firm believers in the importance of education and worked towards that goal with their children. Tim attended Gordonstoun at the same time as Prince Edward, and had some fascinating tales to tell of his time there.

When the Kendalls visited Jim, Ruth and I at our cottage in Carrog, North Wales, we had an exciting moment when Tim, then about six years old, was at the bottom of the steps watching the swift River Dee running past when he heard someone shouting for help. Without a moment's hesitation, he ripped off his shorts, jumped into the river, and tried to get across to the opposite bank to help the drowning man. The distressed person got swept a few feet down the river, and was lucky enough to get caught in some weeds, which stopped his progress. Other folks came running and duly bailed him out of the water. I can remember little Timmy's face, all excited, as he came running back up the sixty-odd steps, stark naked, to be greeted by his stressed out Mum with hugs, kisses, and a dry towel.

On one of Beryl's peripatetic adventures they set sail up a river in Africa with baby Debbie. Upon their arrival at their remote destination they were greeted by a couple of natives, one of whom was called 'Happy'.

Beryl did everything possible to fit into this life. She remembers that one afternoon when they entered their makeshift dwelling, Happy had made up the bed, and there, laid out on the pillow, was a newly washed, neatly folded condom, which he had obviously found amongst the sheets. Now that's recycling for you!

In the early days of her marriage, Tom invited his new boss and wife to visit them for Christmas dinner. This made Beryl very nervous, and she made every effort to prepare a sumptuous repast for them. Imagine her horror, then, when on asking Tom to carve the turkey, he put the spoon into its rear end to remove the sage and onion stuffing, and out came – a tea towel! Yes, when she had cleaned out the bird, she had left the cloth inside, which was by then cooked to a turn, along with the stuffing.

When our sojourn in Australia was coming to an end, as our visas were running out, we were in touch with Beryl in Laguna Niguel in Orange County, California, and she insisted that we come and stay with her while we figured out the next move in our lives.

Lyn and husband Van Kline picked us up at Los Angeles Airport (LAX), and we were utterly bewildered at the traffic. We had never seen anything like the multiple lanes of traffic on the California freeways. We stayed with Beryl and family, where we were made more welcome than anyone could ever hope to be. We lived on our savings (our earnings from the Newtown Photo job) and Beryl offered to take us to Monarch Bank to open an account. We had $2,900 in total and spent $2,100 of that on an orange VW Bug, leaving us with a total worth of $800. No work permits, no prospects, but plenty of optimism.

We had never seen anything like the bank. It was a beautiful open plan office, with candies, balloons, coffee, soft drinks, all for the taking.

Beryl helped us through the process and we opened an account and felt very proud to be a part of the American system. Little did we know at that stage that we would remain here for so long, and even proudly become US citizens further down the line.

Beryl had a Monarch Bank moment of her own. She used the drive-through, which in those days had a gadget you placed your cheque into, it swooshed away down a passage to who-knew-where, a bank teller processed it, and swooshed the receipt back to you. Beryl, in her anxiety to move on to her next errand, drove off with the gadget in her car, and when she got home, found a message asking her to please return it to the bank!

But she got even better at the "drive-by" game. On another occasion, she filled her car up with gas, went inside the gas station to pay, then drove off with the gas pump still attached to her car. Only when she heard a screeching sound did she realise what she had done. She jumped out, removed it, and left it on the roadside, too embarrassed to go back. Next day, when she was passing the gas station, she saw that workmen had dug up the forecourt and there was a lot of activity going on around the pumps. She elected to use a different gas station from then on.

When we lived with her, I was taking a shower one day when, for some reason, the bottom of the bathtub suddenly opened up underneath me (I didn't know I was *that* heavy), and gallons of water poured through into her living room. What a panic that was. After Ruth managed to switch off the water at the main, we rang a local disaster recovery firm who moved in and worked to put it all back together again. I was mortified, but oddly enough, we finished off the day the laughing our socks off – with the help of a bottle of Bacardi, as I recall. It took months for poor Beryl to get it sorted out with her insurance and the Home Owners' Association. But bless her, she didn't hold it against me.

She loaned us her car to drive up to Hollywood to meet folks that our Australian contacts had suggested we contact, which in turn led to a series of events, culminating in Ruth's first marriage to Paul Antonelli, our relocating to Hollywood, Green Cards, citizenship etc., and the rest, as they say...

Beryl sadly left us on June 16, 2012, after a four-year battle with cancer. She was cared for by Tim and Debbie until the end. She was a wonderful woman, a dear friend, and an inspiration to us all.

Ric "Hollywood" Wetzel

One of the most colourful characters in our lives since we arrived in the States has been, and still is, Richard (Ric) Wetzel.

A friend in Australia recommended that we get in touch with a photographer friend when we moved to Los Angeles. During Ruth's first meeting with this chappie at a San Fernando Valley restaurant, they sat at a table close to Richard and his date.

Ric and his friend didn't seem to be getting on too well. When both of the dinner partners went off to the loo, Ric moved over to Ruth and said "Shall we?" Like the nutty gal that she is, Ruth got up and left with him, and went off into the sunset.

As they say in Hollywood, that was the beginning of a beautiful friendship. Shortly after, she invited him to our apartment in North Hollywood and we all got on like we had known each other forever.

The first day I met him he took us all to an afternoon movie and sneaked in a bottle of vino, which we surreptitiously supped from paper cups. That is, until he dropped the bottle. We listened to its progress down the rows of steps in the balcony, clattering on its merry way, a clunk at a time. Fortunately, by the time the lights went up the offending bottle was far away from us.

Ric is one of the most entertaining, talented, funny, and fabled guys that I have ever known. He has done weird things like trying to talk me into getting a tattoo while watching a Gay Pride Parade on Sunset Boulevard. He has driven me, bungee-corded to the back of his motorcycle, into a French restaurant on Ventura Boulevard, and come to "mind" me for an Easter weekend when Ruth went to Cousin Geraldine's wedding in Liverpool. That time he arrived with a bedroll and a huge biscuit tin full of big fat rolled joints. We caroused that evening and around 5 o'clock on Easter Sunday morning, we set off for a sunrise celebration at the Hollywood Bowl on his trusty motorbike. An amazing experience.

We also spent a crazy weekend at a mud baths in Palm Desert, along with his lovely parents, Dick and Evelyn. Like Ric, they used to traverse the States on their motorbike, long into their elder years.

Ric's motorbike provided some interesting moments... like the time he rang our doorbell late at night. When we let him in, his cheek was hanging off and he was in a dreadful way. He wouldn't hear of us taking him to the emergency room. All he wanted was vodka, peppercorns and painters' tape (Yes – that's what we wondered too!). He went in the bathroom, crushed the peppercorns with a pocketknife, and sprinkled them into the open wound. He also took a drop of vodka, poured some on the wound, some down his throat, and stuck it all together with the tape. We winced more than he did. Then, shortly after, he rode off into the night, and was going to an Iranian belly dancing Bar on Ventura Boulevard to meet some people. His pain threshold was something to behold.

Ric is a Vietnam Vet: he has jumped out of helicopters, over the side of aircraft carriers – you name it, he's done it. He even dabbled in the entertainment business, mostly as a hair and make-up artist on movies, commercials, infomercials. He was also the former bodyguard for the Bagwhan Shree Rajneesh, a cult leader who set up camp in Oregon some years back. He (the Bagwhan that is), had twenty-seven Rolls Royces and hordes of followers. It was an incredible run until he was forced to disappear to India, where he died in 1990.

When my sister Joan and husband Peter were visiting from Liverpool, we went to a Hollywood Bowl concert, and Ric sat between Joan and I. She and I were both getting very sentimental and weepy at the music. So what does Ric do? He ripped out the short sleeves of his Hawaiian shirt and handed one to each of us with a flourish to dry our tears.

On a later occasion, he called both Ruth and I at our workplaces and said he was in the Vets Hospital in Westwood, having had another misadventure on his motorbike. Ruth was the closest and got there first. She found him and his pal in adjoining beds, surrounded by takeaway Chinese food containers, smoking joints, and awaiting the arrival of a couple of hookers that they had ordered to come to their hospital room. They duly arrived in their fake fur coats, glittery platform soled boots, fishnets, and a credit card swiping machine. Exit Ruth.

We got another late night phone call from Ric. The muffled phone call began: "Hi, this is Ric. This is my one phone call..." He explained that he had been taking photographs somewhere close to the Reagan Ranch in San Ysidro and had been picked up by the cops. Since he was carrying a gun (he was licensed to do so because of his bodyguard work), they hauled him in. He needed bail money. We got dressed, drove to the nearest Western Union office and wired some money to the police station. His dad (who had worked for "the firm") got over there, bailed him out, and repaid us the money quick smart.

But Ric always paid off in spades. He introduced Ruth to Paisley Productions in Hollywood where she landed her first assignment putting on false fingernails for an actress who had already spent the beauty parlour allowance she had been given on cocaine! That led to a great spell of work, friendships, and adventures for Ruth over a period of several years.

One of Ric's recollections whilst working at Paisley was doing a Bristol Cream Sherry ad with Peter Cook, who he found rummaging around in his make-up kit looking for "stuff". Peter, it seems, finally settled for some nail varnish remover, which he dabbed onto cotton wool balls and sniffed eagerly.

Bless him. Dear Ric still comes to us regularly to cut our hair for a nominal cost of a couple of slugs of Scotch and water. Truly a renaissance man.

Murder I Wrote!

In our early days living in Los Angeles, we became friendly with a writer/actress/voice-over lady named Carol Baxter.

One Thanksgiving when she had Ruth and I as guests in her home, we got to talking about plots, stories and anecdotes. I specifically told her about an old friend of my Mum's, a lady named Mabel Wolf. Mabel had told Mum that she was psychic and when riding her bicycle around Freshfield on the outskirts of Liverpool, she would sometimes hear a phone ring in a telephone box. She would go over, pick up the phone, and receive messages from her long deceased husband, telling her of things that were going on in the village. Mabel fancied herself as an amateur sleuth and would busybody herself into local affairs, worrying the local police to distraction with her theories. She would hear "the voices" and have visitations and apparitions guiding her towards solving crimes. That was far as it went, but it seemed to make for a good outline for the TV series.

With Carol's help and encouragement I created a document, laying down my ideas on paper. I sent it via regular mail to the New York home address of Angela Lansbury.

I was working for RKO Home Video at the time. They had worked on a production of *Sweeney Todd* with Ms. Lansbury, and one of my colleagues knew where she was living. So I sent it off to her, and never heard any more about it. I called it "Cry Wolf" in honour of Mabel. No certified mail, no return receipt. I don't even know if she ever received it. Probably not.

Some months later I read in *The Hollywood Reporter* that a TV series was in the works about a lady writer who sleuthed out suspicious activities. Naturally, I felt that it strongly resembled my story and I called the Writer's Guild (I was not a member) to ask for their advice. They had me send them a copy of my outline and eventually got back to me. They said while there were several similarities, there were not enough for them to take it up on my behalf, which would cost me a fee which was way out of my league at that time. I just dropped it.

But whenever I saw publicity for *Murder She Wrote*, I would always mutter under my breath, "Murder *I* Wrote!"

Note to self: Register all concepts with the WGA!

Earth Girls Are Easy

One of my many jobs in my early Hollywood days was as a production assistant, working under Kim Cooper on a Dino de Laurentiis production called *Earth Girls Are Easy* in 1988. Amongst the performers (who were not yet stars), were Geena Davis, Jim Carrey, Damon Wayans, Jeff Goldblum, and the forever pink Angelyne. It was a comedy about furry aliens who land in a San Fernando Valley swimming pool, and are smuggled into a local hairdressing salon called "Curl Up and Dye" (ouch!) to be de-fuzzed, with some hilarious results.

I worked on post-production with Kim, who, I am happy to say has remained a dear friend. She has moved on at Fox to loftier productions ranging from *Mrs. Doubtfire*, *Fight Club*, *Phone Booth*, *The Devil Wears Prada*, *Titanic* and *Avatar*. Kimmie has certainly run the gamut of genres and directors. Oh, and not forgetting *Alien³*, when I worked for her on the lot and sat through the premiere with my eyes closed. I'm a wimp when it comes to sci-fi and horror movies.

The production manager on *Earth Girls* was Sue Baden-Powell, a descendant of Lord Baden Powell, the founder of the Boy Scout movement in England. So that's a family with a range of experiences. Sue's career has been as varied as Kim's. To my recollection, since *Earth Girls*, she has been involved in the production of such movies as *Equilibrium*, *The Box* (really scary), *The Invention of Lying*, and even a Royal Charity Concert for the Queen and Prince Philip shot in Sydney, Australia. Two very accomplished and busy ladies.

Kim and I still laugh about the way she would "shush" Jim Carrey, who was already showing signs of his great, yet manic personality. She would often tell him to stay in the trailer until he was needed. I'd like to see her achieve that today. Ruth and I spent time with her in her lovely office on the Fox lot in Century City early in 2012, and we always have fun catching up on so many old times. She told us of her new project, *The Life of Pi,* which is the story of an Indian zookeeper's son who finds himself in the company of a hyena, zebra, orangutan, and a Bengal tiger after a shipwreck sets them adrift in the Pacific Ocean! So Kim should have an interesting book to write whenever she slows down long enough.

She and I even made an attempt to drop a few pounds by joining WeightWatchers during post-production on *Earth Girls.* However, we got a little disenchanted when their operators used to stalk us if we missed a meeting. It began to feel a little too restrictive for us, and as we like to relax at the end of the day with a glass (or was that a vat?) of wine, they made us feel guilty about that, too.

I did have a later stint with Nutrisystems, which worked for a time. But I guess I'm not cut out to be skinny. I'm an Earth Girl, but I'm definitely not easy!

Dudley Moore

Ruth briefly dated Dudley Moore during a period when he was between wives, and their British sense of humour bonded them immediately. He had a house on Venice Beach, California, and partnered with producer Tony Bill at a nearby restaurant, 72 Market Street. Unfortunately, it closed its doors a few months before Dudley passed away.

We had some lovely evenings around the piano at his house, and would inevitably finish up being raucous, sharing English ditties and jokes, dissolving into gales of laughter. I could never quite get used to the fact that this lovely man, who was by then a huge movie star, could be a friend of ours.

Sometimes he would ring us on a Saturday afternoon when he was lonely, and we'd reminisce about the old days growing up in England, which hadn't been easy for any of us. I would repeat to him corny old jokes that my father used to tell, which he found hilarious, although they were chestnuts to me. But there's always someone who hasn't heard them.

We were originally followers of his career, starting with *Not Only But Also* with Peter Cook on British TV. I still have their original albums (some rather naughty stuff, too). Then Dudley became a movie star with hits such as *Bedazzled, Foul*

Play, 10, Arthur, and became a beloved household figure to millions.

His musical prowess was a separate talent. He made a lovely album with Cleo Laine and John Dankworth called *Smilin' Through*. The title track was a beautiful old song which my father used to play on the piano and my mother used to sing. We had so many simple, happy times in those days. Dudley was pretty amazed to know that song went back as far as 1919. I still have his 12-inch vinyl album, along with many others that I have carried with me on my travels around the world.

Dudley was particularly touched when Ruth told him he was the reason we originally came to the United States. We were down on our luck, living in London, working several jobs each. One Sunday afternoon we scraped up enough pennies to go to see the movie *Arthur*. That changed our lives. Ruth formed the resolve that we would one day live in America. It took a bit of a detour as we lost our home. We ended up in Laguna Niguel, California, and finally were awarded citizenship of this fine country. Twenty plus years on, here we are (and still crazy after all these years).

Some years back, when Ruth was asking celebrities for recipes for a charity cookbook she was compiling, he sent her one.

Nothing can replace happy memories of such times with gentle people like Dudley. He died on March 27, 2002. The official cause of death was pneumonia, but in truth, he'd been battling progressive supranuclear palsy for many years (although he only publicly admitted to having the disease in September 1999). He was cared for by his dear friend, fellow pianist Rena Fruchter and her husband. The palsy had the effect of making him appear drunk at times and has been described as similar to Parkinson's. In fact, he was fired on the set of *The Mirror Has Two Faces* for consistently not remembering his lines. He appeared to be inebriated, but in fact, it was the onset of this insidious disease.

He was honoured by the Queen as a Commander of the British Empire, and attended the ceremony at Buckingham Palace in a wheelchair, frail, but determined to turn up to accept this award which meant so much to him.

Dudley, with or without the Queen's blessing, was royalty in my book.

Bette Davis

In the mid-Eighties, I was approached by celebrity headhunters, Pauline and Harriet of The Right Connections, to see if I would like to interview for a job as personal assistant to famed actress Bette Davis. I had hooked up with them during my time working for Kim Cooper in the film industry.

I was perfectly happy with my job, but I recommended my dear friend Lora Colvard. She and I had lived through several riotous experiences with *Penthouse* magazine and Jet Records (run by the late Don Arden, father of Sharon Osborne).

Lora was interested and set up an appointment to meet the great, but now rather frail lady. She was hired on the spot.

She took great pains to renew her wardrobe, and was very excited about her new prospects which promised her lots of perks, comfortable quarters of her own in Ms. Davis' West Hollywood home, and various benefits.

But it didn't turn out as she had hoped. "Ms. Davis" (and that was how Lora was told to address her), was monumentally mercurial (which is a nice way of saying she flew off the handle regularly), and would insist on sitting down to a formal dinner early every evening. Her poor housekeeper lived her life like she was walking on broken glass. She and the other staff had to tiptoe around Ms. Davis, and remain silent whilst serving dinner.

One of Lora's first indications that it wasn't going to be plain sailing was when the wrong water glasses were set on the dining table. The boss lady picked one up and hurled it at the poor housekeeper, thundering, "These are *not* the right water glasses!"

I was dying to hear from Lora about her progress. She eventually she telephoned me from a payphone at a nearby Ralphs Supermarket, as she was not allowed to make personal calls from the residence. It seems that Ms. Davis would make Lora get up after retiring for the night to sit and smoke ciggies with her and chat. It wasn't long before poor Lora decided to pack it in and return to her private life and the nice apartment which she had fortunately kept.

Lora, like myself, has lived a peripatetic life, and now lives in the Nashville area. She made a surprise trip to my eightieth birthday celebrations. We speak regularly and reminisce about our colourful times in the wicked world of Hollywood.

At least the old movie stars were larger than life and would hit the headlines without falling out of a nightclub in the wee small hours. The studios were very controlling about their images, and even gay people had to assume fake identities and were provided with "love interests" of the opposite sex to continue the smoke screen with their public. Who would have believed otherwise when watching the Doris Day and Rock Hudson movies?

Ozzy Osbourne

My good buddy Lora Colvard worked for Don Arden of Jet Records in the Hollywood Hills. We formed a bond that would take us through several adventures, and which is still as strong as ever today. Lora's work brought her into contact with such luminaries as Ozzy Osbourne, Lita Ford, ELO, Animotion (formerly Red Zone) et al. Don was the father of Sharon, now Sharon Osbourne who became Ozzy's manager with great success.

Lora introduced Ruth to Paul Antonelli of Animotion, who became Husband #1. Their union resulted in her becoming first a Green Card holder, then a citizen, and enabled me to do the same. At one stage she brought Ruth on board as a temporary assistant, working on a variety of projects, and bringing her into contact with so many people who are still in our world today.

She was in the office on the fateful day when Ozzy was said to have bitten off the head of a dove at the record label's offices. She only became aware of this when all the lights on the switchboard lit up with calls from frantic radio and TV stations and journalists.

That story has become legendary, with so many versions of it appearing in print and on film and video, that it would be crass of me to disillusion the reader with the real truth.

Ruth Killed Orson Welles

When I was working at *Penthouse* Magazine in Westwood, my lovely boss, Wendy Bloxham would occasionally treat me to a meal as a perk for some of the extra hours I would put in which weren't subject to overtime payment.

One of these was the use of her credit card to take Ruth and I out to dinner, which we did on the evening of October 9, 1985, to celebrate what would have been John Lennon's birthday. We went to the swanky Ma Maison in Hollywood, with its trellises, ivy, French provincial style cafe tables and little white lights in the trees, for drinks and din dins. It would be our last time to experience this fine restaurant, which closed its doors a couple of months later.

As we sat having our pre-dinner drinks, who should come lumbering through from the kitchen area but Orson Welles, the great man himself. The waiter told us that he was more comfortable getting in via the back doors which opened wider.

He was seated in a far corner of the bar, and on gaining eye contact with him, Ruth raised her glass and muttered some complimentary remarks about her admiration for his work etc. She offered to buy him a drink. At first, he declined any alcohol citing recent doctor's orders, and settled for a mineral water, but then after some of her usual persuasive banter she said to him, "It would be such an honour to buy you a drink – one little martini isn't going to kill you!" Mr. Welles politely accepted and the waiter duly put one down before him. He lifted his glass and we all toasted one another across the room.

Imagine our horror when, early next morning, we heard on the radio that he had passed away in his sleep that night. Evidently, he had just appeared on *The Merv Griffin Show* on TV, and was feeling unwell. His excessive weight was a serious problem, as we evidenced by his laboured breathing, but it was wonderful to remember that he was ever the perfect gentleman in the way that he acknowledged us.

It is no coincidence that my favourite all-time movie is *Citizen Kane*, and it was chilling to know that we had been in the presence of this great (but much under-appreciated man) in his last hours on Earth, maybe even the last people he spoke to.

I will never forget his mellifluous voice, and particularly enjoyed hearing a story (which may, of course be urban legend) that on one occasion, when checking out of a Hughes Supermarket in North Hollywood, in response to the cashier's "Have a Nice Day," he is said to have responded: "Madam, I've already made other plans."

Starlight Foundation

I spent a couple of years working for Starlight Foundation in Century City, Los Angeles, which was very fulfilling.

We worked with many celebrities, most of whom would participate only if they were guaranteed anonymity, both for their donations, and their visits to sick children in hospitals.

In contrast to his more recent reputation, one of the kindest people we worked with was Bobby Brown, who was then comparatively unknown, and now a worldwide celebrity. He would sit at the bedside of sick children and slip in and out of the hospital unannounced. It's amazing what a difference a few years can make. He was with New Edition at the time.

Fund raising was difficult, and the lady who founded the organization, actress Emma Samms, was very hands on, but at that time was also very busy with her television career, appearing in such epics as *General Hospital*, *Dynasty*, *The Colbys* etc., and she left the day-to-day operations to her cousin, Peter Samuelson, and a very able team of responsible people. I was a general assistant, working on a variety of tasks, from coordinating donation drives to wrangling celebs to accede to the children's wishes, to interacting with the parents, volunteers etc. It was a very interesting job, and made me realise how fortunate I was to have raised a healthy and fulfilled child.

Our friend and client Corbin Bleu is now a supporter of Starlight Foundation, and it is interesting to note that, from the small offices we had when I worked there, they now have a presence in the UK, Australia, Japan and several chapters in the US.

I remember on the run up to a big event that we received huge donations from Lou Diamond Phillips and Michael J. Fox (via their PR people of course), and that when we held an event at Ed Debevic's Restaurant in Beverly Hills, people like Michael Keaton, Dudley Moore, John Stamos, and a host of other celebs turned out to give us their support and star power.

Starlight Foundation does wonderful work, not only in granting wishes to seriously ill children, but in the comfort and support they provide for the parents and siblings of the patients.

George Carlin

I recently re-read *Brain Droppings* by the late George Carlin and was reminded of the time when I answered the phone at Australian American Public Relations in downtown Los Angeles. At the time I was working for Claudia Keech, who now runs the very successful MotherInc.com online publication in her native land of Oz, and oversees the career of her actor son, Callan McAuliffe.

The voice on the other end of the phone said, "My name is George Carlin, and I am a comedian." I was flabbergasted but quickly corrected him. "No, you are *THE* comedian," I replied. He was very flattered. It turned out that he was planning to book some appearances Down Under and had found us through Yellow Pages. He was looking for information on Aussie comedians so he could research their brand of humour. I was able to tell him about one or two that I had personally experienced, like Norman Gunston and Kevin Bloody Wilson, and give him a brief snapshot of their humour. He was very grateful and gave me his private number so that I could feed him more information and funnies as they came to mind. I used to call his machine and leave him jokes and observations, and felt very honoured to do so. For me, he was one of the beacons of observational humour, and he will never be replaced.

Brain Droppings was published in 1997 and here we are, fifteen years later, and it is still as funny and relevant as ever.

Patrick Duffy

Sometime in 1987 I received a phone call one Sunday afternoon from a lady who said her name was Carlyn Duffy, the wife of actor Patrick Duffy. She had been given my name by a mutual friend about a job opening she had as their personal assistant. She didn't tell me who, and I was very curious.

Anyhow, Carlyn invited me to come to their house in Encino a couple of evenings later for an interview. I was pretty excited. Patrick, apart from his fame on the TV show *Dallas*, had been in the headlines recently as his parents were murdered in their Montana Bar by two young men. They were later convicted of murder and sentenced to seventy-five years in prison. One of them recanted years later and admitted that he was the lone gunman, which allowed his cohort to be released from prison. This brought the whole tragic story back into the headlines, no doubt causing more heartache for Patrick and his family.

When I got to the front gate of the house I was buzzed by Patrick himself, who then walked me up to his living room. He asked me to wait there while he got his wife. Imagine my surprise when I saw that their two young sons were watching TV and playing with toy guns. This somewhat shook me, in light of the horrendous murder of their grandparents not long before.

Moments later Carlyn joined us and they both interviewed me. They told me that they travelled a lot and needed someone to be both their personal assistant and oversee the activities of their boys, Padraic and Connor, when they were on their travels, and to sometimes travel with them. This part of the project didn't really appeal to me as I felt I was too set in my ways to take on responsibility for two youngsters. They were most courteous and kind to me, and Patrick walked me out to the gate. I remember how incredibly tall he seemed to my four-foot-eleven-and-a-half-inch frame.

I re-joined Ruth and my friend Lora Colvard who were waiting for me at a nearby bar. I never heard anything more from the Duffys. They had probably sensed that I was not keen to take on the role of babysitter.

In early 2012, I was so pleased to see Patrick as Bobby Ewing again in the revival of *Dallas*. He looked wonderfully fit and handsome at sixty-three. Patrick's one of the good guys and I'm genuinely happy for him.

David Cassidy

David Cassidy was in the UK on tour in 1974 and had an incredible following, the likes of which had not been seen since early Beatlemania.

Like millions of others, Ruth had a monumental crush on David and asked big brother Paul if he could get her an autograph. Paul duly called David at his London Hotel after some sleuthing by his people. When David picked up the phone and heard a voice say "Hi David, this is Paul McCartney." David calmly replied, "Yes, and I'm the Duke of Edinburgh" and slammed the phone down.

When the next call came, he was more inclined to believe it. They evidently chatted for a few minutes, and Paul said his kid sister wanted an autograph. Eventually, Ruth received a big package at Rembrandt, which consisted of several LPs and an autographed photo. It read: "To Ruth, be happy, stay free." She still has it to this day, and that picture, like us, has been around the world a few times.

We remain friends with David and his lovely wife Sue. Ruth convinced him that he needed one of these new-fangled things called a website many moons ago. He was our second client. The site has lived through many incarnations and is now being run one by one of his fans in Australia.

When David was living in L.A., he and Ruth literally bumped into one another and hung out for a time. Then later, when he was married to Sue, and their son Beau was born, Ruth and Martin visited them in Las Vegas. Martin did an astrological chart for little Beau, who's not so little now.

Ruth and Martin were invited to be a part of David's fiftieth birthday celebrations in Vegas where the guest list included his stepmother, Shirley Jones, Dave Madden (their manager on *The Partridge Family*) and many, many more friends and loved ones.

Sue started a children's charity named Kidscharities.org in 1999, and Ruth served on the advisory board, contributing Internet-related guidance. In many different ways, our paths have crossed over a long period of time.

Sue hosted an early group meeting of her Arbonne cosmetic interests at our home in Playa del Rey a couple of years ago, and has since gone on to great heights with this company, being their ENVP. She was honoured at a big event in Los Angeles in late 2011.

We have always gone to see David's shows whenever possible. His popularity still remains with fans old and young alike.

Germany and Russia

After Ruth had met and married Husband #2, Dieter Bockmeier, on a commercial for toothpaste in California and a wedding in Las Vegas at The Little White Wedding Chapel, she visited his family in Munich and somehow got involved with a local TV station, and in turn, with a Record Executive from Virgin Music. He said that if she could provide him with a demo, he would help her to get a record deal in Germany.

So, nothing ventured, nothing gained, she dashed back to base in the San Fernando Valley, had me resign from my job, made a demo and sallied forth to Germany (with her ever-loving Mum in tow), and by the time we got there, this guy no longer worked for the TV station, so we were up the proverbial creek without a paddle, and living with Dieter's lovely parents on the outskirts of Munich.

The day after we arrived, Dieter went away on assignment to a far-flung island, in his capacity as a gaffer, to film a movie, leaving us to our own devices and phrase book.

Ruth, whose German was sparse, to say the least, began looking in the Yellow Pages for record companies, not knowing they were called Schalplattenfirma, and eventually picked on a phone number for something called Jupiter Records. She got herself an audition, and was off to the races once again with a record deal, a producer, and connections to folks who wanted her to tour Russia, Siberia, and all the countries that ended in "...stan" like Uzbekistan, Turkmenistan, Tajikistan. You name it, if they had a stadium and a sound system, she played there. It was an amazing time in our lives. I followed along as the "stage Mum" and general dogsbody.

We had an armed bodyguard at all times named Sasha who would sit on a chair outside our hotel room all night in case anyone tried to kidnap us. I don't know who they think might have paid the ransom!

What's in a Religion?

When Ruth and I moved to Germany, we were obliged to register at the police station. For visitors, it is mandatory to let the authorities know at all times where you are living. So off we trotted to the Polizei, passports in hand, to explain that we were visiting with the Bockmeier family as Ruth had a potential offer from Virgin Records for a contract.

"Name, Address, Religion..." I was asked by a very stern looking woman in uniform.

Being a naive Brit, I was horrified by the last question. When I asked why I needed to give my religion, I was told they needed an answer immediately. She certainly didn't look like she was playing games. I panicked and gave her a totally left-field answer.

"Callithumpian," I said.

"Vos is dis Callithumpian?" she asked.

"It is an ancient Scottish sect," I countered. "Have you not heard of it?"

"How are you spelling Callithumpian?" came her response. I spelled it out for her.

To this day I am on the Deutsche records as a practicing Callithumpian. (Look it up on Google some time – it makes fascinating reading!)

Ruth followed my lead and having overhead my conversation, she announced herself as being a "pedestrian".

I found out later why it was a requirement. The Catholic Church made deductions from wages at source for their funds. If you were baptised a Catholic and did not donate to the church from your earnings, you would not be permitted to be married or buried on consecrated ground. How Christian of them.

I figured the Catholics had enough money of their own and could probably get on without a piece of my pay cheque.

Alvin Ailey Dance Theatre

In 1989, while we were living in our fifth floor flat on Leonrodstrasse, I got a phone call from my friend, Joanne Fish in Los Angeles, saying she was working with The Alvin Ailey Dance Theater of New York, and they were planning a visit to Munich, but that the logistics were proving problematical. She wondered if I had any suggestions. So I rallied the troops, including Dieter Bockmeier, (Ruth's Husband #2) who was a gaffer, and Ruth's then-manager Warren LaRose and his business partner, Dieter Lück. They were all wonderful in helping to set this up, culminating in a very successful show at the Deutsche Theatre in Munich.

The choreographer of the piece to be featured, Barry Martin, was in a wheelchair, having had an accident in South Africa some time previously. Alvin Ailey was debuting a piece called *Chelsea's Bells*, in honour of Barry's niece, Chelsea, which was set to a Melissa Etheridge song. It was performed by Aubrey Lynch, and in all, the party consisted of ten people, which included two assistants for Barry.

Anyway, finally the day dawned when they arrived by train into the Hauptbahnhof, and we were all there to greet them and help with their luggage and equipment, which was pretty considerable. I was amazed at how they had been able to prepare for such a mammoth trip, with carnets, travel documents, medical coverage etc., but somehow, Joanne had pulled it off.

Language had previously been a concern. Bavarian (spoken in Munich) is a dialect and often runs far from the High Deutsche German language of the land, but Dieter and his band of helpers took care of that, overseeing the paperwork and formalities until the tired group finally landed in their hotel, exhilarated that they had made it, and were eagerly looking forward to rehearsals and finally a performance in Germany, which is home to so much art and culture.

We had managed to secure permits for them to film in the streets of Munich. Shortly after their arrival, the Berlin Wall started to come down on November 9. It was a very exciting time for us all, and needless to say, the performance was stunning. Ballet is such a hard life as a chosen career and seems to have faded from popular culture nowadays, but with the advent of shows on TV by dance aficionado Nigel Lythgoe, maybe it will have a well-deserved renaissance?

How to Get Thrown out of a German Beer Garden During Oktoberfest

During our stay in Munich when Ruth was recording at Ralph Siegel's Jupiter Records, we welcomed a visit from Mick Flinn. He was an old friend from the

Aussie group The Mixtures from way back in the Rembrandt days. Ruth was introducing him and his pal Hattie to famed music producer Harold Faltermeyer.

As the weather was lovely, we decided to take the U-Bahn to the Seehaus in the Englischer Garten, and show them the delights of German beer and pretzels. We had a great old time of it, reminiscing, and drinking more beer than we realised. When the local oompah band began playing "New York, New York" (I can't imagine why!), we all clambered up on the long wooden table and began belting it out, Liza Minnelli style. The place was packed.

Small surprise, then, when one of the large dirndl-clad Frau who had been serving us came over and asked us to leave. I think there should be a special award for anyone who can be considered as being too loud in a beer garden.

The Seehaus is one of the largest beer gardens in Munich. They have capacity for something like 2,500 guests outside and another 320 in the restaurant. Nice to think we stood out from the crowd.

On another occasion when my sister Joan and her husband Peter came to visit us in Munich, we went to Oktoberfest, another ball game entirely. Oktoberfest drives a lot of the locals out of Munich as they prefer to stay as far away as possible from the drunken English and South Africans – the two groups they reckon are the worst boozers. Ruth's mother-in-law, Fannie Bockmeier, worked every year at Oktoberfest and could carry four of those enormous steins in each hand.

A job there is a coveted position and people are put on the waiting list for years. Others, I am told, can pass the job on to their daughters when they can no longer manage the heavy loads.

And did you know, they can get three-half chickens out of every one chicken! Don't ask me how, but they do.

AAFES, Munich, Germany

When I moved to Munich I needed to be gainfully employed. My German was very limited, but I managed to land a job at the McGraw Kaserne, the US Army base. I enjoyed my time there and didn't especially mind that it took me three forms of transport to get to and from – two buses and an U-Bahn trip.

I worked as a secretary in the contracts department. Even though I had received my Green Card, I was still deemed a "foreigner" so was not permitted to shop at the post store. However I could usually get my workmates to buy me things such as chocolate, *Billboard* magazine, or snacks, all of which were a joy.

That was right about the time the first Gulf War broke out in 1991. I remember the first day as I went through the gates. The soldiers patted me down (always enjoyable), searched my handbag, even plunging a knife into a jar of face cream to make sure I was not smuggling in Semtex. For the folks that drove onto the base, there were armed guards with mirrors on sticks, investigating the undersides of the vehicles.

The troops were, of course, American, but most of the maintenance workers on the base were German. The first morning I arrived I had to enter through the canteen. There I was astonished to see them all drinking beer at 7:30 a.m. Evidently it is the law in Bavaria that people may have beer, sausages and pretzels for sustenance throughout their working day. Now those were lawmakers I could respect!

I worked for Chuck Lamoreaux, a civilian who headed up the contract division, then later for another lovely man called Ray Ziembinski. They were both really kind to me and I had some wonderful experiences there.

As the troops in the Gulf were limited in what they were allowed to receive in their care packages, I started a library in my office. It consisted of paperbacks, novels, comics, sports magazines, which I would box up and ship out to the boys in the Middle East, with just one or two copies of *Penthouse* and *Playboy* on the bottom. I was very popular because of that.

At one stage I was due to fly out there for a short trip for training, but darned if the building didn't get hit by a missile. That sorta put an end to my plans. I did, however, receive an award for services to the troops in battle. The large gilt medal, which I have to this day amongst my treasures, is one of my proudest possessions.

The US military moved out of this facility in 1992 and it is now the Bavarian Police HQ.

That meant I was off to another job and another adventure.

Hannah Grace

One day in the canteen at the McGraw Kaserne, I was carrying a copy of *Billboard* magazine when a young girl approached me and asked me where I bought it. She was a young American and we chatted. She told me she was in Munich from Kentucky, as she had landed a recording contract with Ralph Siegel of Jupiter Records. Coincidentally, Ruth had just done the same thing, and was recording in his studio with her producer, Andi Slavik. Hannah was able to enter the base at the invitation of a German friend who worked there.

So I made the connection with Ruth. We all got together for dinner at our place, and she and Ruth became fast friends. Also in our musical circle was Martin Nethercutt (now my Son-in-Law #3). He was working on music at the Baldham Studios, run by music producer Harold Faltermeyer (*Top Gun*, *Beverly Hills Cop*).

Ralph Siegel had provided Kate (professionally re-named Hannah Grace) with a place to live in a house on the outskirts of Munich in a remote spot. There came a time when she was missing. We were told by the locals who worked with her that she had somehow become involved in what seemed to be a cult and was going through emotional difficulties, suspecting that there was an evil leader trying to shape her life. Then came the sad news that she had wandered out into the woods and laid down, just before a heavy snowstorm. Her body wasn't found until the snow melted.

Ralph Siegel kindly made all the funeral arrangements and flew Kate's parents in from America. In an effort to help and comfort them, he enlisted Ruth and Martin to act as translators at the service. This is how Ruth and Martin met.

To this day when people ask her where she met him, she says she picked him up graveside, not kerbside!

From Russia With Love

When Ruth was invited to go to the Soviet Union as a performer, we thought it was going to be on a very small scale. Waldemar Pokromski, a make-up artist in the film industry, invited her to be his "date" to an event in Munich, Germany, where she met various Russian promoters and a singer from Moscow named Natalia Lapina. They suggested to Ruth that if she could send them a video clip of herself, they would run it on Russia's one and only TV channel, generate some interest, then get her invited to perform over there.

Dieter Bockmeier, Ruth's second husband, drummed up a crew and they shot a guerrilla video to a song called "Locked in the Shadows of Love". This was sent, and in no time we began receiving telephone calls on very static laden phone lines, indicating that the 'Russkies' were ready to organise a tour for Ruth. (And to bug our phones).

Always the crazy child, she was all for it. The first trip involved our dear friend and her M.D. Barry Coffing, who flew from Los Angeles to Munich, armed with cassette backing tapes of some of the songs they had worked on together. One was called "Russian Nights", which ultimately became a video.

The concert promoter had lined up six beautiful boys from the Bolshoi Ballet to be her backing dancers, and a variety of supporting acts. They included a body-builder, a fire-eater, and various other colourful entertainers.

Ruth had acquired the services of a Russian manager, Nazim Nadirov, who was a gay Kurdish ex-ballet dancer. He was a hilarious young man who spoke little English but was always armed with a phrase book and copious amounts of vodka.

He introduced us to Savita Poornam, a delightful translator, who turned out to be lots of fun. She was of mixed Russian and Indian parentage, and we were astonished to find that racism was alive and well in the USSR. Sometimes, she would try to book tables for us in restaurants after the show, and they treated her very badly, even to the extent of not giving her a menu when we all sat down to order. We made it very clear that we wouldn't tolerate this behaviour.

When Ruth would announce onstage what her next song would be., Savita stood at the side of the stage and translated what she had said to the audience before the performance began. She (Savita that is), spoke about twelve languages – which was pretty amazing, for someone raised in a country that was so underprivileged at that time.

This motley crew finally got on the road to perform in places like Moscow, St. Petersburg, Kiev, Beriosova, Minsk, Nizhnevartovsk, Noyabirsk and Salekhard in the 60-degree Arctic Circle. On the first night we arrived in Russia, the airport was thronged with lights, cameras and paparazzi. Ruth wondered what celebrity was on the flight. She thought it must at least be Michael Jackson or someone of equal stature. Then we saw the banners and heard the chants of "McCartnya, McCartnya..." Ruth thought, *Oh these poor devils, they must think it's Paul who's coming.* But no, it was for her. Due to the limited choices television viewers had – one station for all of the USSR, which was government controlled – they had seen Ruth's music video on maximum rotation for weeks, sometimes up to fifteen times a day. Those lovely communists already thought she was a ready-made star.

From there we were taken to our hotel to check in, hand over our passports (a nerve-racking experience to say the least), got changed and were taken to the wedding reception of a very high ranking and powerful senator – we had no idea who he was. Our host turned out to be Vladimir Zhirinovsky, the rebel politician who was holding forth in Russian throughout the dinner. He pretended not to speak English but we later realised that he understood every word of what that was said.

We were invited to move out of the hotel and stay at a *dacha* (a country home) in a gated, military guarded compound where politicians, KGB heads, diplomats and other important dignitaries lived. As this area was off limits to civilians, we had to get down under grey blankets in the back of the vehicle each time we went in and out of the compound.

It was warm during this time of the year and there were armed guards outside all night, and two lovely ladies who cooked and did our laundry. There was a huge communal *banya* (a bathing area with dark brown cloudy water), where everyone stripped, dipped, drank vodka, conversed, laughed and sang.

We were picked up daily by an assigned driver named Rasputin and driven to God knows where. We were told he had just been released from prison after serving eight years for murder. Splendid.

One day we were told that Ruth was going to do a live cooking show on a Moscow TV station. She suggested shepherd's pie, a simple dish that maybe the locals would be able to buy and prepare for. All that was needed was ground beef, a couple of onions, salt, some brown stuff which we hoped was gravy browning, and lots of vodka. But no hot water! So we drank lots of vodka, as did the crew and the audience, and mocked up this incredible looking dish.

The stadiums (yes, you heard correctly – stadiums!) we played at were vast, and the people stood in line very seriously and quietly. The front of the orchestra pit would be lined with soldiers who faced the audience, who stared blankly and sat emotionless throughout the performance. It was very nerve-racking at first, until you realised that they were not encouraged to applaud or make any sound until the performance ended. Then they showed their enthusiasm in great strides.

In most towns after the show we were invited to dinner with the local dignitaries and their wives and children. How these delightful people do it I will never know, but their spirit is indomitable, and we were always made so welcome.

In all, Ruth made eight tours of Russia and Siberia, the final one being in 1997.

We emerged from Russia with a lot of wonderful experiences, knowing the difference between good and great vodka... and with a lot of love.

Showering with the Soviets

Ruth called me from Moscow and asked me to bring a shower rail for her manager, Nazim. He had a bathtub with a showerhead, but when he took a shower he had to rig up a piece of wire, some paper clips and plastic bin liners.

When I boarded the flight, the cabin staff looked at me a little oddly when I carried a telescopic shower rail in my carry on, which I duly stowed in the overhead bin. When we Ianded at Sheremetyevo Airport in Moscow, I was greeted by Ruth, Nazim and a cast of thousands!

Word somehow got out about my contraption and the Soviets were anxious to view the new prized possession. As I alighted, it was triumphantly borne aloft. Then strapped with rope on the roof of Nazim's car until it reached its destination, where it became the town's main attraction. Nazim's friends and neighbours all gathered to celebrate, toasting the new arrival with copious amounts of vodka, sitting on the toilet and perching on the sink.

The Soviets launched a dog in space, built nuclear arms to obliterate the world, but went ballistic at the sight of my little shower rail. Go figure.

Siberia. Yep. I said Siberia.

Surprisingly enough, the simple hotels in Siberia were not as bad as we had feared. They were not luxurious, but reasonably equipped with bedding without any holes! Clean too, with water that was not too scary, although in most places it had a greenish tinge. But we travelled with plenty of hydrogen peroxide, which we put in the tub, and used as a mouthwash. You just can't be too careful in these places. This was a few years back, and I am sure things have improved a great deal since then.

One morning before our handlers arrived, Ruth and I managed to sneak out of the hotel. We explored and came upon an open air/smog market where the locals were haggling with stall holders for varied goods like used books – many were dog-eared, filthy paperbacks – CDs, used underwear (yes, really!), and dead, scrawny chickens. We bought a couple of children's books, which we still have.

One enterprising woman combined her inventory. She stood alone apart from the main marketplace, holding a chicken aloft in one hand, and in the other a greyish frayed bra in an extremely large size. Up to the time we left she hadn't had any takers. Not surprising, but she definitely had our vote for Entrepreneur of the Year.

We met an amazing variety of people. One was a group of guys who had been shipped out from Sweden on a sort of "probationary period". They all had offences such as unpaid parking violations, unpaid child support etc., and instead of being imprisoned, their government devised a scheme of sending them out to tough countries to do manual work on the roads, mending fences etc. It gave them a sense of satisfaction that they were putting something back, and they knew that their records would be wiped clean if they fulfilled their tasks satisfactorily.

Another bunch of young men we met were from Doctors Without Borders, out there to help in some of the poorly equipped hospitals and institutions. This scheme also provided help on both sides to the coin. A remarkable system.

Soviet "Gavlets"

In one remote Siberian eatery our taste buds were assailed with suspect looking little brown rolled up "thingies".

I asked one of the our Bolshoi Ballet boys, who spoke a little English, what it was we were ingesting. He replied "gavno", which I later found translated to faeces, or the literal translation: shyte.

This ultimately became "gavlets" – our equivalent of cutlets. As the tour progressed I unwittingly caused great hilarity whenever I ordered gavlets. Somehow they always seemed to bring me a reasonable facsimile of the original.

USA – Take 2: 1993 to 2012

When we finally returned to our beloved America, and tried to settle down (who were we kidding?), we spent time acclimating to this wonderful country, finding various jobs, domiciles, vehicles, relationships, etc., and finally getting our Green Cards, then citizenship, driver's licenses, being able to vote (although we sometimes wondered why) and pay taxes. Truly living The American Dream.

To this day, when I hear people complaining about their lot in life in this incredible country, I can only tell them to travel, see how the other half lives, and be thankful for the amazing freedom they have to like, to disagree, and to protest if they want to, without the fear that so many people have on other continents. It is so true that travel broadens the mind (as well as the backside from sitting on too many planes, trains and automobiles).

We learned about this amazing new thing called the Internet – learned, and are still learning – started a little business, established ourselves in cyber world, where we are still happily ensconced and hope to be into the next millennium.

Now, put that in your pipe and smoke it!

Los Angeles Riots and How To Gain a Duck

The riots started on April 29, 1992, after a jury trial resulted in the acquittal of four LAPD officers accused in the videotaped beating of motorist Rodney King following a high-speed car chase. Thousands of people throughout the Los Angeles metropolitan area rioted over the six days following the announcement of the verdict. Widespread looting, arson, burglaries and murders occurred during the riots, and estimates of property damages topped one billion dollars. The rioting ended after soldiers from the California National Guard, along with US Marines from Camp Pendleton were called in to stop the rioting. A total of fifty-three people were killed, and over two thousand injured. The hospitals were groaning at the seams and emergency workers worked around the clock. The Red Cross was desperate for blood donations, and I was happy to be able to give them some of mine. The mayhem lasted for six days.

Ruth was still winding up her life in Germany and I had just returned from Munich and had a job in downtown Los Angeles in Koreatown, working for a man who had previously been a co-worker in our *Penthouse* Magazine days. I was living in the converted garage at the rear of Barry and Megan Coffing's house in Los Angeles, and they were away, as Barry was singing at a royal wedding in the Middle East.

My friend Richard Keech who had met me at LAX, rented a car for me on his credit card, until I could get on my feet. You don't find many friends like that. I tried to get to work the next morning but was turned back by the police who told me it was too dangerous to even try. I was scared stiff, being alone on the property. My good pal Lora Colvard said I should come and stay with her up in Burbank, which was a good few miles north of the troubles, so off I set. She and I sat up night after night, glued to the telly, clasping our handbags, car keys etc. until things settled down.

My boss, (yes Ron, you know who you are), was in New York at the time, and was not very sympathetic when I called and told him I couldn't get to work. He obviously hadn't realised how serious it was. I remember him saying, "Get over yourself Ange, remember, you live in a very violent city." So I resigned, and started looking for another job. Crazy woman. I didn't even get a paycheque for my final efforts.

After combing the *Los Angeles Times* jobs section daily, I was fortunate enough to land a job with *USA Today* working for Eric Belcher. That was the beginning of a long and beautiful friendship, which continues to this day. I later worked for Eric again at Hollywood Online and we still have a working relationship with him in his present company.

A young lady, who worked for my landlords Barry and Megan, found a lost duck waddling round the streets on her way to work one morning during the riots, so she picked him up, put him in a cardboard box, got on the bus and brought him with her. As you do. Looters had broken the windows of a pet store and he had made his escape. Barry's girls just loved him, so the plan to take him to an animal shelter never materialised, and they named him "Looty". He soon established his residence as the family pet in a blow-up paddling pool in the back yard.

Valerie St. John

During my time working at my next job at *USA Today* in Los Angeles I became friends with Valerie Singleton, later to be known as Valerie St. John, a successful journalist. Valerie was a wild child – she bungee jumped off bridges and out of aeroplanes, interviewed a dangerous criminal in jail. She was a go-anywhere, do-anything kind of a girl.

In her early television days she was an online TV anchor in a remote part of Iowa. Prior to leaving Los Angeles she interviewed Ruth (for her demo reel) at our apartment at The Summit in Woodland Hills to talk about her career. That interview can be seen today on www.YouTube.com/ruthmccartney and we are very proud of what Valerie has achieved.

She later went on to producing segments for all the major TV networks and several cable channels, too.

As I write this, I have just heard from her on her return from a trip to Italy with the family, and she is now communications director at a prominent research company.

You've come a long way baby!

Northridge Earthquake 1994

We were living in the same condo in Woodland Hills at the time of the Northridge Earthquake. Martin was living with us, although he and Ruth were not yet married.

Ruth and I had just returned from a trip to Russia and Siberia. On Sunday, January 16, 1994, I went into my office at *USA Today* to play catch up. Before leaving for home, something made me dig out the "earthquake preparedness" document, make several photocopies and put them on everyone's chairs. I called Ruth to say I was about to leave, and she too had had the same premonition. She had just been to the local drug store and bought batteries, ring pull cans of food, water, first aid stuff, and perhaps the most important item of all – a plastic bottle of scotch.

That evening the three of us watched television. When it was time for bed Martin roused Ruth to go upstairs and settle in. For some odd reason she said she'd rather stay downstairs, but he persuaded her, and off they went. I retired to my bedroom on the ground floor.

At 4.31 a.m. on Monday January 17, I woke up, sat on the side of the bed, and saved my life. At the very second I sat up the quake happened. A big picture which hung over my bed crashed down, shattering in shards of glass which even embedded themselves into the duvet and mattress. If I had still been lying down I'd have been done for. It was recorded as a 6.7 on the Richter scale – a biggie!

A bookcase on my bedroom wall shattered into pieces, with the shelves flying everywhere, and books hitting the opposite wall. We also had a bookcase halfway down the stairs which was unrecognizable after the dust settled. It was pitch black at the time and we had torches (flashlights) bedside, which every self-respecting California resident always does, plus shoes, car keys, and a fireproof box with passports, legal documents and all the other important stuff. Still do!

Martin had never experienced an earthquake before and was thrown out of bed and across the room, landing in a unit that held Ruth's collection of cactus plants. He was sleeping naked. Never again. Ruth spent the next few days gingerly picking cactus plant stingers out of his naughty parts with tweezers:

not an enjoyable experience for either of them. His first instinct was to reach for a cigarette until Ruth yelled at him not to strike a match in case there was a gas leak.

The death toll came to a total of fifty-seven people, and there were over 8,700 injured. In addition, the earthquake caused an estimated $20 billion in damage, making it one of the costliest natural disasters in US history.

Ruth had been due to appear on the Michael Jackson radio show that day and the freeway she would have travelled was completely obliterated, killing a policeman who was on his way to work.

The next few days were like something out of a horror movie. Our little Ford car in the garage was turned into scrap metal. The kitchen stove and fridge met in the middle of the kitchen. If anyone had been in that room they would have been wiped out. The aftershocks continued for days. The phones were off, the power was out, and in those days, most people didn't have cell phones. The toilets backed up and flooded. It was a nightmare.

We and most of our neighbours took to the car parks, sat on tarpaulins under the stars, talked with one another, and took stock of our lives. We had a second car, which we slept in for the next few nights. We had to drive to a restaurant several miles away to use a toilet and have a wash... talk about survival. Rapper Snoop Dog, er pardon me, Snoop Lion, was living in one of the condos and his limo driver appeared in the parking lot with all of the headlights on and music blaring. It's always party time in California.

I was eventually able to telephone Eric Belcher, my lovely boss, and tell him I was OK. My family in England and Australia were frantically trying to reach me as was Martin's Mum from Germany. It was almost a week before we were all in touch.

Then came the decision to go back to work – but which route to take? It was quite an adventure, getting to and from Woodland Hills to Santa Monica Boulevard in Beverly Hills. Eventually I managed to do it, but it became a two-hour journey at least every morning and night.

After lengthy negotiations with FEMA (the Federal Emergency Management Agency), I eventually received a cheque for $200. They said I should use it to buy a phone and a television set and keep the receipts for seven years. Yet an undocumented lady that I knew (a housekeeper to some friends), got $5,000.

She didn't have a Social Security number, but she just filled in the paperwork with all zeros in the spaces, and duly received a cheque from them. Yes, your tax dollars at work!

We were all so unnerved that we decided to move away. I asked Eric if the Gannett newspaper group could transfer me anywhere else. He arranged a phone interview for me with *The Tennessean* in Nashville, who offered me a position as Assistant to the Manager of Advertising, Mary Ella Hazelwood.

I flew down, Ruth and Martin packed up the truck and the cat box, and humming our Willy Nelson anthem, "On the Road Again", drove to Nashville. Off we went on another adventure, which thankfully continues to this day.

The Birth of McCartney Multimedia

We rented an apartment in a complex on a golf course called Deerfield, and Ruth and Martin made inroads into getting jobs locally. Martin worked for Nippon Airlines at the airport, using his skills as a forwarding agent.

About this time, Martin began planning to record his first tracks in Nashville, which were at least a diversion for him during his transition. I remember going with him (along with Louise Harrison who was visiting), to a studio to record "Rain Dance" when we had the most torrential downpour I had ever experienced, and we literally did our own rain dance, bailing out water throughout the session.

Ruth got various jobs, temping, writing songs, and generally became acclimatised to the different pace of life in the South. She did catering on music video and movie sets. One notable experience was working on the Sharon Stone movie *Last Dance*, as personal assistant to Peter Gallagher. This stark movie about a Death Row prisoner took them on location to an actual Death Row prison in Kentucky, which was a harrowing experience for all the cast and crew.

When Ruth and I had to go out of town to appear at a Beatlefest, Peter kindly agreed to have Martin deputise for her and take care of squiring him around, and even having some down time (fun time) out of our Deerfield Apartment together, where the Deerfield golf course wound through the complex. This in turn led to Martin being re-hired in various positions as the movie progressed, from which he learned a lot about movie production, and intently studied every aspect of it, which would be beneficial to him throughout the coming years.

We were fortunate enough to make many friends in Nashville, including Bob Mather of EMI Music Publishing, Bob Krusen and wife Ann Stokes, in whose studio Martin made his first demos, and a variety of music-related people, grafting away at their craft.

The norm then was for songwriters to report for duty daily, sit locked away in their little caves grinding out songs for a weekly pittance, then sign over all their writers' and publishing rights to their employer.

One of our former Australian friends said Ruth should meet up with Brian Cadd, a prominent Aussie rocker who was staying out in Franklin, close to Nashville, so off she went, accompanied by my sister Joan who was visiting from Liverpool.

Caddo was (and still is) a wonderful colourful character, and took them for shepherd's pie to the Bung-a-Nut Pig pub, where they cemented their friendship in grand style. During their time together, Caddo asked Ruth if she had ever heard about "a Yahoo"? She had not, at this point, but he whetted her appetite about this new technology which was emerging, which led her to ask the local library if they had any books about the Internet. The lady there was bewildered at the question, thumbed through her cardboard box of Rolodex cards and, not coming up with any answers, said she would send away to Knovxille Branch Library to see what she could find.

The librarian called a few days later saying she had some information, so Ruth trotted off to the library and came home armed with a stack of books about this mystical new "hypertext mark-up language". Or HTML. She and Martin hunkered down, ordered pizza, and settled in to learn the wonders of this emerging technology which had begun developing through the auspices of Al Gore's father in Advanced Research Projects Agency, which I believe, created the first available-to-the-masses computer networking system. Previously, it had only been used by the military, and in relation to space-related technology. Everyone said was a flash in the pan and would never last. Aha!!!

I was busy integrating into my new job at the newspaper, and made friends with several of our advertising clients, one of whom was Robert Hendrick, who headed up a company called Creative Syndicate, a techy company which brought computer users into the twentieth century. I didn't understand much at first, but I certainly learned a lot.

A little while later, Rob offered me a job to move over to his nearby Brentwood offices to be General Office Assistant, keeper of the timesheets, nightly shredder of unwanted documents etc., and from there, I too learned more about computers, the Internet, email, even scanners – I was sooo impressed with this incredible machine that could take a picture of your document and send it to your computer. Robert was kind enough to let Martin come into the office in the evenings to learn a little more about all of this new technology, which was to prove invaluable to him in his quest for knowledge.

I withdrew the princely sum of $100 from my meagre savings and we formed McCartney Multimedia, Inc., a Nashville Corporation (later to become a California Corporation). Still crazy after all these years. Whoda thunk it?

Rob Hendrick helped us land our first website clients, as I recall, a pair of Australian brothers, the LaGarde Twins, who had their own little theatre on Music Row. Martin built them a website. Ruth decided to get in touch with old friend David Cassidy and convince him that he needed to have a website to publicise his career moves, and he generously complied.

Those beginnings helped us gain entry into a world which is still expanding. I looked at our client list yesterday, from the beginning, and it's currently thirteen pages long. We have had a colourful and varied roster of clients, ranging from musicians, writers, actors, photographers, cosmetics creators, restaurants, medical groups, the Royal Navy, government departments, film commissions, small businesses, the MGM Grand and related Las Vegas hotels, lawyers, entertainment managers and agents, automobile giants, celebrities, events coordinators... You name it, we've worked on it.

We eventually became a Woman Minority-Owned Business (to which dear Martin kindly acquiesced), which enabled us to pitch for government jobs, public utility projects and large publicly traded companies who have a diversity vendor program. From sole proprietors and entrepreneurs to multi-national corporations, no project is ever dull!

Check us out at www.McCartneyMultimedia.com

Steven Tyler, Aerosmith

When I worked at *The Tennessean* in Nashville, one of our advertising clients would give us tickets for shows at the local Starwood arena in Antioch.

One night, we were invited to an Aerosmith gig, which I was delighted to accept. Ruth, Martin and I were huge Aerosmith fans. The night of the show my somnambulistic instincts overcame me, and I nodded off right in the front row, with Martin sitting beside me. (Ruth was in the row behind). Martin told me later that, much to his embarrassment, while Steven Tyler was doing his massive strutting stuff onstage he spied me, pointed an accusing finger and waggled the mike stand at me for a brief moment, before resuming his posture with flowing locks, mike stand, and mandatory scarf.

As usual, I woke up just before the end of the show and asked "Was it good?" You know, I have been able to sleep wherever, whenever, for the greater part of my adult life, which has probably stood me in good stead. Six years of the Luftwaffe seems to have been a good rehearsal. I've even bought expensive theatre and cinema tickets and snored my way through the best part of the show. And even at an Ozzy Osbourne concert! (Don't tell Sharon).

Sometimes I don't know why I even bother.

United Cerebral Palsy and Wheels for Humanity

We at McCartney Multimedia Inc. are proud to support United Cerebral Palsy and Wheels for Humanity, which has come a long way. We first met David Richard, founder of Wheels for Humanity, in 1996 when he was working out of an old garage in the San Fernando Valley.

In those days it was just David, his brother and a few volunteers who ran the entire operation. They would forage for old beat-up wheelchairs, refurbish them, and then redistribute them to less fortunate people. They were really struggling in those days. We too were running our business out of our garage at a little house in Playa del Rey, so we could empathise with them. We used to give them any odds and ends of office supplies that we didn't need, and they were grateful for any help they could get. They gradually expanded and became a centre for donations of wheelchairs after folks passed on and their families found a group of people who were glad to receive them.

Over the years their contributions to the disabled around the world have been more and more recognised. Today they have combined forces with United Cerebral Palsy, having helped more than fifty thousand people with disabilities in approximately seventy developing nations, helping them gain increased mobility and dignity.

Take a look at their website (www.ucpwfh.org) and you will see some amazing stories unfold. They often take trips to countries where landmines still do their horrendous damage to people's lives.

They have a volunteer programme too, so if you ever feel you want to do something worthwhile, give them a ring and see how you can lend a hand. And tell them Angie sent you!

Benny Mardones

For a number of years we have been friends with the very talented Benny Mardones. He first came to fame in 1980 with his recording of "Into The Night", which has been dubbed the song most featured at weddings and other romantic celebrations. It was also one of the few songs to ever ascend twice to the Top 20 of the *Billboard* singles charts.

He wandered into our offices in Playa del Rey one day when we were meeting with a very religious group of potential clients. Benny being Benny ambled into Ruth's office and was blasting off some comments about a traffic problem he had just encountered, his vocabulary peppered with some of Syracuse, New York's favourite choice words. Ruth tried to give him the fish-eye, the "shut-up-Benny-and-mind-your-language" look.

He realised he was interrupting a meeting and apologised. Ruth, in her embarrassment, told her guests that he was Benny Mardones, famed for his song "Into The Night". One of the ladies in the strictly Baptist group melted, and said, "Oh, I'd love to meet him! I danced to that song on the day I was married." So Benny was duly called back in and redeemed himself by singing a few bars for her. She melted. We landed the client, got the job, and all was well.

Score one for Benny!

As told to us by Benny, he got caught up in the vagaries of the music business. Despite being hailed as one of the best voices by many top people in the music industry, he fell into drugs for a time and lost much of his position in the business. But he eventually felt a tap on his shoulder from a greater power. He got himself back together and back on the road again.

In 2011, Usher recorded a version of "Into The Night" with different lyrics, which encouraged Benny to get moving again.

Benny suffers from Parkinson's but he will tell you that once he goes on stage and begins to sing, the shaking goes away. He recently married a lovely lady, Jane Braemar, and they are very happy together. She takes good care of him. He actually proposed to her at a live gig much to her astonishment. He invited her up on stage, got down on one knee and asked her to marry him. There wasn't a dry eye in the house.

Early in 2012, he recorded an incredibly romantic ballad, "I've Got You", which received great airplay, and is, of course, available in iTunes. The world hasn't seen the last of Benny. In addition to his music career, he is very active in helping to find the cure for Parkinson's, closely following Michael J. Fox in his endeavours.

You can keep up on Benny by visiting www.bennymardones.com/movie.html. In the meantime, we'll keep working on his salty language.

Christian Volquartz aka Boy Genius

When we moved back from Nashville to Los Angeles in 1997, we rented a house in a sleepy little community called Playa del Rey, close to LAX and Marina del Rey, and for a time, worked out of our garage, where our dear friend Ric "Hollywood" Wetzel built us a vocal booth. We enlisted the services of Peter "Dr. Atomic" Harris, who used to come to work on his recumbent bicycle, and moved from his little apartment near Capitol Records to room with our Brit friend Tony Baily who had a house nearby. (Tony later moved on to Queensland where he is thriving).

We gradually re-integrated back into the Hollywood working scene, and eventually got a small office in Playa del Rey, next door to a Hamburger joint called The Shack, a few steps away from the Pacific Ocean.

Thus began the next phase of our adventures. Shortly after, we attended an event at Loyola Marymount, which was showcasing the talents of their film and technology students. This resulted in an application to become an intern from Christian Volquartz, who has stood the test of time and is still with us to this day, and is now Vice President of Operations. We "upgraded" from the little upstairs office to the ground floor of this building, an old red brick, Coastal Commission-protected property, ably run by our great and supportive landlord, Gary Entrekin. It may not be Disneyland, but it is one of the happiest places I have known to work at. Martin has built a recording studio in the back of the building, which is where he spends many hours working his magic on recording, video editing, helping me create voice-overs, and producing others for clients. Whenever he is missing in action, we always know where to find him. It's his own little "man cave".

We enjoy the ambience of Playa, which is still a comparatively unspoiled little spot, with many great watering holes and little local stores. It is truly a pleasurable place to live.

Christian is not only a valued member of our motley crew, but additionally, is an incredibly talented photographer – a skill which he no doubt inherited from his late father, the Danish photography legend Per Volquartz.

He, like the rest of us, works tirelessly to endeavour to meet the needs (and foibles) of many of our clients, some of whom figure that we never need to sleep, and cell phones, emails, Tweets etc. often continue long into the night. This, of course, is partially due to the fact that we have clients in so many time zones and spots on the globe.

Peter Atomic has travelled since then too. First to Beijing, then Brisbane, more recently to Bristol, and soon to Berlin. (What is it with the "B" thing, I wonder?)

Over the years, as technology has advanced, Christian has been an avid follower of all the new bells and whistles of our business, and we call him "gadget boy" as he loves keeping up with all the new stuff which seems to be coming at us almost daily. Me? I am just a plain old bookkeeper and office grunt; seems some things never changed. When I was young, my only ambition was to be a good secretary. Still working on that one!

John Cleese

In 2004, McCartney Multimedia was delighted to be recommended to John Cleese to create his first website, which proved to be the biggest project we had handled up to that time. Ruth and Martin had numerous discussions with the great man, both at our Playa del Rey offices and at his ranch in Montecito. I was happy to be a part of some of those visits, where we had a fantastic time with all of his amazing animals: llamas, peacocks, horses and chickens.

John was a wonderful host, and would leave us the run of the house, whilst he stayed down at the beach at another of his properties. We spent many wonderful evenings together when he would cook dinner and regale us with numerous stories of his young life, his career, his aspirations, his incredible knowledge of wines, and his literary experiences.

We built him a green screen in one of the property's barns so that he could do his "rants" any time something occurred to him, and then have us fill in the appropriate backgrounds at a later stage.

When we eventually launched the website, he suggested we throw a little party at the office so that he could meet the many folks who had worked on his site. This was a great success.

Tim Brown, the photographer who was documenting this occasion, said he would have to leave by a certain time for his next assignment and wanted to get a photo of me with John. John was deep in discussion at the time, so I began plucking at his elbow (about eye level to little me). After a few moments, he looked down on me and said, "Woman, if you don't stop it, I will have to put the cover back on your cage!" Truly a Kodak moment.

He used to love staying at our local Inn At Playa del Rey, where they even got a longer bed especially for him. We would all have long lunches at Cantalini's next to our office, where he was most engaging with not only our staff, but with the restaurant folks, too. They loved having him there.

For a time we employed his beautiful daughter Camilla as an intern to learn some of the background to our business. She was the apple of his eye (and still is), and was prone to the Hollywood nightlife, hobnobbing with her friend Paris Hilton until the wee small hours of the morning, frequently losing her cell phones, or at least one if not both of her designer shoes. Evidently, the girls would kick off their shoes to dance in these hot spots, then sometimes forget to go looking for them before driving home in their luxury vehicles. I don't know if she learned anything from us, but she certainly had the attention of our male staff, turning up at the office looking like a movie star. We had to keep extra cold drinks in the cooler on the days she was around and watch the thermostat on the wall!

In return, Camilla told us some hilarious stories about her father. Like the time he told her they bought her at Harrods, and she believed him for quite a few years. Then, when the kids were asked to take part in a "show and tell" at her posh London school, and to bring in a photograph of their parents, she took in one of John in full female attire, curls, lipstick, eye shadow and all. That evidently went down like a lead balloon. But there is no doubt that she and John have a great relationship, and she later travelled the world with him appearing on stage in many venues.

As I write this, John is still making appearances all around the world, and I hear from my Australian relatives that they have been captivated by his shows recently. John, as is his gift, can make any nation laugh.

John married his fourth wife, jewellery designer, British-born Jennifer Wade in August 2012 on the island of Mustique, a favourite getaway haven for Princess Margaret, and sometimes visited by the Queen and Prince Philip.

Steve Tyrell

In early 2006, we had the good fortune to be introduced to Steve Tyrell, the incredibly talented singer, arranger, producer, who continues to go from strength to strength with his mastery of the Great American Songbooks, with legendary albums and music for movies, and production of other artists, evening garnering a Grammy for his Rod Stewart album production.

If you want to smile, take a look at this video link to Rod presenting Steve with the Jazz Man of the year outside a little hostelry: www.youtube.com/watch?v=FrViVbMulmQ Beware photo bombers bums in the background!

Steve and Stephanie visited our humble pad in the days when we were planning his website, and we all had lunch in at La Marina in Playa del Rey, where Steve was impressed when they were playing his music as we entered the restaurant. Our working relationship and friendship have continued over the years, and he has gone from strength to strength in all aspects of his career over these years. It's hard to imagine that in mid-2012 he became a grandfather, when his lovely daughter, Tina, the talented photographer, gave birth to a little darling in New York.

His early beginnings in the music business ranged from Texas, where he was born, to A&R and promotion at Scepter Records. There he was mostly behind-the-scenes, producing hits for popular recording artists and movie soundtracks. When he was only nineteen years old he first began producing with the likes of Burt Bacharach and Hal David. He worked on several Dionne Warwick hits such as "The Look of Love" and "Alfie". Together with B.J. Thomas, he worked on the Bacharach-David song "Raindrops Keep Fallin' on My Head", which went on to win the 1969 Oscar for Best Original Song (*Butch Cassidy and the Sundance Kid*).

And since then he has consistently pursued his talents, from writing music for TV shows ("How Do You Talk to An Angel" with Barry Coffing for *The Heights*) to his initial foray into performing in *Father of the Bride*, and producing soundtracks for such diverse projects as *The Brady Bunch Movie*, *The Partridge Family* movie, and numerous others.

His contributions to the film industry include *Mystic Pizza*, (Ruth even had a clip of her music in that one), *That Thing You Do*, *Father of the Bride*, *The Brady Bunch Movie*, and *Out of Sync*. Steve also worked in television and did the music for *California Dreams*, *The Heights*, and *Frank's Place*, among others.

His collaboration with the Sinatra family led to his beautifully performed and produced album. Steve was so honoured to be approached by them to make this record, helped and encouraged in this daunting task by Nancy, Tina and Frank Junior, who actually collaborated with him on the production. One evening when we were at a Hollywood venue, Steve proudly announced from the stage that Tina herself was there to watch his performance. I am sure this must have been both rewarding and unnerving for him.

As a music supervisor and music producer for film and TV, Steve has worked with such distinguished directors as Steven Spielberg, Tom Hanks, Nancy Meyers, Steven Soderbergh, Betty Thomas, and Charles Shye.

His songs have been recorded by such revered artists as Ray Charles, Diana

Ross, LL Cool J and Elvis Presley, and "How Do You Talk To An Angel "was a number one pop hit in 1992. Aside from being a Grammy Award winner, Steve has earned two Emmy nominations, three Ace Nominations, 2004 American Society of Young Musicians "All That Jazz Award", 2004 The Wellness Community "Human Spirit Award", 2006 Society of Singers "Lifetime Achievement Award", and 2008 Los Angeles Jazz Society's "Jazz Vocalist of the Year". Truly a living legend.

I feel it's a privilege to know him, and he always makes me so welcome when I am able to visit him appearing in Hollywood. Keep it up Steve – you have a great future ahead of you.

Mel Haber

Mel ("Call me Mr.") Haber is one of life's incredible characters. He is the owner of The Ingleside Inn in Palm Springs, California, which includes the celebrated Melvyn's Restaurant.

We at McCartney Multimedia Inc. have taken care of Mel's website and social media needs for some years, and it is always a pleasure to spend time at his timeless Inn.

You really should take a look at www.inglesideinn.com. You'll be glad you did. I describe it as the happiest place on earth – never mind Disneyland!

It's steeped in history and a great place for celeb spotting. Frank Sinatra held his pre-wedding dinner there before his marriage to Barbara Marx. June Alysson is quoted as saying, "Everybody should get married there at least once." Schwarzenegger used to hang out there before he became The Governator. Mel deservedly has a star on the Palm Springs Walk of Fame, and is a great philanthropist, as well as an amazing host.

He has written two books: *Bedtime Stories*, which contains some hilarious revelations about his foray into the hospitality business; and *Palm Springs a la Carte* with the very talented Marshall Terrill. Both are highly entertaining. and regale the reader with stories of Mel's early days in the "nodding dog and furry dice" business, all the way through to the opening night of Melvyn's Restaurant where he failed to recognise Steve McQueen and Ali McGraw on their Harley

Davidson and turned them away for being underdressed. Ooops! If anyone deserves the title "raconteur" it's our Mel.

You mustn't visit Palm Springs without experiencing The Ingleside, and in particular, Melvyn's. The menu is without parallel, the service flawless, and as for Brian Ellis, the Maître d'... well, what can I say? His stories alone will have you on the floor. Their Sunday afternoon jazz sessions have to be seen to be believed. McCartney Multimedia shot a pilot for a TV series there called *Early Bird Special*, about old farts trying to find love again. It was hilarious, and a wonderful experience. Mel and all of his fabulous staff were involved and made it the smoothest ride you could ever wish for. It is my number one spot for an R & R getaway, and I can always be assured that Armida, Karen and Hal will take care of me as if I were at home.

They hold weddings in their lovely back garden courtyard, including a number of same sex marriages, as Palm Springs has become a haven for the GLBT community. And as it is only a leisurely drive from Los Angeles, it is an enormously popular venue.

Mmm... writing this is making me want to jump in the car... get in my robe and order a drink. I'll be back in a second...

Roseanne Barr

We had the good fortune to become friends with Roseanne Barr a few years back. It turns out that we're neighbours and we've shared many fun evenings together, both at her house and ours. Despite her fame, Roseanne is a very approachable gal, and although I was a little in awe of her at first, we soon found we had a few things in common, mainly our sense of humour. Her boyfriend Johnny Argent and my son-in-law Martin also enjoy a musical rapport.

On one of our Vegas trips she invited us to see her one-woman show at the Sahara. And afterwards, we all piled into a limo and went to an absinthe bar across town. I had never drunk absinthe before *or* since. I have very little recollection of the end of the night, or of the next morning for that matter.

For such a busy lady, she sure makes time to take care of people when they need her. Ruth broke her leg a while back and was confined to bed, and very frustrated. Roseanne would frequently pop around with homemade chicken soup (what else would you expect from a Jewish mother?), with offers to take care of anything Ruth might need doing. That was at a time when she was up the wall with work, family related stuff, and her own busy life, but it didn't stop her dropping by our place with sincere offers of help.

We were doing a photo session at our house one evening when she dropped in, along with her mother, Helen. We were privileged to be included in the wedding of her son Jake to his lovely wife Alicia, and have all celebrated birthdays together. She and Johnny taped a little piece for my eightieth birthday video, which Ruth and Martin secretly put together, including friends and family from all around the world. When Ruth sent out my birthday party invitations, she said that I didn't want any gifts, but that people could buy me a Lottery ticket. Roseanne bought me eighty – one for each year. I didn't win any huge prizes, but the net result of the mountains of Lottery tickets I got that night bought me a camera, an iPod, and yes, *more* Lottery tickets.

Roseanne's personal assistant is a wonderful lady named Becky Pentland. Becky married Bill Pentland, one of Roseanne's ex-husbands on *The Roseanne Show*, and they live and work close by. Becky is *the* most efficient and loyal lady anyone could ever hope to have working for them. Ruth often says that she wishes she could steal her away to work for us, but I know her loyalty is so strong that we never could.

A while back, we were all invited to Roseanne's place, but I had had a long day and chose to go to bed early instead. Not long after they had walked around the corner, Ruth and Martin called me and said, "Bed be damned, get your arse over here and meet Phyllis Diller!" So I did just that: walked around in my jammies and my JC Penney dressing gown, and put on a tiara (to be a little festive), and was glad I did. Miss Diller was wonderful.

I told her that I was still using an old gag of hers: "You know you're getting old when your liver spots show through your gloves." She had forgotten that one, and said she would resurrect it. Evidently, when Ruth had walked in and gone over to her and offered her hand, and was about to say "It's a privilege to meet you Miss Diller," she shoved an empty martini glass in her outstretched hand and replied, "Cut the crap kiddo and get me a f***ing Martini." I have a delightful picture of Roseanne, Phyllis and myself – me resplendent in my jammies! I recently read Diller's book *Like a Lampshade in a Whorehouse* and found it fascinating.

I wonder how on earth did these gals find the time to write books when they lead such full lives. It has taken me over eighty years to get to this stage with mine!

It was with sadness that we learned of the passing of Ms. Diller on August 20 2012, resulting in tremendous tributes to her from around the world. I am so glad that I was privileged to meet her, she was truly a gem, talented, warm, kind, and oh so funny. Ruth and I spent that evening finding many of her wonderful YouTube videos.

Angie's 'ead

On February 11, 2008, I had a mental lapse for about forty-five minutes and didn't know who or where I was. Fortunately Ruth was around and rushed me to Daniel Freeman Medical Center in Marina del Rey. They ran lots of tests and eventually allowed me to go home. At their request I saw my general practitioner the next day, Dr. Firoz Sheikh, who referred me to a neurologist, Dr. David Keradyer. He ran more tests and had me undergo an MRI, the end result being that I had not had a stroke or a heart attack, and that all that was wrong was a severe Vitamin B12 deficiency.

As Mike McGear would have said, "Yer 'ead's gone, Ace."

It was a "phew" moment and a relief to discover that it was nothing more than that. Our good friend and neighbour, Dr. Tony Strickland, has suggested using me for some research into the brain activity of mature people who live a very active life. So I am going to be a guinea pig for their research team sometime soon. Should be interesting! Tony heads up the Sports Concussion Institute in Los Angeles, which examines, researches and treats the effects of sports-related injuries, which can cost a promoter, a team or a franchise a fortune when their valued players are rendered incapable of playing for extended periods of time.

I now take liquid Vitamin B12 every morning. They reckon the brain lapse condition comes about through not eating sufficient red meat and dairy, which is no doubt why lots of famous vegans and vegetarians have regular B12 shots to make up for the deficiency. It certainly helps stave off memory loss.

The famous "they" (who conduct surveys on all manner of things) have recently discovered that Alzheimer's does not affect American Indian tribes, and it's interesting to note that they eat a lot of vegetables and pulses, and spices like turmeric etc. which may have a beneficial effect on their health.

I managed to rock through the night of my eightieth birthday, and for my eighty-fifth I'm looking forward to going bungee jumping in Vegas. And Martin says he'll spring for a tattoo for me as well. Lovely boy. It's now 2012 and I'm still rockin'! Or, at least I think I am...

Paul Antonelli, Son-in-Law #1

When I had my knee replacement in 2006, my dear ex Son-in-Law paid me a visit in recovery – dressed in one of my old bathing suits naturally! I have no idea what Ruth did or did *not* do to him while they were married, but for the past fifteen years he has been living happily with his lovely partner Paul Adent and is well, loud! A brilliant musician and an even better human being. There's always room for these Pauls in this family.

Jonas, my Pet Rock Star
(And Personal Handyman)

Jonas and The Massive Attraction is their official title, headed by the delightful Jonas Tomalty, a wonderfully talented and warm Canadian friend whom Ruth and Martin discovered North of the Border, and who has integrated into our "family" big time.

You just have to witness him performing his magic (or putting up shelves) to know the wild musicianship (and craftsmanship) of this boy, he's not averse to doing a few tasks around the house whenever he stays with us. In fact, when I know he is coming to Los Angeles, I start making my "Jonas to do" list. It always seems a bit hokey to me that one night he can be playing to thousands of adoring fans, the next day going with me to Home Depot to buy curtain rails – and he is as handy with an electric drill as he is with a guitar.

We have had some pretty wild nights with him, along with other muso friends, at the Casa in Playa del Rey, and he always connects with our friends around the globe when he tours Europe, Australia or Germany. It's great the way our extended family just keeps on growing.

Find him on Facebook, YouTube, and his website at: www.jonasandthemassiveattraction.com.

I always tell his Mum, Rhonda, that she did a wonderful job raising him, he is so house trained, particularly for a rock star. He even makes his own bed and folds his laundry. What a wonderful catch he will make for some lucky lady one day.

David Archuleta

I was pleased to meet David Archuleta for the first time at one of the Britweek opening parties at the Residence of the British Consul. Producer Nigel Lythgoe brought him, along with the other *American Idol* finalists to be introduced to a slice of British life. He was absolutely charming and rather shy, as I remember. He kindly posed for photographs with everyone who asked him, including moi.

At a later event, a Britweek occasion to honour Sir Richard Branson, I briefly met up with him again. David was about to perform "Imagine", which was a very moving performance. In the May 2008 season, he finished as the first runner-up, receiving 44 per cent of the 97 million votes cast.

I have since followed his progress, as he moved into the spiritual area of music and is active with his church. He continues to be very concerned and supportive of many charities. It's so warming to find a young, successful man like him caring so much for others. He truly believes in giving back. I know he will have a long career ahead of him, and he is such a sincere person. The way I see it, he can only spread more goodwill and cheer as he goes through life.

"From The Reverend Angie McCartney"

As an ordained minister I am available for weddings and other ceremonies. I always find it most helpful to have a few facts at my fingertips.

For example, did you know why June is considered the most popular month for weddings? In the olden days (when Adam was a lad), most people got married in June because they took their yearly bath in May, and still smelled pretty good by June. However, by the next month they were starting to pong a bit, so brides carried a bouquet of flowers to hide the smell. Hence the custom today of carrying a bouquet.

There are lots of interesting wedding traditions worldwide. For example, in Italy, wedding festivities usually kick off in the morning, ideally on a Sunday. According to regional Italian folklore, you should never marry (or leave for your honeymoon) on a Friday or Tuesday, or you're bound to have loads of bad luck while Saturdays are reserved for widows getting hitched to husband number two (or three, or four...).

Fathers once used their daughters as currency to a) pay off a debt to a wealthier landowner, b) symbolise a sacrificial, monetary peace offering to an opposing tribe, or c) buy their way into a higher social strata. So when you feel all soppy and sentimental about Daddy walking his little girl down the aisle, remember that it's just a tiny hangover tradition from the days when daughters were nothing but financial investments to dear Papa.

And as for wearing a veil over her face – that was so the groom wouldn't know if he was stuck with an ugly one until it was time to kiss the bride and too late to back out. There is also some superstition about warding off evil spirits. Personally, I prefer the first option.

And as for the Best Man? I have read that he was like the second shotgun, to stand guard over the proceedings in case anyone tried to kidnap the bride, or some even worse fate might rear its ugly head. Now it has merely become a symbol (or the guy who goes out with the groom the night before and gets shit-faced and finishes up with the strippers). All he has to do is not lose the wedding rings.

Something old...This dates back to Victorian times in England. The "something old" was meant to tie the bride to her family and her past, and the "something new" represented her new life as the property (yes, property!), of a new family. The item "borrowed" was supposed to be taken from someone who was already a successfully married wife, so as to pass on a bit of her good luck to the new bride. The colour blue (Virgin Mary-approved) stood for all sorts of super fun things like faithfulness, loyalty, and purity. My, my, how times have changed.

Something new...I was delighted to officiate at the marriage of my very dear friends, Tim Arendt and Donald Dale when same sex partnerships first became legal in California in October 2008. They were married on the porch of their beautiful Playa del Rey home, surrounded by friends and family, and they hosted a beautiful reception at the Ritz Carlton in Marina del Rey. It was a truly memorable occasion. Martin supplied the music, and Ruth and Christian Volquartz took pictures.

And I got to marry two wonderful people who are in love... and have been for over thirty years!

Chef Anthony Bourdain

A couple of years ago our friend Madge Claybion suggested that we present Mrs. McCartney's Teas at a UCLA event she was organising for a group of hospitality students from the university. It was held at a Century City Hotel and Anthony Bourdain was the guest of honour. Ruth, the chief "foodie" of the family, was more than willing to accept the invitation.

We set up our wares and duly entered into the luncheon to witness our hero in action. He was, as we had expected, highly entertaining. He railed against various things that irked him and concentrated his efforts on a particular chain of family friendly restaurants, obviously unaware that these people were sponsoring the event and were responsible for paying his not-too-shabby fee.

It turned out that the group on the next table to us was from that very organisation, and they all got up and walked out in the middle of his rant. We knew why – he didn't. After he finished his presentation, he threw it open to the crowd. "Any questions?" he asked. His request was met by a deathly silence.

Since Ruth had read all of his books, including the *New York Times* bestseller,

Kitchen Confidential, she had a good background knowledge regarding some of his escapades and adventures. She stood up and asked him a couple of questions about the stinky fruit durian and whether or not he had really enjoyed a steaming floor massage in Uzbekistan, which got the ball rolling.

His sardonic wit is part of his charm, and you can get an idea of his not-so-subtle take on TV chefs, award shows, the Food Network, and restaurant chains by checking out his ten favourite insults online at The Ten Most Insulting Things That Anthony Bourdain has said about Food Network.

And he's *very* tall.

The First Man on the Moon

At one of the Britweek launch parties at the Residence of the British Consul in Los Angeles, I met former astronaut Buzz Aldrin. He was a delightful gentleman with many a tale to tell.

When I shook him by the hand and said how proud I was to meet the first man on the moon, he corrected me. "Oh no, that would be Neil Armstrong," he said. I was sufficiently brave to question this well-documented fact and asked him, "But how? If there was a picture of Neil Armstrong taking the first step for mankind, then who was the man already standing on the moon holding the camera that took the picture?"

He just smiled wryly, patted me on the hand, and said how happy he was to meet me. The question remains in my mind. Who was *really* the first man on the moon?

And then in August 2012, we lost Neil Armstrong, a loss greatly felt by his fellow space travellers, and Buzz promptly posted a tribute to him. They had all hoped to participate in the fifty-year anniversary of that first monumental landing on the moon in the year 2019 together.

I was shocked to read that they did not have life insurance when they took off for the moon. At a yearly salary of $17,000 they couldn't afford it. So, before take-off, they sat in a Plexiglas room and signed autographs on envelopes, which were then stamped and mailed on the day of the moon landing, thus making them valuable collectors' items. Some of them were up on eBay at around $5,000 each shortly after Neil passed on.

I read that Neil Armstrong wanted his ashes to be scattered at sea. Interesting to note that he went to the moon, and finished up at the bottom of the ocean.

There has been an urban legend (or untrue story) floating around the Internet since 1995, but due to the fact that the perpetrators inserted so many little "factoids" into the lie, it circulated like wildfire as if to be true. So, for what it's worth, here it is.....

When Apollo Mission Astronaut Neil Armstrong first walked on the moon, he not only gave his famous "one small step for man, one giant leap for mankind" statement but followed it by several remarks, usual communication traffic between him, the other astronauts and Mission Control. Just before he re-entered the lander, however, he made this remark "Good luck Mr. Gorsky."

Many people at NASA thought it was a casual remark concerning some rival Soviet Cosmonaut. However, upon checking, there was no Gorsky in either the Russian or American space programs. Over the years many people questioned Armstrong as to what the "Good luck Mr. Gorsky" statement meant, but Armstrong always just smiled.

On July 5, 1995 in Tampa Bay, Florida, while answering questions following a speech, a reporter brought up the twenty-six year old question to Armstrong. This time he finally responded. Mr. Gorsky had died and so Neil Armstrong felt he could answer the question.

When he was a kid, he was playing baseball with a friend in the backyard. His friend hit a fly ball, which landed in the front of his neighbour's bedroom windows. His neighbours were Mr. & Mrs. Gorsky.

As he leaned down to pick up the ball, young Armstrong heard Mrs.Gorsky shouting at Mr. Gorsky. "Sex! You want sex?! You'll get sex when the kid next door walks on the moon!"

Nigel Lythgoe

Producer and director Nigel Lythgoe has become pretty much a household name in America, due to his hugely popular shows such as *Pop Idol, American Idol, So You Think You Can Dance, Opening Act* and many more.

Another "local lad made good" – from Merseyside, Wallasey to be precise – he began with tap dancing at a very early age, and went from strength to strength, becoming a very successful choreographer in London.

He used to occasionally be involved with the dancing school in Wallasey where a pre-teen Ruth first became bitten with the showbiz bug. It was with great amusement that they ran into one another again in recent years at the Britweek events in Los Angeles.

He and his schoolmate Ken Warwick opened a winery together in the Napa Valley, and made a short-lived TV series called *Corkscrewed: The Wrath of Grapes*. It was highly entertaining, and highlighted many of the challenges they faced as outsiders to the wine world.

They have both remained active in 19 Entertainment, as well as diversifying into numerous other entertainment related ventures. They both remain "vewwy Bwitish", and their sense of humour is untarnished, I am happy to say. Nigel is also co-founder of Britweek.org – Ruth is on the digital committee. Britweek is held each April/May in California and celebrates British and California ties with various events, ranging from soccer and cricket matches to a five-star gala, art shows, fashion shows, tastings and car rallies. It's great to see the Union Jack waving all the way down Wilshire Boulevard thru Beverly Hills. Poet Rupert Brooke was right... "That there's some corner of a foreign field that is for ever England."

Ruth and Martin recently worked with Nigel and Ken on *American Idol* and *So You Think...* by bringing in an amazing technology we represent called Mativison. It is a 360-degree film capture system that produces a "bubble" of film so that when you view it on a smart TV or online, you can use your mouse or even your iPad like a gyroscope to navigate 360 degrees inside the film. Don't we wish they had had those in the Abbey Road days? They just filmed Slash in the studio making his new album and it's even available as a 360 app. To think I was born into a house with gas lighting and an outside loo and now I can rock out to Slash on my iPad. As you do.

Nigel's success hasn't gone to his head, and he is still the same, boyish, charming, affable personality that he was as a young dancer from way back in Wallasey. (Boy, am I angling for free case of Villa San Juliette wine?).

Anna Griffin

Anna is a fellow Brit, a dear girl, whom we met at the launch of Virgin America's inaugural flight to Fort Lauderdale, Florida. We hit it off immediately, with matching senses of humour and work ethics.

She is the publisher and Editor in Chief of Coco Eco Magazine, a revolutionary step into the online publishing world which is available not only online, but in print, and is known as the primo multimedia publication that celebrates the life of beautiful and ethical products, people and places.

She kindly featured Mrs. McCartney's Teas in her magazine, and even more importantly, introduced me to the world of John Paul DeJoria, of Paul Mitchell Systems Hair Care, and Patron tequila fame, who then included my teas in his online sustainable website, JP Selects. This in turn led to me being invited to participate in his Annual Gathering at The Aria in Las Vegas in 2011. John Paul introduced me to his 4,500 guests onstage, and even included a box of my teas in every one of their gift bags. Truly a memorable occasion for me, which I talk about a bit more later.

And now this book, the result of several years of my random jottings, is being published by one of John Paul's companies, ROK, so I have much to be grateful to Anna for. (Never end a sentence with a preposition).

In addition to be a gorgeous young lady, Anna has the biggest heart in the world when it comes to rescuing animals (both of the canine and human variety).

At Coco Eco, they take environmental and social responsibilities seriously and in an effort to only bring their readers authentic content, they rigorously research the brands they partner with to ensure their core ethics. They promise never to sell out and promote companies other than those who legitimately share their philosophy, ecological commitment, and philanthropic principles.

Anna is also a frequent contributor to the Huffington Post, and manages to cram about twenty-eight hours into every day.

I like their motto: Coco Eco Magazine. Smart. Sustainable. Sexy.

Just like Anna!

Mrs. Angie McCartney's Teas

All my life the staple sustenance has been a good old pot of tea. My earliest recollection is of my Mum brewing a good old cuppa in a brown teapot. It was from her that I learned the adage: "To obtain tea hot, first warm your pot."

Tea is the second most popular drink on the planet, I'm told. It is even creeping up in popularity close to coffee in the United States. But in my younger days, tea bags had not been heard of, and later, when we began to see American films, we were interested to see tea bags being used. It would be several years before they became popular in England.

The history of tea has always fascinated me. And now, here we are in the twenty-first century with such a plethora of flavours. A good friend of ours, Kerry Dunne, was visiting from Arizona one day and asked aloud, "What's more British than a cup of tea? What's more British than the Beatles?" The proverbial light bulb went off in me head and Mrs. McCartney's Teas (www.mrsmccartneysteas.com) was born... in America of all places!

We spent many long hours researching and sourcing teas to ensure everything is Fair Trade, and hooked up with a local distributor. He actually gets the tea off the ships in Long Beach, California, and packs it in his facility in Orange County. He then delivers it to the World Headquarters of Mrs. McCartney's Teas – my garage! We decided to kick off with English Breakfast (my personal favourite), Earl Grey, Green Tea and Rooibos, a red South African blend.

Ruth and Martin built me a nice website, and Andreas Slavik of Vienna recorded a jingle for me with the Vienna Symphony Orchestra as a gift and a contribution to the project. I got myself a Facebook page and voila, we were in business!

I'm happy to make donations to the Linda McCartney Cancer Centre in Liverpool, and have been fortunate enough to be featured in the JP Selects catalogue.

There are moves afoot for me to host afternoon teas and tell stories about "the old days" which I am quite excited about.

My son-in-law Martin has made me an electronic press kit, and I even have my own app on a video badge from the company called Salespoint Networks. The company is run by Jeff McQueen in Los Angeles, so I am becoming quite the electronic octogenarian.

Time Warner Cable shot a piece about me at our McCartney offices, and Ruth and my dear friend Don Dale provided the comestibles (sandwiches and cakes) for our little tea party which is out there on YouTube.

The American Red Cross bought 4,500 variety packs (they contain five bags of each of the four flavours) to give away as incentives for people to donate blood. Will donate for tea.

There are lots of interesting stories about the history of tea, which I sometimes talk about at various gatherings. The Americans are always fascinated about anything British and love our anecdotes. There is so much to talk about, including the protocol of serving afternoon tea. I have been fortunate to obtain a nice collection of teapots, silver teaspoons, tea strainers, and other accoutrements such as china dishes, two-tier cake stands, cake forks, and cake tongs, which lend a nice atmosphere at any tea party.

The origin of people putting the milk in a cup of tea first or last was because after the plague in England, when disease was rife, and people had to boil water to make tea. The rich (posh) people would put the milk in last to ensure that the tea had brewed sufficiently. They, of course, used fine bone china cups. The poor people, who had less fine vessels to drink out of, were scared of the boiling water cracking their cups, so they put the milk in first to diffuse the heat.

We at Mrs. McCartney Teas don't care which method you use, as long as you drink up our brand (wink, wink, clink, clink).

Connect Codes

We began seeing these codes, squares of black and white, aka QR Codes, at the end of 2010, and on delving into a spot of research, discovered that they had long been in use in Japan, originally pioneered as bar codes by the Denso Wave Corporation, and were gradually creeping into the cyber consciousness of Europe and America.

We learned that these codes has originated when an auto manufacturer had found that, due to the number of parts in every vehicles shipped, the regular bar codes on the documentation just wouldn't cut it. Then someone came up with the idea of placing layer upon layer of bar codes on top of one another, and condensing it into a small square, and this became a most acceptable alternative. Ruth and Christian got their heads together on this with some of our crack programming team, on the basis of four brains being better than one, and came up with a DIY version for everyone in the world to be able to build a mobile website and generate a code to act as their "digital fingerprint".

Ruth contacted Paul Reitz in Texas (a former owner and client from Two Bunch Palms Resort in Desert Hot Springs, CA), who was interested, and contacted an investor, and they formed a Texas Corporation called Connect Code Media, Inc. www.connectcode.mobi. (Mobi meaning for mobile applications, as opposed to just websites). Even I as an octogenarian accept that people are spending more time on their mobile devices now, as opposed to sitting at a desk in front of a computer, and that something needed to be done to address this technology on a grander scale. The actual statistics are 4 to 1 when it comes to time spent on mobiles versus computers.

Ruth and Paul made a connection to RE/MAX in Denver, CO, the Real Estate leader in the States, and thus began a relationship, with ConnectCode becoming their approved supplier for their 200,000 members and their subsequent house signs. Ruth has been making presentations, speaking to groups, seminars, webinars, etc. to guide people into using this technology. And in 2011 President Bill Clinton adopted our technology for his Clinton Foundation to be able to drive mobile donations with the click of a camera.

By degrees, we are beginning to see Connect Codes in grocery stores, in gas stations, on hotel websites, and many other areas. Unfortunately, when you scan them with your Smartphone, they often don't connect as one would hope, but in many cases, just connect you to a Flash website, which of course doesn't work on a cell phone. But our internal genius bar has figured it out, so now if you are a small business, a college campus, a non-profit organisation, or just a person who wants a business card, you can go to www.connectcode.mobi, and in a few clicks create your own mobile web site and get a QR / ConnectCode to unlock the pages on smart phones. It's easy, cheap, saves trees, and you can change it any time.

It's all a smidge complicated to me, but not to Ruth and Paul, who confer daily on the ramifications and potential of this great technology. We can only hope that the world catches up. After all, remember, they said the Internet would be a flash in the pan!

At least, I know that *my* Connect Code works! But then, I am fortunate enough to have the in-house expertise, and at the right price too.

Callan McAuliffe

I have known Callan since he was a toddler, way back in Australia, through my long time connection to his Mum, Claudia Keech. As I have written elsewhere, Claudia and I have had numerous relationships spanning umpteen years.

I worked with her first husband, Richard Keech, at Penthouse/OMNI/ NewLook magazine group, the Bob Guccione empire based in Los Angeles, then later, when she and Richard parted, she went on to open an online publication, *Mother, Inc.* which is still going strong, and I worked for her when she ran Australian American Public Relations in downtown Los Angeles.

Somehow, during all this, she managed to give birth to her fantastic son, Callan, who is a young Aussie actor of note. In addition to his many Antipodean successes, he has appeared in more recent American movies such as *Flipped*, *I Am Number Four*, *The Great Gatsby*, (playing the young version of Leo DiCaprio's adult Gatsby), a made-for-TV movie about Julian Assange called *Underground* and is currently working on a feature called *Blue Potato*, due to be released in 2013. He has already worked with such notable directors and producers as Rob Reiner, D.J. Caruso, Steven Spielberg and Baz Luhrman. Not a bad track record for a seventeen year old.

He is more than an actor: he's an animal activist, concerned for the welfare of wolves, an extremely humorous young man, and has an enquiring mind that even *The National Enquirer* would be excited to learn about.

He manages to juggle completing his education whilst globe-trotting between his native Australia, Europe and the USA. We were last all together at our Casa in Playa early in 2012 when he and Martin disappeared into the man cave to make music together. I know that one day we will be seeing him at the Oscars, although he hates fuss, and deep down is a really unassuming and lovely lad.

(He will probably want to make a doll of me and stick pins in it for that last sentence.)

John Paul DeJoria

In early 2011, we were introduced to John Paul DeJoria by our friend Anna Griffin, Founder and Editor of the highly successful online magazine CocoEco.

We were invited to take tea with him, his delightful wife Eloise, and their children, at their Malibu home. We prepped the usual comestibles for an afternoon tea spread and set off. When we arrived John Paul was completing a video shoot for JP Selects, an online daily deals site for green, glamorous and sustainable products. It was just one of his many interests within the ROK Empire. To his credit, he also is a giver and is quite active in charities, helping the less fortunate, having risen from the ranks of being homeless in Los Angeles, to now being featured in the *Forbes* lists. I particularly like his slogan which is, *Success unshared is failure.*

He made us feel so welcome. In no time we were all regaling one another with tales of our early days, our struggles, our achievements, although his far exceed ours. Before we got too deeply into the afternoon tea, the Patron was introduced, thus encouraging us to relax have a lovely warm exchange of stories and laughter.

We did the deal with a handshake, and he also suggested that he put a box of my variety pack in each of his goody bags at the upcoming annual Paul Mitchell gathering to be held at The Aria Hotel in Las Vegas in July 2011. He also invited me to make an appearance at the launch, which I was delighted to do.

This resulted in a flurry of activity at the world headquarters of Mrs. McCartney's Teas, which was our garage. Al Scherner, my tea supplier in Orange County, made sure all was ship-shape in time for the big event.

We duly organised for him to pack and ship 4,500 boxes to their transportation people in time to be packed into the gift baskets which were then given to all the beauticians and hairdressers from around the world who attended this annual shindig.

It was a memorable occasion for me. My suite at the Aria was an exercise in cyber awareness. There was a console beside the bed which controlled the curtains, the TV, the temperature, the room service, etc. I was greeted on arrival with a lovely fruit basket and a bottle of Patron, plus a nice welcoming note from John Paul. Ruth and Martin had a nearby room, and we all basked in the luxury of everything.

We had an early call on Monday morning, and I got up in the wee small hours to do a bathroom run (almost needed to call a cab to get there), and decided to take my daily meds with what I thought was a mouthful of water from a small bottle in the fridge, which turned out to be vodka! Oops. Good way to start the day. And on an empty stomach too.

My delightful "minder" Anja from Paul Mitchell Germany, turned up, together with two security men who kept talking into their wristwatches about our progress, and off we went. We walked through the bowels of the hotel, kitchens, and security elevators to the area where all of the participants were being beautified for the show. Some of John Paul's ladies did my hair and make-up while Ruth and Martin mingled with the video camera, capturing some of it for us to enjoy later.

I was seated at the side of the runway next to Eloise, who was as warm and delightful as ever.

The show was opened by John Paul paragliding in – never a man to miss a good PR opportunity. He then opened the show by talking about his forthcoming JP Selects and saying how he had chosen as his first brand, "Mrs. McCartney's Teas". He then invited me up on stage where we exchanged a few words and a few laughs. You can see the result on video by scanning the ConnectCode on the back of this book with a free QR Reader app on your Smartphone.

The participants dispersed after the show for their various training and instructional classes all day. That evening he was hosting the annual White Party. John Paul asked me if I might drop in for a few minutes, to which I replied that I would be there "till the death". As indeed I was, as it was about 3 a.m. before I finally got back to my suite. We had a wonderful time and were welcomed by literally hundreds of young and not-so-young Paul Mitchell people.

I had the time of my life, and my tea continues to be featured on www.jpselects.com, where I make regular sales. This in turn, enables me to send donations to The Linda McCartney Cancer Centre in Liverpool.

A lot of my Facebook friends have also become tea fans, which is nice. I wish one of those hairdressers would move into my guestroom!

More recently I have been in contact with some other prominent members of his group of companies in England, such as ROK Comics. I am currently working on a project with the wonderful Jonathan Kendrick, who has been instrumental in generating interest in the publishing of this book.

Lang may yer lumb reek Jonathan! (That's Scottish for "long may your chimney smoke.")

Royal Wedding 2011

As expat Brits we still have close ties with England, and many happy memories of our lives there. Like so many others, we were delighted at the plans for the Royal Wedding on April 29, 2011. We knew that when Prince William exchanged nuptials with Kate Middleton, it would boost the spirits of millions around the world.

Due to the time difference in California, we were tuned in to the BBC to watch at 1 a.m. Ruth and I had logged in couple of hours naptime and were in our jammies when the broadcast came on. We added our headgear, (me, a tiara; Ruth a big purple floppy hat), and set ourselves up in her big bed upstairs. We had prepared cucumber sandwiches, scones, biscuits (or cookies to the Americans), and a nice pot of Mrs. McCartney's Tea, with just a wee drop of whiskey in it!

Martin set up the video camera in the corner of the room and recorded our reactions to the television coverage. We were pretty much unaware of him, and prattled on to one another in our usual silly fashion, and found out later he posted it to YouTube.

What a simply splendid and delightful occasion it turned out to be, and www.youtube.com/mccartneystudios is where you can find this and several other of our forays into the media world.

Great Britain, Australia and Canada's Elizabeth II; Margareth of Denmark; Beatrix of The Netherlands; Sophia of Greece and Spain; Noor of Jordan; Elton John and David Furnish.... The Abbey was full of old Queens.

The Speakmans

My great niece in Manchester, Steph Elmore, is a TV host and introduced us to Nik and Eva Speakman. They are top British TV psychotherapists who were in L.A. to shoot a TV pilot.

We met briefly at our home in Playa del Rey, along with their two delightful children, Olivia and Hunter. They were on their way to LAX to fly home, but we all felt like we had known each other a lifetime.

Ruth told Nik about her fear of falling downstairs since she had broken her leg a couple of years previously. He spent about ten minutes with her in Martin's office, then she went upstairs, put on a pair of her highest heeled shoes, and walked downstairs without holding the banister, or even looking down. He had cured her of her fear. She is still fine to this day.

A friend was visiting at the time and told Nik of her phobia about cockroaches. Again, after just a few minutes with her, she too was cured. I learned recently that she is still in good order in this regard.

My main fear (apart from fire), is of not being able to swim. Nik and Eva have promised that the next time we can spend a little while together, they will help me overcome that.

We do keep in touch and I see their TV segments all the time. I don't know how they do it, but they do! So I'm hopeful that when we see them again soon so they'll be able to wave their magic wand over me.

Then watch out Michael Phelps!!

Model Citizen

After being a Green Card holder for the requisite number of years, I was eventually called to Memphis, Tennessee, to take my medical exam and answer questions to qualify my eligibility for citizenship.

I had been eagerly studying the citizenship test, burning the midnight oil and nearly tearing my hair out in anticipation of the ordeal. We were living in Nashville at the time (where we had moved after the 1994 Northridge earthquake) so Memphis was the chosen spot.

Ruth, Martin and I set out the night before, and took advantage of some of the fantastic jazz clubs. We caroused a little longer than we should have before falling into bed at our crummy little motel.

The next morning Ruth and Martin dropped me off at the appointed place, where I nervously awaited my name being called.

Eventually the big moment came and I was ushered in to a small room with a very serious gentleman who took my papers and examined them. His first question was, "Mrs. McCartney, I see you were born in Liverpool. Have you ever met any of the Beatles?" My answer nearly blew his socks off. He spent most of our time together asking me questions about the boys, assuring me that his wife and kids would never believe he had been talking to me. He called them on the phone while I was there. Yada, yada, yada.

As far as I can recollect, I only had to answer a smattering of the questions about the constitution. The many subjects that I had been poring over for weeks and the interview soon came to a close. It was a great relief I can assure you.

I became a US citizen in the Nashville courthouse in July 1996. It puzzled me that when the court bailiff would call out the name of the next person in line, several times, there was no response. When it was my turn, I asked the Clerk of the Court what that was all about? She told me that in many cases new citizens didn't speak English and didn't understand when their names were called. That shook me because at the beginning of my trusty book, *Our Constitution and Government* (a Federal textbook on citizenship), it indicated that in order to apply, citizens would need to read, write and speak English. In those far off days, America was still primarily an English-speaking country.

On a side note: when Ruth sat for *her* citizenship test, she was asked to complete an English test! Yes, really: born and bred in England, yet required to fill out this form, which had several typos and spelling errors, which Ruth duly marked with a red pen. Oh, and yes, she passed with flying colours.

I would later also find out that one can sit for a driving license in several languages such as English, Spanish, Tagalog, Vietnamese, or Korean. What interests me is how do people who do not speak or read English recognise traffic hazard warning signs? Ah well, they tell me I am becoming picky in my old age.

Martin Nethercutt:The Man and his Music

In addition to creating five libraries of Netloopz for the McCartney Multimedia Inc., Music Library, and scores of other music related projects for clients, my son-in-law Martin Nethercutt has worked for some five years on his personal dream project, www.geistmusik.com.

When it was nearing completion in late 2011, he took it to famed music producer and old friend Niko Bolas at Capitol Records to be mixed. Niko happened to be working with a very famous multi-platinum-selling rock star, who heard it and was impressed. He asked if he too could work on the vocal mixes, as he thought the quality of Martin's voice was close to his own. A great compliment indeed, and one well deserved as far as I am concerned. However, as this gentleman didn't want to draw attention to himself, he insisted that the only thanks to him in print were to be addressed as "Vladimir Johnson", a nom de plume. So he and Niko got cracking on *Geist* and an incredible album resulted. It is available on iTunes.

Martin worked with several local musicians and the end result is an amazing collection of mostly self-penned songs, along with a book, wonderful images and graphics, rounding it out as a fantastic collection of his music, lyrics (with a little help from Ruth), and photographs. Truly a big journey in his life.

As I have said before, Martin, Ruth and I, all live and work together, in perfect harmony (well nearly all the time!). The only possible exception is when his German national team is playing soccer on telly, against England. That's when Ruth and I don our crash helmets.

While he's the big strong, strapping German, who swims, runs, and performs all manner of exercise, behind closed doors, he's a closet cat lover, and has a soft centre. But don't let him know I told you that.

As I write this, he is producing a hip hop group from Detroit, a really talented and interesting threesome, and he's spending long hours down at our studio working on their tracks.

Start Spreading the News

In researching for this book, it's interesting to think back on how we got the news over the years. When I was a little 'un, my Dad used to bring the *Liverpool Daily Post* home on workdays. And on Sundays he would go across to Scargreen Avenue and buy the *Sunday Express* from a man who stood on the corner of Utting Avenue East. Now it's Google Alerts.

Dad always encouraged me to do the Skeleton crossword puzzle, which I grew to love. My eldest sister, Mae, used to do the fashion competition. She won a couple of prizes for her selections. She was very proud of her success.

I still love crossword puzzles and buy them by the book! I even do the crappy ones at the back of the scummy magazines. And of course, it's so easy to find them on the Internet and in the App Store. My generous daughter Ruth recently bought me a large print (thanks for the hint that I'm getting long in the tooth), crossword puzzle book from the Dollar General store for the princely sum of $1. It says printed in China so maybe "across" means from right to left and "down" actually means up. Time will tell.

One of my favourite magazines nowadays is called *The Week*, which encapsulates headlines from worldwide news. It is a great resource for quickly finding out what has been going on all around the globe. It's also useful for me when I plan for my weekly radio spots with Pete Price at Radio City, Liverpool, as it enables me to sound knowledgeable and well read. It's not all serious either, and I find plenty of amusing stuff in there. And yes, I read it on my iPad.

Fred and Mary Willard

To celebrate America's birthday in 2012, we started off the night before with a delightful party at the home of Mary and Fred Willard in Encino. Fred is known and loved by many for his appearances as the eternally vague and bumbling guy in such movies as *This is Spinal Tap*, *A Mighty Wind*, *Best in Show*, and *Waiting for Guffman*. In his seventies, Fred is still very active, constantly making new movies and appearing on TV shows and just signed on to co-star in a new Christopher Guest project for HBO called *Family Tree*.

Fred and Mary run sketch comedy workshops in Hollywood, which are a hilarious opportunity for budding performers to interact with professionals and hone their skills. Mary is also very active in several prominent charities benefitting both humans and animals, which is how Ruth and I met her when presenting our Connect Code technology to help them with online donations. Mary is also a successful playwright and has published numerous comedies, skits and scripts.

But back to the party... The house and garden in the San Fernando Valley were magnificently decorated with flags, bunting, lights, a myriad of ornaments, posters, tsotchkes, memorabilia, etc. There was also a gargantuan buffet, a never-ending bar, and boxes full of noise-makers, funny hats, masks, and feather boas, which we were all encouraged to don for the big parade around the tennis courts at the end of the evening. Everyone entered into the spirit with gusto, and we were accompanied by traditional John Philip Sousa marches and American music, young and old alike. What fun it all was.

We rubbed shoulders with many familiar faces from the world of movies, radio and television, including Ed Begley Jr., Jeff Garlin, Ted Lange, Jo Anne Worley, Leonard Maltin, and Peter Marshall, the TV host who worked with Ruth, (together with Leslie Uggams) on her first-ever appearance on NBC Television when we first arrived in America. It was years since I last met Leonard Maltin when I worked for Michael Rollins at Hollywood Online, and he hadn't aged one bit. Must be doing something right, I guess.

Many of these folks had worked with Andy Griffith and to mark his passing, we all stood up, toasted his memory, and whistled the theme tune to *Mayberry R.F.D.*

Also joining in the festivities were The Right Honourable Bob Peirce, the former British Consul, and his charming wife, Sharon Harroun Peirce. We all had almost too much fun. It was Sharon who first introduced us to the Willards, for which we are very grateful.

Then came the fireworks, tended by several of the young men in the party, and aided (or were they?) by Fred himself, brandishing a cigarette lighter. We held our breath, hoping that he wouldn't step too near the rockets being launched into the night sky.

But earlier in the evening Mary brought everyone to attention before introducing to the stage a selection of the guests, each of whom read a quotation from a famous speech by a politician, a president, or a movie star. The quotes were from a much earlier time, but they were relevant to today's events and attitudes.

Some things just never change.

Mary and Fred are involved heavily and have been honoured by several charities including Big Brothers Big Sisters of Los Angeles, Actors and Other for Animals and have introduced us to so many people doing great things for the non-profit world. We are working with ConnectCode's capabilities to create a secure mobile donation platform for any charity that wants it. We just completed a Code for the Clinton Foundation and also attended the ABC John Wayne Cancer Foundation luncheon recently which honoured Kris Jenner – "Momager" to all those Krazy Kardashian Kidz!

We have begun working on a couple of projects with Mary and look forward to some fruitful conclusions.

Daily Word

Many years ago a friend gave me a little inspirational booklet called *Daily Word*. It is Christian-based, but more or less non-denominational.

As a "loose" Christian, I took the gift and didn't pay much attention to it at first. Every so often I would take a casual look at it. Then by degrees, I began to see a great deal of relevance in the messages. So when the book ran out of pages, I decided to subscribe and have done so now for years. I also buy a subscription for friends and relatives when they are going through health or emotional problems. They too have said quite often said how "on the nail" the daily thoughts can be.

You can also call or email them and ask them to pray for someone who is in a bad place, and I have done this many times, too. It's a handy dandy pocket size, fits in your purse, glove box, beside drawer – even under the pillow.

I don't want you to think I am going all 'Holy Joe' on you, but it really does works for me. In fact, today's message tells me I can make a positive difference because I am the light of the world. So that's inspired me to make a difference by telling you, dear readers, about my powerful little book. The back page of this month's says, "Let go and let God."

Go on, I dare you.

Angie's Bucket List

1. Become a published writer (duh, if you're reading this...)
   OK, then substitute:
   Stop being a wimp, take life by the throat

2. Learn to swim

3. Meet Betty White

4. Become Miss Universe (just kidding)

5. Have belly button piercing and all tattoos removed

6. Become financially independent

7. Find Ruth a new daddy (kidding again)

8. Sell Mrs. McCartney's Teas to China

9. Cancel hang gliding appointment with George Clooney

10. Write a sequel within the next eighty years (Book II is already percolating)

Thank so much for reading this book.
Sincerely,
Angie.

Acknowledgements
In alphabetical order, to be politically correct

Andi Slavik
> *who created the music for my jingle on my website*

Anna Griffin
> *for not only being a True Brit friend, but for introducing me into the John Paul DeJoria world which led to me becoming a published writer*

Ashley Walls
> *for the introduction to my stealth editor*

Babs and Will Crawford and their darling families
> *who gave us a home when we ran away to Australia*

Barry & Megan Coffing
> *for turning their garage into a guesthouse and their entrance bell into a whistling fest*

Benny Mardones
> *whose company I have enjoyed over many an afternoon tea, and whose music just gets better all the time*

Beryl Kendall (RIP) and The Kendall Cousins
> *who gave us our first home in America and helped us make a new life*

Betty White
> *who proves you can just keep doin' it!*

Bill Clinton
> *for being my motivation to become an American Citizen*

Bill Kelly, Esq.
> *for all the legal eagle advice and rum drink recipes*

Bill Miller
> *My very favourite Virgin (ahem) person, who started so much*

Chris Alan
> *for keeping me in bandwidth*

Christian Volquartz
> *who takes so many calls, nurses my computer, helps to organise my life, and who took so many photographs to make me look good (all smoke and mirrors)*

Cynthia Lennon

a lasting friend, who agreed to write the foreword

Dale & Vicki Jensen

For your faith and support. And oh, those rides on your private jet!

Dawn Bowery

my lovely British photographer friend, who photographed my cover picture

Dieter Bockmeier

my second son-in-law who videoed me in the early days, and whose parents opened their home to us in Munich and taught me how to speak Bavarian (wo sind meine Brille?)

Don Woods

My magnificent Wirral song writing buddy whose video clips of Merseyside and the Wirral on YouTube constantly remind me of home

Edana Corbin, CPA

for not cooking the books

Eric Belcher

for hiring me not once, but three times and letting me quit instead of getting fired!

Freda Kelly

another stalwart from the early Beatles days who agreed to let me write about her despite her yearning for privacy over the years

George Harrison

for showing Ruth that learning to play piano could be fun.

Jim McCartney

who took us into his life and made a new world for us beyond belief

Joan Archer

my big sister who taught me to be resilient in the face of a good air raid and a bristlescrubbing brush and who inspired me by recording her first CD at eighty-two.

John Hewston

for his help in the making of this edition

John Lennon

for always being the true voice of reason in a mad, mad world

John Paul and Eloise DeJoria

for the Vat of Patron, the support and the recognition I deserve, dammit!

Jonathan Kendrick
> *of ROK who made it all possible, and the JP Selects team for promoting my Organic Teas*

Karotti & HD Schmitz-Nethercutt
> *for the gift of your lovely son Martin in our lives*

Kerry and Cynthia Dunne
> *who encouraged me to start Mrs. McCartney's Teas. See – it's all your fault*

Louise Harrison
> *for hanging in there, and being a fellow member of the Beatles' survivors club*

Marshall Terrill
> *my loyal, stealth friend, for advice and guidance*

Martin Nethercutt
> *my beloved son-in-law, who has guided me throughout this project, and my life for the past umpteen years, with tolerance, kindness, loving support, and a dang load of technical know-how to bring it all together*

Mary & Fred Willard
> *for both being the Best In Show*

Mel Haber
> *for the old-fashioned, 5-star innkeeper standards at The Ingleside Inn in Palm Springs and those heavy pours at Melvyn's*

Michael Raven
> *for the Swiss chocolate supply and the never-ending love of kittens!*

Mike McCartney
> *for helping us ease into the craziness, and for the humour, support, and love over the years*

Mr. and Mr. Tim and Don Arendt-Dale
> *a pair of splendiferous chaps! for inviting me (The Rev. Angela McCartney) to officiate at their wedding, and for being an outstanding couple*

Nashville Natives
> *Bob Mather, Blaine Hayes, Rob & Sally Hendrick, Ann Stokes and all the "deep fried pie" aficionados at South Street and Sammy P's.*

Pat Roxworthy
> *You know what you did!*

Paul Antonelli
my first son-in-law – you know what you did, you crazy little kumquat!

Paul McCartney
for all the love, help and acceptance in those far off days

Paul Reitz
for being a great coach and a good solid friend!

Pauline Sutcliffe
for her encouragement, and help with Stuart's early artwork and fonts

Pete Price
my inspiration for writing this book in the first place, and for featuring me so much in his Name Dropper book, and every week on his radio show where I'm not allowed to say "crap"

Rachel Jones
our lovely Vet who takes such good care of our kitties, and is always willing to go the extra mile. (How about putting in a good word for me with your Dad, Quincy, to produce my next album? Just kidding)

Ray Connolly
my rare and trusted journalist friend, for his encouragement

Ric Hollywood Wetzel
whose genius with my hair and make-up could make a goddess from a sow's ear. And did.

Richard Oliff
for helping me remember to clean with... and not drink white vinegar

Rikki Klieman & Bill Bratton
a woman of strength and humour who should run for President, with a husband who looks really good in uniform!

Ringo Starr
who talked Jimmy Mac into my first dishwasher

Roseanne Barr
who laughs at my jokes at our Friday Shabbat get-togethers

Ruth McCartney
my beloved daughter, my reason for living, my pal, my inspiration, my Digital Diva and fellow laundry folder

Shelly Goldstein

>*for her early encouragement, guidance, honey, and loving support throughout the project*

Steve Tyrell

>*for what else? the music!*

Team Paisley

>*Tony & Carol Busching, Alisa Allen, Kevin Stofer-Smith, Mr. & Mrs. Farrow (finally!) and all the crazy kids who taught me about lights, camera and in some cases ACTION!*

Timothy Wentworth-Brown

>*who patiently archived my old video clips and researched history*

Tony Barrow

>*who also knows the true stories, and who gave me so much support in reviving my memories*

Xavier Autrey

>*for believing in ConnectCode Media and connectcode.mobi*

Zebedee

>*because I don't know anyone else whose name begins with Zed*

And all my loving friends, family, neighbours, Beatles fans, Tea fans, Facebook buddies, your never-ending warmth and trust in me has helped me to keep going, often when I felt like giving up. But there 'ain't no stopping me now. I'm already working on Book II – *Weird S**t from Outer Space or How to Clean your Dishwasher for 14 cents*

>**Angie the Fearless!**
>*Four Feet Eleven and a Half inches.*
>*And you'd better not forget the half-inch!*

About the Author

Angie McCartney was born in Hoylake, Wirral, Merseyside on November 14, 1929 to Edith and Robert Stopforth, the youngest of four children (or "the shakings of the box" as her Mother would describe her). At age three she moved across the river to Norris Green, Liverpool and was beset with lung problems, suffering pleurisy and pneumonia every winter. This delayed her starting school until she was six, and by nine, World War II broke out, further disrupting her education. When the May 1941 Blitzkrieg almost flattened the city, her school, St. Teresa's, was commandeered for the homeless. Students gathered one day a week elsewhere to check the roll call (register) and exchange tales of their experiences, but little real education happened after this time.

She managed to deliver morning newspapers to earn a few shillings a week to pay for piano lessons, and would practise diligently for about four hours a day. She achieved her Teacher's Certification a few days before her fourteenth birthday.

She worked as a junior (dogsbody as she calls it) at various offices and factories in and around Merseyside and developed a variety of secretarial skills.

She has lived and worked in England, Australia, America, Germany, and her travels as "stage Mum" to daughter Ruth took her several times to Russia, Siberia, and lots of the "-stans" (Turkmenistan, Uzbekistan, etc.) broadening the mind (and the backside as she was oft heard to say), culminating in being one of the founding members of McCartney Multimedia, a Los Angeles based online digital agency, where she still works full time, as book-keeper, Administrator, and, as she puts it, "I got me old job back" as dogsbody to fellow workers, clients, the tax man, and myriad characters in this never-dull world.

On the run-up to her eightieth birthday, she began her organic tea company, www.mrsmccartneysteas.com, which introduced her to a world of research, history of tea ceremonies, etc., and many of her 5,000+ Facebook friends are her customers. She is happy to be able to donate to the Linda McCartney Centre in Liverpool, her hometown.

She lives and works with daughter Ruth and son-in-law Martin Nethercutt in the little town of Playa del Rey in Southern California.

She retains her love of music, reading, humour, cats, and life in California, and to quote her, "It's better than working for a living."